CRIMES OF COMMAND

In the United States Navy
1945-2015

By Michael Junge

Copyright © 2018 by Michael Junge

All rights reserved. This book or any portion thereof may not be reproduced or used in any manner whatsoever without the express written permission of the publisher except for the use of brief quotations in a book review.

Printed in the United States of America

First Printing, 2018

ISBN 978-1721230068

Contents

Acknowledgements i

Illustrations ii

Introduction iii

1: The United States Navy and Command 1
Navy Culture 3
The Search 24

2: 1945-1965 30
USS Indianapolis - 1945 30
USS Queenfish and Awa Maru 43
USS Brownson and USS Charles H. Roan - 1950 62
USS Wasp and USS Hobson - 1952 68
USS Bennington - 1954 74

3: 1965-1985 79
USS Hartley and Blue Master - 1965 81
USS Frank E. Evans and HMAS Melbourne - 1969 85
USS Belknap and USS John F. Kennedy - 1975 95
USS Ranger - 1983 107

4: 1985-2015 115
USS Stark - 1987 117
USS Indianapolis - revisited 124
USS Cole - 2000 134
USS McFaul and USS Winston S. Churchill - 2008 142
USS William P. Lawrence - 2013, and unfinished 148

5: The Reasons 159
Overall reasons or issues 160
Rickover's Technocracy 179

6: Towards Forgiveness 206

Conclusion 253

Bibliography 263

Acknowledgements

Thank you to Dr. Ivan Luke, Dr. Paul Povlock, and Steven Forand for their advice and encouragement in this endeavor. Proofreading assistance from Michael Boucher, Commander, United States Navy (Retired), Captain Chris Rawley, United States Navy, and argument honing with the folks at SailorBob.com was invaluable.

Great thanks to Commander Douglas D. Henry, United States Navy (Retired) for use of his father's letters and files in chapter 2 and to Commander Reo Beaulieu, United States Navy (Retired) for use of his letters and files in chapter 3. If only more officers were as good at keeping, and sharing, history as these two are.

Thank you to the crew of USS *Whidbey Island* (LSD 41) from 2007 to 2009 for helping me keep the bottom wet and not scratching the paint.

Thank you to Lenny, Vinnie, Hank, and Buttercup for not caring that I was working and reminding me there was more to life than books and the computer.

Thank you to Ella, Eva, and Paulette, for caring that I was working and still reminding me there was more to life than books and the computer.

And thank you to dog father, friend, confidant, philosopher, and life-long saint – Dr. Eric Shaw, Captain, U.S. Coast Guard (retired)…everybody's boon companion. You are missed.

Begin at the beginning and go on until you come to the end; then…

Illustrations

Figures
Figure 1. Annual per-capita courts-martial and nonjudicial punishments 23
Figure 2. Number of commanders removed between 1998 and 2015 . 25
Figure 3. Total courts-martial and non-judicial punishment (NJP) from 1977 to 2014 176

Tables
Table 1. Cardinal Virtues and Deadly Sins 220
Table 2. Langford's distinctions between autonomous and heteronomous behavior 237

Introduction

In 2004 I was done with my executive officer tour in USS *The Sullivans* (DDG 68) and working at the Headquarters, United States Marine Corps. The previous year or so had a spate of commanding officers gracing the cover of Navy Times and the Navy's Chief of Naval Information (ChInfo) released a story detailing a comprehensive report done by the Navy Inspector General. ChInfo's offices were down the hall and around the corner so I wandered down and sweet talked a copy from the lieutenant who had it on his desk.

I read through report and thought "this is it?". There were some great nuggets, and some lessons to be learned, but nothing. Nothing salacious and nothing of import. Basically, the commanders were removed from command, there were no common characteristics and that was that.

Six years later I was done with my own command tour. There'd been a spike in removals, another report, and at a Surface Navy Association luncheon I sat next to a recently retired Captain who commanded twice at sea. The topic came up and I asked him about the current official line that only about 1% of commanders were being removed. He scoffed and said something to the effect that 1% is too many, no one should be getting fired – they all know what the rules are.

From there I thought and wondered. The new report was also pretty empty; except for the comment that most of the identified lessons from 2004 had not been implemented. I began my own tracking list and thought some more. Finally, I wondered, if 1% is an acceptable number and we only have 300 ships, then what was going on when the Navy was over a thousand ships? Shouldn't we have heard something about how many commanders were removed from command? Something didn't make sense.

Over the next ten years I collected stories of commanders removed from command. Some I knew, some were friends; none of the stories were good. At the very least a career was over. Sometimes a sailor was dead. Sometimes a ship damaged very badly. And sometimes, rarely, something bad happened and the commander wasn't removed and moved on and up. What? Something didn't make sense.

As I read more and looked for past issues I came across the sinking of USS *Benevolence* (AH 13). *Benevolence* sank in 1950 after colliding with a freighter in heavy fog off the coast of San Francisco. Twenty-three sailors and civilian crew died. The captain was court-martialed and convicted of hazarding a vessel. But, Barton E. Bacon, Jr. retired as a rear admiral!

Well, my shock was somewhat misplaced. Admiral Bacon retired as a rear admiral because contemporary law allowed post-retirement promotion for recipients of combat valor awards. Bacon commanded a submarine in World War II, receiving the Navy Cross – the second highest award for valor. Still, he'd lost a ship, sailors died, but we didn't know about it.

Eventually, I found a list of incidents someone else cataloged and digitized it. I searched and added to it. I found names and ranks and stories and tried to figure out what happened then and compare it to what was happening now.

In the beginning I had some ideas and preconceptions that matched the current beliefs and feelings of officers and sailors in the Navy and Coast Guard. By the time I was done, those ideas were turned on their head.

Historically commanding officers are the sole word of authority aboard ship. Every decision rests squarely on the Captain's shoulders; they are metaphorical pillars of leadership and integrity. I had command of a landing ship dock – USS *Whidbey Island* (LSD 41). Command is both a heady feeling and a crushing weight. At no point did I ever feel above anyone else, and often I felt shackled by the responsibility. One of the things that shackled me was the modern ability for instant and constant communications. Even with instantaneous communication, the Navy advocates a culture of autonomous operation. "Command by Negation," a concept unique to navies, allows a subordinate commander the freedom of judicious operation. While subordinates inform superiors of decisions taken, those decisions are the default action unless, and only if, the senior clearly and positively overrides it. The United States Navy is the only service with the acronym UNODIR (UNless Otherwise DIRected) by which a commanding officer informs superiors of a proposed course of action that will occur unless overridden. The subordinate is informing the boss, not asking permission. This concept dates to the age of sail when ship captains were dispatched throughout the world and given simple, yet clear, orders to act in the best interests of the king, or of the country. UNODIR provides a firm foundation for naval command; a firm foundation for the pillar that is a commanding officer.

That same modern communications technology allows seniors to reach ever deeper past the chain of command to issue, approve, or countermand the most banal order, and the concept of command by negation is eroding. This erosion creates a commensurate decay in the traditional authority of command. At the same time, increased scrutiny allows for an increase in the accountability of command. Technology is aiding that scrutiny but is not alone in causing the erosion. Captains are still pillars but are standing on less firm foundations than they once did.

While a Captain's specific powers have declined over the centuries, the idea that a commanding officer is 'the closest thing to God on earth' remains. Public myth, the press, and even Navy publications, portray Captains as solely responsible for everything within their command. Where a captain's authority once equaled this responsibility, the authority has eroded, but the responsibility remains. This divergence, great responsibility without equal authority, engenders problems. Every few months there is a national news story about the U.S. Navy removing a commanding officer from command for one reason or another. A common question raised in these instances is "why?". Why was that commanding officer removed? What incident led to the removal? Was it a personal failing? An operational accident?

Something in between?

The Navy does not ease the understanding. Citing privacy concerns, Navy leaders rarely provide a full accounting of why a commander was removed. In 2018, the Navy ended the common practice of providing press releases when a commander was removed from command. This lack of openness inevitably produces conjecture and rumor. Conventional wisdom holds that society changed and the Navy was slow to catch up. This is not the entire story. Many of the actions in these firings are commonplace in society. Alcohol abuse, adultery, and theft occur with regularity and rarely lead to automatic dismissal in the civilian workforce. When an officer was removed before 2018, and after the mid 1990s, it was normally public, open, and announced, but also shrouded in secrecy. The now former commander was pilloried between the shame of open censure and the Navy's insistence that privacy concerns for the disgraced officer overrode transparency. Rumors flew, stories were told, but the whole truth rarely came out. With the end of press releases the problem is worse. Now friends of the commander don't even know unless that commander reaches out – and very few do.

For almost every removal, especially those involving personal indiscretion, two competing narratives devolve down to the same phrase: *what was he thinking*? What was the fired officer thinking when he committed the act, and what was the senior thinking when he removed that officer for committing the act? These competing narratives indicate the societal change impacting the Navy is not complete, and likely that society does not fully comprehend the rules under which military officers operate.

Motivation plus action equals behavior and while some behavior is based on conscious reasoning some may result from unconscious drives. When unconscious drives combine with action we find it difficult to assign moral attributes to the result.[1] This provides a second challenge. We know the behavior, sometimes we know the action. What was the motivation? Modern rules are steeped in tradition and modified by a changing society. Civilian societal norms are not the only changes that affect perceptions of leadership and authority. Civilian ideals of military life also play a significant part.

There is a different way to ask this question: *Why does the Navy remove commanding officers?* In a non-military job few, if any, of these incidents result in job termination, especially for a subset of transgressions known as *crimes of command*. Crimes of command are specific violations of law, such as hazarding a ship through collision or grounding, which have no real counterpart outside naval command.[2] The two most common – collision and grounding – have specific definitions and understanding within maritime law. A *collision* is any time two ships strike each other, and both are underway (not anchored, moored, or grounded). Essentially, two moving ships strike one another. Collisions may be glancing blows, generally with little damage. Or, they can occur perpendicularly where the bow of one ship strikes the other in the side – commonly called a broadside or "t-bone." Collison contrasts *allision* wherein a moving ship strikes a non-moving object, a moored ship, pier, piling or buoy. A *grounding* is when a ship strikes the bottom of the ocean, intentionally or not. While some landing craft intentionally ground themselves as part of their mission, they are designed to do so; most ships are not. Likewise, some submarines might ground themselves as part of their mission or seek to blend with the ocean floor and escape detection. However, any unintentional grounding, or grounding outside of mission requirements, is a crime of command. In both cases, collision or grounding, contact may range from slight and

---

[1] Harold F. Gortner, "Values and Ethics," in *Handbook of Administrative Ethics*, ed. Terry L. Cooper, 2nd ed. (New York, NY: Dekker, 2001). 513.
[2] See Fidell, Eugene R., and Jay M. Fidell. "Loss of Numbers." *Naval Law Review* 48 (2001): 202.

glancing to catastrophic. The level of damage is not a factor in deciding whether a grounding occurred, though often the level of damage is tied to the severity of punishment. In all cases, the commanding officer is called to account for the actions of his ship – whether he had control at the moment of impact, or not. There are no clear civilian analogies to crimes of command; the closest lies in parental responsibility for children or vicarious responsibility within a corporation. However, even these analogies fall short when applied to crimes of command.

Even without direct analog, the U.S. military is a reflection of the society it draws from and as American society has changed, so has the Navy. And to some degree, as the Navy changes it also changes society. Today there are actions, once condoned, or even celebrated, which lead to removal from command but do not lead to dismissal in civilian society. Has the Navy always removed commanding officers for drinking too much, for adultery, for striking their subordinates, for running a ship aground or into another ship?

The Navy has officially examined command removals, twice; once in 2004 and again in 2010. Two naval officers, Captains Mark Light and Jason Vogt, wrote monographs in 2011 and 2014 respectively and examined the issue from a moral perspective. Each report, 2004, then 2010, then 2011 and finally 2014 built from each other but also to varying degrees used essentially the same data sets of officers removed from command between 1999 and 2013. The data were the officially tabulated numbers from the U.S. Navy Bureau of Personnel. Essentially, all four studies came to similar conclusions - removals are rare, largely for individual behavioral problems, and there are no links related to race, gender, age, naval community or career path. Each report assessed that all 300 reliefs might be cast as anomalous. Given an overall data set of almost 2,500 command positions with the record removal rate in 2011 of 26, the transgressors number 1% of all commanding officers. That normal or acceptable number that still made headlines. Why would anyone spend time concerned about 1%?

In short, because the United States is a maritime nation. The world relies on the security provided by the United States, and the United States Navy, and Navy commanding officers. All officers are commissioned by the President on behalf of the nation because of a "special trust and confidence in the Integrity and Ability" of the officer. Even 1%, in a modern world of nuclear weapons and guided missiles, is worth study.

However, I knew that this 1% number was a problem when you moved back in time. Of today's 2,500 command positions, only 300 are ships. At the end of World War II, the Navy had over 6,000 ships - 20 times as many as today. If the ratio of ships to overall commands held true, then in 1945 wouldn't you expect a potential removal rate of 500 commanding officers – each year? If 26 removals make headlines today, what would happen with 500? How valid is that accepted number of 1%?

This raises the next part of the question. First, I asked – *why does the Navy remove commanding officers?* Then, *has the Navy always removed as many commanding officers as it does today?* Even a cursory review of history shows that many naval heroes lost their ships to war or nature. In 1803, Commodore William Bainbridge grounded USS *Philadelphia* off Tripoli, was captured and imprisoned. Today, USS *Bainbridge* (DDG 96), an *Arleigh Burke*-class destroyer, is the fifth U.S. Navy ship named for him. In 1778, Commodore John Barry ran USS *Raleigh* aground during combat action and then abandoned the ship. The British captured and refloated her. John Barry, because he possessed the first United States government commission as a naval officer, is considered the "Father of the Navy" and USS *Barry* (DDG 52), also an *Arleigh Burke*-class destroyer, is the fourth U.S. Navy ship in his honor. In 1908, Ensign Chester W. Nimitz was court-martialed and removed from command after running USS *Decatur* (DD 5) aground in the Philippines. In 1944, this same Nimitz became the Navy's third Fleet Admiral, supervised the Pacific Theater of World War II, became Chief of Naval Officers and the aircraft carrier USS *Nimitz* (CVN 68) is named in his honor. In some cases, officers were removed from command, but quietly, without public notification and without censure.[3] Obviously not every commanding officer is either removed from command, or the U.S. Navy, for crimes of command.

An examination of all incidents over 242 years is unrealistic. Using just a few would provide insufficient data to draw any real conclusions. If one looks at the Navy's historical size, World War II is a clear anomaly. In 1940 the Navy had less than 500 ships. By 1942, just under 2000 ships. By 1945 - 6,768 ships. Since 1945 the U.S. Navy has experienced a slow, sometimes steady sometimes precipitous reduction in naval forces. This steady decline, when combined with the technological and administrative changes after World War II, provides a starting point. The ending point of 2015 was arbitrary. It made for a good even number, was current, and let me stop the numbers somewhere.

A way to address the question: *Why does the Navy remove commanding officers and has the Navy always removed as many commanding officers as it does today?* is by taking all U.S. Navy incidents and accidents between 1945 and 2015 and then determining what impact, if any, that presumed crime of command had upon the commanding officer and his subsequent career. Research ultimately provided over 1,500 discrete incidents for quantitative analysis. The data shows that the Navy acts differently than before. The change is identifiable, but not discreet. Like the proverbial frog in a pot of boiling water, the change was slow and gradual – and largely unnoticed. In fact, so unnoticed that even presented with quantitative data disputing the modern concept of "command accountability" officers, current and retired, will dispute it and insist that the tradition is as it always has been.

From those 1,500 incidents fourteen case studies were

---

[3] Gregory L. Vistica, *Fall from Glory: The Men Who Sank the U.S. Navy* (New York: Simon & Schuster, 1995). 11.

drawn for qualitative analysis. The sinking of USS *Indianapolis* in the closing days of World War II and USS *Queenfish*'s tragic, and illegal, sinking of a Japanese mercy ship earlier that year; the investigations into fires aboard USS *Bennington*, and USS *Ranger*; collisions involving USS *Brownson* and USS *Charles H. Roan*, USS *Wasp* and USS *Hobson*, USS *Hartley* and Motor Vessel *Blue Master*, USS *Frank E. Evans* and HMAS *Melbourne*, USS *John F. Kennedy* and USS *Belknap*, and USS *McFaul* and USS *Winston S. Churchill*; the attacks on USS *Stark* and USS *Cole*; and an aircraft accident aboard USS *William P. Lawrence* provide insight into how the Navy handles crimes of command, and how today's actions differ from past years.

While there are some who place the onus for change on American society, or the introduction of women to the Navy, or the great and terrible weight of nuclear weapons, and still others who ignore change insisting on a "tradition older even than the traditions of the country itself," the clear and irrefutable fact is the modern Navy removes, and discards, commanding officers more than any other time in the past seventy years.

Why? Because a lack of naval war experience combined with a technocratic concept of responsibility and accountability warped Navy culture from one capable of understanding and practicing the *art* of leadership into one that worships the *science*, and infallibility, of technology. The paradox of great responsibility without equal authority now combines with a false ethical binary of only one right answer, which is at odds with a world where ethical decisions are as gray as the ships these officers command. The Navy's own writings, shown in the fourteen cases highlighted here, show that change. That very language traces back to the Navy's greatest technocrat, Admiral Hyman Rickover, the father of the nuclear navy, who in 63 years of naval service commanded at sea for three months, in 1937.

Acknowledging change is only part of the overall analysis. Even if Admiral Rickover provided the impetus, why has the Navy changed? What traditions or processes propelled the Navy towards a deviant form of accountability? What can

been, a natural nexus of man and machine. Many individual human beings crew each navy ship, but a single person leads those ships in a historical hierarchical manner: the Captain. If the global order relies on America and her Navy, then her Navy relies on leadership from her captains. Admirals make and set policy, but on the seas, the lieutenants, lieutenant commanders, commanders and captains in command of ships are the ones providing and enforcing security.

In leadership circles, there are few myths as strong as that of a ship captain. From explorers Christopher Columbus and Vasco De Gama to warriors John Paul Jones and Francis Drake, diplomat Matthew Perry or even starship captains Jean Luc Picard and James Tiberius Kirk, the myth pervades life and art. Aphorisms like "women and children first" combine with the historical understanding that a ship captain is the sole word of authority aboard ship and every decision, large or small, rests squarely on the Captain's shoulders. A captain's impact lasts long after a command tour is complete. Promotions, evaluations, special selection programs, officer and enlisted retention are all impacted by the commanding officer. Every sailor keeps something of the captain for the rest of that sailor's life. Knowingly or unknowingly a captain's strengths and weaknesses are eventually spread into other commands.[1]

Within the Navy commanding officers are seen, known, and conceptually understood, however, there are still very few of them. In the 2018 Navy there are fewer than 300 ships – and commensurately fewer than 300 commanding officers of ships - commonly called 'Captain' regardless of rank and sometimes more informally called 'Skipper.' In a country of over 300 million, Navy ship commanding officers make up roughly .0001% of the population. Captains are in command for roughly two years, are in their early forties and live at least 30 years after leaving their command tours, which means that the overall population of former commanding officers is still only .001% of

---

[1] Robert B. Hunt, "Monsarrat Was Wrong," *Proceedings*, February 1997.

the U.S. population. In other words, of every 100,000 people, there is one current or former Navy ship captain. Yet, everyone has a concept of a ship's captain, a general knowledge of their existence, their power and their responsibility. Some from history books, but far more from fiction – both literary and theatrical; book, play, and film. While one may debate the accuracy of a Kirk, Picard, or even Sparrow we cannot escape the reality that most Americans never meet, much less know, a ship captain and those fictional portrayals are what shape their opinions and those opinions end up shaping culture and law.

Navy Culture

Navy culture builds on traditions of the sea and seafaring in a nearly unbroken line from the British Empire through today's modern ships of steel and nuclear weapons. One common saying is that the United States Navy is "over 240 years of tradition, unaffected by progress;" clearly not fully true, however, tradition is a such a cornerstone of naval life that the word is an unofficial fourth core value and the single most common rationale for any action. "Tradition" is used in many ways and forms and often interchangeably with custom and routine.

However, tradition is not the bedrock historical habit commonly believed. In reality, cultures usually invent traditions, consciously creating and adapting them for unique and specific reasons. "The term 'invented tradition' is used in a broad, but not imprecise sense…[and].. includes both 'traditions' actually invented, constructed and formally instituted and those emerging in a less easily traceable manner within a brief and dateable period..." The purposes of these "invented traditions" are to "inculcate certain values and norms of behaviour [sic] by repetition, which automatically implies continuity with the past."[2] These creations are "responses to novel situations which take the form of reference to old situations"[3] where tradition differs from convention or routine (lacking significant ritual or symbolic function) and custom (which is flexible where tradition is not).[4]

This created tradition appears and reappears in naval thinking. The most commonly cited form comes from one of the cases later discussed. Following a 1952 collision at sea in which an aircraft carrier cut USS *Hobson* in half killing 176 sailors, including her captain, the *Wall Street Journal* published an editorial which reads in part:

> On the sea there is a tradition older even than the traditions of the country itself and wiser in its age than this new custom. It is the tradition that with responsibility goes authority and with them both goes accountability. This accountability is not for the intentions but for the deed. The captain of a ship, like the captain of a state, is given honor and privileges and trust beyond other men. But let him set the wrong course, let him touch ground, let him bring disaster to his ship or to his men, and he must answer for what he has done. No matter what, he cannot escape...[5]

This article has been reproduced and repeated so often that the lessons within are now mythic in nature and scope. Adherents, especially those with limited understanding of history, are unaware that the lessons are more modern than mythic. The lessons are relevant, but they are not as clear as some profess, or even as well understood as some interpret. In fact, in "Hobson's Choice" we have the first mention of "a tradition older even than the traditions of the country"- the

---

[2] Hobsbawm, E. J., and T. O. Ranger. *The Invention of Tradition* (Cambridge: Cambridge University Press, 1983). 1.
[3] ibid 2.
[4] ibid 2-3.
[5] "Hobson's Choice." *Wall Street Journal* (1923 - Current file): 10. May 14, 1952. ProQuest. Web. 10 Dec. 2013.

origination of "with responsibility goes authority and with them both goes accountability;" two ideals firmly embedded in today's Navy.

Modern Navy culture is largely affected by two concepts – women and World War II. World War II looms large over modern naval thinking. At the United States Naval War College, Pacific battles against the Japanese are studied and dissected. Novels of the war, including *Mister Roberts, The Caine Mutiny, Winds of War,* and *War and Remembrance,* are favorites among officers and sailors alike. Women are the modern impact, with female service at sea allowed in two periods - aboard non-combatant ships in the early 1970s, aboard combatant surface ships since 1995, and submarines since 2015. The period between women first embarking ships in the 1970s and embarking surface combatants in 1995 was one of Navy leadership's most turbulent times, and a time oft written about.

The 1991 Tailhook Scandal provides a central core of writings. More than 100 women, both civilian and active duty, were assaulted at a naval aviation convention in Las Vegas, Nevada. The incident was a social watershed, not only for what happened in Las Vegas, but what happened afterward. The scandal and botched investigation directly claimed the careers of a Secretary of the Navy, a Chief of Naval Operations, at least three admirals, and almost a dozen other officers. The scandal tarnished the reputations of many others, and "tailhook" remains shorthand for an embarrassing, and revealing, chapter in naval history. However, writings on Tailhook deal more with the investigations, or recommendations for the future of women in the service than they do with any crimes of command. Sexual assault, drunken debauchery, botched investigations, and general incompetence[6] may be crimes, but they are not crimes of command. Crimes of command, in their purest sense, are

---

[6] Browne, Kinglsey. *Military Sex Scandals from Tailhook to the Present: The Cure Can Be Worse than the Disease* (Detroit: Wayne State University Law School, 2147483647) and Vistica, Gregory L.. *Fall from Glory: The Men Who Sank the U.S. Navy.* (New York: Simon & Schuster, 1995)

solely related to being in command. Crimes of command occur when a commander violates the ideal of command.

'Command' in the United States Navy

Navy culture in turn begets and rises from, a subculture of command. While there are only 300 ships, there are more than 2,500 commanding officers. However, the responsibility, authority, and risk for commanders ashore are unequal to commanders at sea. Command of an aircraft squadron and command of a ship are command. However, they are not identical. In understanding the concept of command, a broader review provides context. While the risks are less, the selection process and legal regime for command at sea and command ashore are identical.

In the past decade, almost 300 senior Navy officials were removed from their positions of authority. A "senior Navy official" denotes someone in a position of extraordinary trust, authority or responsibility. A legal term, the concept is generally accepted to mean an admiral, senior civilian executive, commanding officer, executive officer, or senior enlisted advisor. 300 is a large number providing the perception that larger numbers of officers are being moved from their jobs. The reasons for those removals range from operational errors and accidents to sensationalist personal peccadillos. To understand why they were removed, we much first understand why they were there. What is a Navy commanding officer? How is a commanding officer selected? What laws govern the commander?

One place to begin understanding what a Captain is and does is the United States Naval Institute's manual on *Command at Sea*. First published in 1943, *Command at Sea* is now in its sixth edition. This unofficial publication is the only definitive guide for Navy commanding officers. Despite its unofficial status, the book is issued to each new commanding officer graduating from the Navy's Surface Warfare Officer School

Command. The core language on command has changed little since the third edition (1966). Tellingly, the first edition (there is no second) does not address the independence of command; a concept first addressed in the third edition with "More often than not, commanding officers are directed to accomplish a mission without being told specifically how to do so." The fourth edition (1982) expands the discussion with an entire section on "The Independence of the Commander" that, unsurprisingly, follows the section on accountability. The previous comment of being told what to do but not how to do it remains but is modified by the following statement: "In recent years ... traditional independence has been modified in practice. The issue today is not too much liberality, but rather a growing tendency of high command to exercise control in too great detail." This caveat remains in the current edition, over thirty years later. Of note, the fourth edition, published in 1982, predates or presages, the ubiquity of modern communications.[7] In January 1941, future Chief of Naval Operations, Admiral Ernest King issued a message to the Atlantic Fleet regarding the "exercise of command" wherein he detailed what he saw as an excess of detail in orders and instructions. Predicting America's entry into the war, King urged commanders to stop telling subordinates how to do things, instead urging them to recall and leverage the "initiative of the subordinate" closing his message with this guidance:

> (a) adopt the premise that the echelon commanders are competent in their several command echelons unless and until they themselves prove otherwise;
> (b) teach them that they are not only expected to be competent for their several command echelons but that it is required of them that they be competent;

---

[7] Cope, Harley F., *Command at Sea* (Annapolis, Md.: United States Naval Institute, 1943), Cope, Harley F., and Howard Bucknell. (3rd ed. 1966), Mack, William P., Albert H. Konetzni, and Harley F. Cope. (4th ed. 1982), Stavridis, James, and William P. Mack (5th ed. 1999), Stavridis, James, and Robert Girrier. (6th ed. 2010) Note: there is no second edition.

(c) train them — by guidance and supervision — to exercise foresight, to think, to judge, to decide and to act for themselves;
(d) stop 'nursing' them;
(e) finally, train ourselves to be satisfied with 'acceptable solutions' even though they are not 'staff solutions' or other particular solutions that we ourselves prefer.[8]

The two most recent editions of *Command at Sea* open with a quote from Nicholas Monsarrat's *The Cruel Sea*, a 1951 novel about Royal Navy sailors in World War II's Battle of the Atlantic.

> The Captain carried them all. For him, there was no set watch, nor any established time to rest and retreat from the harsh conditions of the sea. He was wonderfully reliable, uncomplaining, and ready to take any watch, no matter the hour or the situation. He was the kind of Captain to have.[9]

The quote is a superb introduction to a chapter filled with words like 'burden' and 'heavy.' Long quotations from law and regulation. Expansion of "the responsibility of the commanding officer for his or her command is absolute" and treatises on accountability, including portions of the Wall Street Journal editorial on USS *Hobson*, frame a Captain's role as all-encompassing, never-ending, complete and total. A heady task for someone human, possessing neither omniscience nor omnipotence. Monsarrat, while writing fiction, well-articulated the ideal of a commanding officer at war, but only if that commanding officer is at war, and at sea. And possibly a little more than human. Or maybe even a little less.[10]

The United States Naval Institute publishes a number of

---

[8] King, Ernest. CINCLANT SERIAL (053) of January 21, 1941 Subject: Exercise of Command — Excess of Detail in Orders and Instructions
[9] Monsarrat, Nicholas, *The Cruel Sea* in Stavridis and Mack (5th ed. 1999), 5 and Stavridis and Girrier (6th ed. 2010), 1.
[10] Hunt

other semi-official books and guides like *Command at Sea*. The *Bluejacket's Manual* provides guidance for enlisted sailors, the *Newly Commissioned Naval Officer's Guide* for officer candidates and newly commissioned officers, the *Division Officer's Guide* for group leadership at the junior level, the *Watch Officer's Guide* for shipboard officers, and *The Naval Officer's Guide*. The *Newly Commissioned Officer's Guide* was first published in 2009 to provide additional information not found in the other books. *The Bluejacket's Manual* and *The Naval Officer's Guide* provide both core and generalist information for officers and enlisted sailors where *Command at Sea* is solely focused on command. *The Bluejacket's Manual* was first published in 1902 and the *Naval Officer's Guide* in 1943. The other manuals followed between 1952 and 2009. All remain in print, however only *The Bluejacket's Manual* and the *Naval Officer's Guide* provide sufficient information between 1945 and 2015 to illuminate the Navy's changes, and only the *Naval Officer's Guide* addresses command, albeit in less detail than *Command at Sea*.

The 1943 First Edition of *The Naval Officer's Guide* provides a wartime focus for the naval officer recognizing that officers assuming command in war likely have less sea-going experience than officers in the peacetime Navy.[11] This edition also restates and explains Navy Regulations with an emphasis on the former. The chapter on *Assumption of Command* mentions responsibility a dozen times, accountability three times and each mention is in relation to financial accounts. The closing chapter is a treatise on leadership from Chief of Naval Operations Ernest J. King, originally delivered during the U.S. Naval Academy class of 1942's graduation - six months after Pearl Harbor.

King's speech was titled "The Responsibilities of Leadership." In it he reminds the graduating midshipmen that

---

[11] Arthur A. Ageton, *The Naval Officer's Guide*, 1st ed. (New York, NY: Whittlesey House, 1943). 227.

war remains a human endeavor, reiterating themes from his January 1941 message to the Atlantic Fleet on "exercise of command." He also makes an interesting commentary on traditions, calling them "no more than testimonials to the successes of our predecessors." [12] Though two more editions of the guide were published by 1946, the sections on command and King's speech remain unchanged.

These books and manuals use naval language and concepts for command; a distillation of that information provides a common understanding of the command ideal and how an officer rises to that position. To be sure, command is a lofty position; sometimes also described as lonely. Captains have some material perquisites or trappings of command – good reserved parking spaces, individual cabins, and reserved personal chairs on the bridge and bridgewings number among them. Leading some of the best trained men and women with the highest character and motivation for service also provides a real and very personal sense of accomplishment.[13]

What is a command?

The easiest command to comprehend is a ship - be it a destroyer, cruiser, battleship, submarine, or aircraft carrier. The Navy also has shore commands, in this case, naval bases and naval stations are the easiest to understand, but sometimes a single naval base has multiple commands within its boundaries. Any boater understands the responsibility of seafaring, especially the solo sailor who can rely on no one else. However, regardless of the crew size only one person can decide and direct the path of a ship. Whether that individual directly controls the wheel and engines, rudder and sheets, or paddles or does so indirectly with force of personality, leadership, and law, only one person can be in charge at sea. An aircraft carrier at sea has up to, or even more, than seven commanding officers aboard.

---

[12] ibid. 502.
[13] Hunt

However, only one of them is captain of that ship. The others command the air wing, individual aircraft squadrons, or a group of ships also known as a squadron. Each ship has only one captain, one person with overall authority for the ship and its crew. Traditionally even superior commanders are reticent to challenge the authority of a subordinate commander over his ship, crew, squadron, or base.[14]

How do officers rise to command?

There are some important prerequisites for officers are not just given command, they are selected from among those who meet very specific requirements. First, one must seek and earn a commission in the United States Navy. Afterwards, the new officer selects a warfare community. There are over two dozen distinct communities across four larger groups - the Unrestricted Line who command ships, aircraft, and submarines; the Restricted Line who supervise maintenance and personnel commands and activities; the Staff Corps who are the Navy's externally licensed professionals including doctors, dentists, nurses, and lawyers; and the Limited Duty Officer who are prior enlisted sailors commissioned into specialist roles. For this discussion, career training is limited to the Unrestricted Line, as only they can command at sea. Members of the Unrestricted Line are called "line officers."

Current line officer career progression models stress generalization; however, that generalization also contains significant specialization. All line officers must gain some level of proficiency in management, fleet operations, and equipment operation and maintenance. Officers are encouraged to broaden their experience through tours that span the spectrum of operations and equipment within their medium (air, surface, subsurface) and even across geographic locations. Each of these

---

[14] Robert F. Dunn, *Gear Up, Mishaps Down: The Evolution of Naval Aviation Safety, 1950-2000* (Annapolis, MD: Naval Institute Press, 2017). 49.

communities follows a similar path of increasing responsibility from division officer to department head to executive officer and finally command. Each of these tours is separated by assignment to shore duty to allow for maturation and broadening experience between operational tours. The primary differences occur in timing, selection flow points, and retention percentages. The broad experience gained in these career paths is the underpinning of the commanding officer's ability to understand in the broadest sense how the command operates.

Aviators undergo basic flight training, then an initial operational tour within a squadron. A support tour in either a training squadron, teaching new aviators, or in some other shore support role follows the operational tour. A "disassociated" tour is next as aviators go to sea in broadening roles as division officers in aviation focused ships or staffs. A department head tour and, hopefully, a rotation among the major departments (maintenance, operations, training) within the squadron is the last operational tour before command. A second shore tour brings staff experience followed by command screening and assignment as executive officer with subsequent command of the same squadron.

Submariners and surface warfare officers follow a similar path. Initial training is followed by division officer tours. Surface warfare officers serve aboard ships in either an operations, combat systems, or engineering billet for twenty-four-months with a transfer to a second ship and broadening tour in the "other" specialty. Submariners (ideally) rotate among submarine departments over a thirty-six-month tour. Basic qualification as an officer of the deck and warfare qualification occur during this tour. Both move to shore duty in either training, education, or staff commands followed by department head tours. Surface warfare officers do back to back tours, specialize within one of the major departments (operations, combat systems, and engineering), and qualify as tactical action officers (TAO). Submariners serve a single longer tour leading one department (navigation, combat systems, or engineering). A second shore tour provides staff experience and, following screening for executive officer, assignment as second in command. A third shore tour is an opportunity for assignment to additional staffs or the War College. Command screening brings the now specialized officer to command with minimal experience in two of the major shipboard departments. While the specific schools, length of instruction, and tour-length vary, the patterns themselves are remarkably consistent since World War II.[15]

Selection to command

The command selection process between 1945 and the mid-1970s was poorly documented. Groups of senior officers met in Washington, D.C. where they reviewed officer records and selected future commanding officers. In some cases, officers applied for command, in others they were simply selected from an available pool. There were clear instances, especially in the rise of the nuclear Navy, where individuals were specifically chosen for specific commands. However, unlike today, no clear process, timeline, rules or regulations for command selection were employed.

The modern selection process began in the mid-1970s and is generally consistent since then. Over time each warfare community (air, surface, subsurface) makes minor alterations, however the core remains the same. Arriving in command is part of a long process of education, training, experience, and evaluation,[16] and command remains the apotheosis of a naval career – especially command at sea. Officers compete for command as department heads and are selected to command somewhere in their fifteenth year of commissioned service and arrive in their first command somewhere close to their eighteenth year of service. In general, commanding officers are

---

[15] See Ageton and subsequent editions for more detail.
[16] Terrance J. McKearney, "The Path to Command," *Proceedings*, March 1978.

around forty years old. Captains in command are five years older, lieutenant commanders in command five years younger. Chief of Naval Operations James. L. Holloway wrote of his squadron commanders when he commanded USS Enterprise (CVN 65) in 1965 and 1966:

> A profile of the squadron commanders who served on board the Enterprise on the 1965-66 deployment would be typical of that found in any naval air wing at that time. All were mature officers, in their early forties, with more than twenty years' experience as commissioned officers, most of it flying planes off carriers. About half were graduates of the United States Naval Academy, and the others were products of the Naval Aviation Cadet Program at Pensacola, Florida, and the "regular" NROTC program. More than 60 percent had advanced degrees, mainly master's degrees in personnel management, aviation ordnance engineering, and aeronautical engineering.[17]

Aviation squadrons are invariably commanded by officers at the rank of commander and this profile is appropriate to commanders who today command ships, submarines, and aviation squadrons. Commander command being the center, captains in command are in their "Major Command" tour while lieutenant commanders in command are in "Early Command." The process for selection, however, is virtually identical.

Selection for Commander Command is predicated upon a single thing – performance as a Department Head at sea in a submarine, ship, or aircraft squadron with such performance clearly and well documented in an officer's fitness reports. The most important part of that documentation is how the individual officer ranked against peers. Officers ranked 1 of 4 are likely to screen for command. Officers ranked 3 or 4 of 4, unlikely.

The basic process by which a board selects a record is

---

[17] James L. Holloway, III, *Aircraft Carriers at War: A Personal Retrospective of Korea, Vietnam, and the Soviet Confrontation* (New York: Naval Institute Press, 2011). 188.

the same for command selection boards (screen boards) and promotion (statutory boards). The laws governing the boards are the same. The only differences lie in the information within the official record considered by the board to be important enough to warrant selection and the number of officers that can be selected.

The selection board meets in a room called "the tank." Board members present records to the other members and members then vote on those records. Individual fitness reports are not normally read or reviewed by the board when voting. The record is reviewed, in its entirety, by a board member known as the "briefer." This board member reads fitness reports, any letters to the board, and reviews any other information in the record. When presenting the record, a summation screen is shown on large display screens, and the briefer provides pertinent details. The briefer makes annotations on the summation showing performance trends or important distinction within the fitness reports…but the briefer has sole discretion in what is annotated.

When voting there is a small period for discussion (in many boards it can be less than two minutes). During that discussion any question can be asked about the presented record. Any officer with personal knowledge of positive or complimentary information may introduce that information at this time. Adverse information not contained within the official record cannot, by law and regulation, be presented to the board. No stories of "I heard that ship ran aground" or "Wow…why isn't that DUI showing up" or "Odd, I don't see the results of that IG investigation." If something is not in the record, it does not exist. It never happened and cannot be discussed. The Navy has a phrase: "boards pick records, not people." Of the records seen by selection boards over the past four decades, less than half are selected for command.[18]

---

[18] McKearney

By the time an officer takes command today, that commanding officer has experience at multiple positions and ranks.[19] A competitive board process selects every commanding officer. Every commanding officer attends some level of specific tailored training before taking command. Which should be expected. Commanders have much authority and discretion. Commanders must have the confidence of their subordinates and superiors.[20]

The Legal Regime

Today's laws and regulations did not exist when Monsarrat wrote - in either the U.S. or Royal Navy. While Monsarrat codified something many felt, but few articulated, after World War II a variety of laws and regulations moved what was once implicitly understood to something explicitly stated.

Current military law, the Uniform Code of Military Justice (UCMJ), was established in 1950 to link and codify disparate military justice systems into a single one, still administered separately by each service. Before the UCMJ, the Navy operated under regulations nicknamed "Rocks and Shoals" (the formal name was *Articles for the Government of the United States Navy* and later *U.S. Navy Regulations*). Modern *Navy Regulations* are subordinate to the UCMJ, but are codified within the Code of Federal Regulations, making them not only regulation but also Federal Law. From 1913 to 1947 *Navy Regulations* underwent 22 minor changes. In 1948 the Navy published completely new regulations, substantially altering over four decades of operations and guidance. The changes are easily seen in the language around the commanding officer, his authority, and his responsibilities. *Navy Regulations* since 1948 provide clear guidance on the responsibility and accountability of the commanding officer. The current version, published in

---

[19] ibid
[20] Matthew Dolan, "The Heavy Responsibilities of Command - Lessons to be Learned," *The Virginian-Pilot* (Norfolk), March 10, 2004.

1990, provides an entire chapter on the roles and responsibilities of the commanding officer. At 20 pages the guidance is five times greater than that for the Chief of Naval Operations, the Navy's senior most officer. The very first line of direction is clear "The responsibility of the commanding officer for his or her command is absolute."

However, that line is not present in *Navy Regulations* dated 1941 or prior. The closest comparable line relates to delegation. The 1941 edition reads: "The officer in command of a ship of war is not authorized to delegate his power except for carrying out the details of the general duties to be performed by his authority." It's 1948 companion reads: "While [the commanding officer] may, at his discretion, and when not contrary to law or regulations, delegate authority to his subordinates…such delegation…shall in no way relieve the commanding officer of his continued responsibility for…his entire command." The concepts are similar, but the language is significantly different.

Today's commanding officers work within a legal regime that requires they "shall use all proper means to foster high morale"[21] and in doing so may not "injure their subordinates by tyrannical or capricious conduct, or by abusive language."[22] Federal law further requires that

All commanding officers and others in authority in the naval service are required to show in themselves a good example of virtue, honor, patriotism, and subordination; to be vigilant in inspecting the conduct of all persons who are placed under their command; to guard against and suppress all dissolute and immoral practices, and to correct, according to the laws and regulations of the Navy, all persons who are guilty of them; and to take all

---

[21] United States, Department of the Navy, *Naval Regulations* (Washington, DC, 1990). Article 0820
[22] *Naval Regulations*, Article 1023

necessary and proper measures, under the laws, regulations, and customs of the naval service, to promote and safeguard the morale, the physical well-being, and the general welfare of the officers and enlisted persons under their command or charge.[23]

It is these laws that commanding officers are subject to - these laws seen through the lens of an invented tradition.

Investigations, Administrative and Legal Proceedings

The other side of the legal regime is the quest for truth, accountability, or blame. The *Manual of the Judge Advocate General* (JAGMAN) governs modern naval investigations, supplementing the *Manual for Courts-Martial*. Within this document are the procedures for everything from nonpunitive corrective measures through courts-martial involving the death penalty. Chapter II provides procedures for "Administrative Investigations." This chapter provides commanders the authority and guidance to investigate, and dispose of, crimes of command (and other crimes, of course).

The first step in determining whether an investigation may be required is a *preliminary inquiry*. The preliminary inquiry serves to establish a timeline of events, as well as identify and interview witnesses. A written or oral report to the commander directing the preliminary inquiry informs the commander in how to proceed. That commander may take no action, record a Line of Duty determination, conduct a command investigation, convene a litigation-report investigation, or convene a court or board of inquiry.[24]

The option to take no action is self-explanatory. A Line of Duty determination relates to individual injury or death. The remainder, command investigation, litigation-report

---

[23] 10 U.S. Code § 5947 (1956).
[24] United States Navy, Office of the Judge Advocate General. *Manual of the Judge Advocate General* (Washington, DC: U.S. Dept. of the Navy, Office of the Judge Advocate General, 2012). 2-7 to 2-9.

investigation, and court or board of inquiry all begin in the same way - with a decision by the commander, known as the convening authority, and a subsequent order. The convening authority designates an individual or group to conduct the investigation, and the type of desired investigation is part of that order. The convening authority selects investigating officers who are "best qualified by reason of their age, education, training, experience, length of service, and temperament...[who are] senior in rank to any individual whose conduct is subject to inquiry."[25] The order provides the purpose and scope of the investigation, requires findings of fact which explain the event, directs the investigator to seek advice and assistance of a judge advocate and specifies a completion date. The convening authority may amend his order at any time, changing board membership, investigators, scope, and completion date or simply to provide more instruction to the investigator.

Administrative investigations are not courts-martial, the standard of proof is much lower, and commensurately the potential penalties are expected to be lower. For administrative investigations, a "preponderance of the evidence" or a "more likely than not"[26] finding by the investigator is sufficient to establish fact. Administrative investigations vary in format but usually include a preliminary statement, findings of fact, opinions, and recommendations. The preliminary statement provides a summation of the investigation's results, the nature of the investigation, and any difficulties the investigator encountered.[27]

The lowest level investigation for crimes of command is the "command investigation." The command investigation is the most common and sometimes called a "JAGMAN investigation." Command investigations are appropriate for ship grounding, shipboard flooding, fires, or collision and aviation mishaps so long as they are not identified as major incidents.

---

[25] *Manual of the Judge Advocate General*, 2-11.
[26] ibid, 2-13.
[27] ibid, 2-17.

Major incidents are

> An extraordinary incident occurring during the course of official duties resulting in multiple deaths, substantial property loss, or substantial harm to the environment, where the circumstances suggest a significant departure from the expected level of professionalism, leadership, judgment, communication, state of material readiness, or other relevant standard. Substantial property loss or other harm is that which greatly exceeds what is normally encountered in the course of day-to-day operations. These cases are often accompanied by national public and press interest and significant congressional attention. They may also have the potential of undermining public confidence in the Naval service. That the case is a major incident may be apparent when it is first reported or as additional facts become known.[28]

This definition is quoted in its entirety for a reason. All fourteen cases presented fit the criteria for a major incident which in turn should prompt a court or board of inquiry, however, in recent decades the resulting report was a command investigation under which a single investigating officer collected and selected information to create a final report.

On completion, the report is delivered to the convening authority who has 30 calendar days to act on the recommendations of the report. The convening authority may decide the investigation has no interest outside the command and file it, or may choose to endorse the report, in writing. The endorsement must recommend approval or disapproval of the findings of fact, opinions or recommendations. It may also add, delete, or modify findings of fact, opinions or recommendations. The convening authority should comment on any corrective action either taken or recommended, and whether any form of punitive or non-punitive action should result from the incident.

---

[28] ibid, A-2-a to A-2-b.

If endorsed, the convening authority forwards the investigation, via the convening authority's chain of command, to the next superior general court-martial convening authority.[29] The intermediate endorsing office must also recommend approval or disapproval of the findings of fact, opinions or recommendations.

Command investigations are retained by the convening authority's command for two years after which they are forwarded to the Investigations Branch of the Judge Advocate General (Code 15) for filing. Not all command investigations are retained, not all are filed with Code 15, and not all commanders removed from command are investigated via command investigation (or any other).

A litigation-report investigation is next in the hierarchy. The litigation-report is solely for incidents that may end in claims or civil litigation for damage or death by Navy personnel within the scope of their official duties. Litigation-reports are specifically excluded from incidents involving active-duty deaths, or in major incidents. Litigation-reports are also protected under attorney work product and therefore exempt from release under the Freedom of Information Act.[30] One way to keep investigation reports from public release is to create them under the litigation-report guidance, even where the JAGMAN specifically prohibits their use. As the litigation-report is not releasable as public record they were not used for data collection or analysis in this study.

The next level of investigation is Courts of Inquiry and Boards of Inquiry. These investigative bodies are for the express purpose of major incidents, or "serious or significant events."[31] A separate Judge Advocate General Instruction titled *Procedures Applicable to Courts and Boards of Inquiry* provides specific guidance for their conduct. A Court of Inquiry has at least three commissioned officers and appointed legal counsel.

---

[29] See JAGMAN appendix A-1-y for a list of GCMCAs.
[30] *Manual of the Judge Advocate General*, 2-18.
[31] ibid, 2-28.

The court uses hearings to obtain information; individuals under suspicion of misconduct are designated as 'parties to the court' and granted specific rights, including legal counsel. The court may also order military personnel to appear and testify and may issue subpoenas to civilian witnesses. The Board of Inquiry differs only in that it may not subpoena civilian witness, but may compel naval personnel to appear and testify. The report review process is identical to the command investigation.[32]

The JAGMAN dates to at least 1961 replacing the earlier *Naval Courts and Boards* published in 1937. While *Naval Courts and Boards* provides more detailed information for conducting the same fact-finding bodies, the core authorities, powers, and requirements are the same as the modern JAGMAN. Therefore, while some administrative changes arrived between 1945 and today, the general requirements for naval investigations remain unchanged. However, the implementation and execution of those general requirements changed significantly between 1945 and 2015. Court-martial rates dropped after World War II before rising in the 1960s and 1970s then dropping again. Figure 1 collates data from the Annual Report of the Code Committee on Military Justice filed with the Congressional Committees on Armed Services for the years 1952 through 2014 and information gathered via Freedom of Information Act requests.

At the height, the Navy annually court-martialed up to 4% of its sailors. Since 1994 the number lies around one percent - for the last decade below one percent and in recent years less than one-tenth of one percent. Nonjudicial punishment, which does not have the same legal standards or same legal review, sat at roughly 25% from 1977 to 1983 before also steadily falling to roughly five percent in recent years.

---

[32] ibid, 2-29 to 2-31.

Legal reforms made courts more public and the public nature of the courts, and commensurate costs, drove more cases towards administrative solutions. Over that same time frame Navy culture, regulation, and law regarding hazing, sexual impropriety, sexual assault, alcohol, drugs, and homosexuality have all changed. What courts-martial of the 1960s saw as "horseplay" is now seen as sexual assault.[33] What was once determined via a Court or Board of Inquiry followed by Court Martial is now handled via Command Investigation and Non-Judicial Punishment or other administrative means. As the likelihood and severity of punishment rose, the formality of investigation decreased.

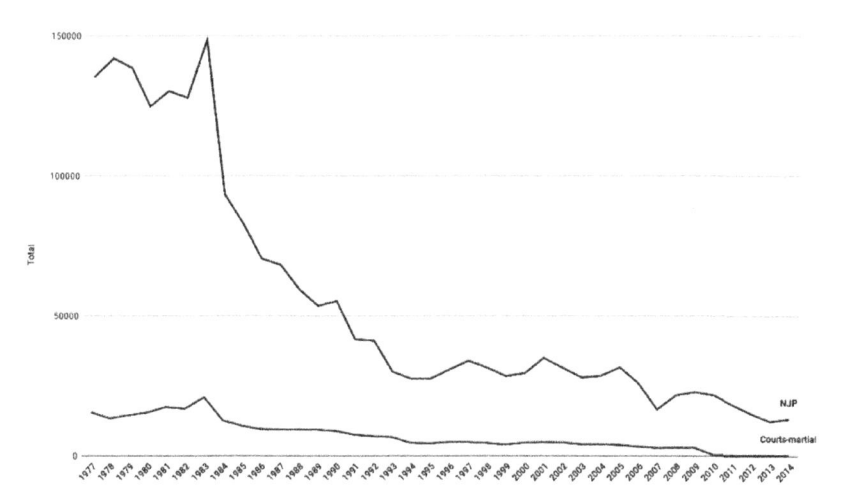

Figure 1. Annual per-capita courts-martial and nonjudicial punishments

---

[33] Elizabeth Lutes Hillman, *Defending America* (Princeton, N.J.: Princeton University Press, 2005).

The Search

Twice this century the Navy sought answers to command reliefs; once in 2004 and again in 2010. The 2004 study by the Naval Inspector General examined cases of officers formally detached for cause (DFC) from 1999 through 2004 after a perceived increase in command removals. The findings included revelations that the Navy does not track removal from command, that when commanders conducted investigations those reports were not retained more than three years, and that personal behavior, often including alcohol or adultery, was the most prevalent reason for removal. The study found no systemic issues or significant commonalities in the reliefs or why the Navy saw an increase of reliefs. In all, the study found that less than one percent of commanding officers were removed from command each year.[34]

Between 2004 and 2010 removal from command dropped from the 2003 high of 18 to 9 in 2005 and 8 in 2006 before rising to 17 in 2007 and reaching 24 in 2010. Working from where the 2004 study left off, a new review looked at all removals between January 1, 2005, and June 30, 2010 - 87 individual cases. From those 87 the study again found "no correlation between CO DFCs and career paths, personality traits, accession sources, time in command, or year groups."[35] The study also found that the recommendations from the 2004 study had "no discernable impact"[36] on the rate of removal from command. The lack of correlation was attributed to "the very low rate of approximately one percent of COs being relieved annually...[compared to] the relatively large sample size

---

[34] United States, Department of the Navy, Naval Inspector General, *Report of Commanding Officers Detached for Cause* (Washington, DC, 2004).
[35] Ibid.
[36] United States, Department of the Navy, Naval Inspector General, *Report of Commanding Officers Detached for Cause* (Washington, DC, 2010).

(approximately 1,500 COs) and the small variance in the number of DFCs on a year-to-year basis prevent making statistical inferences with any significant degree of confidence."[37]

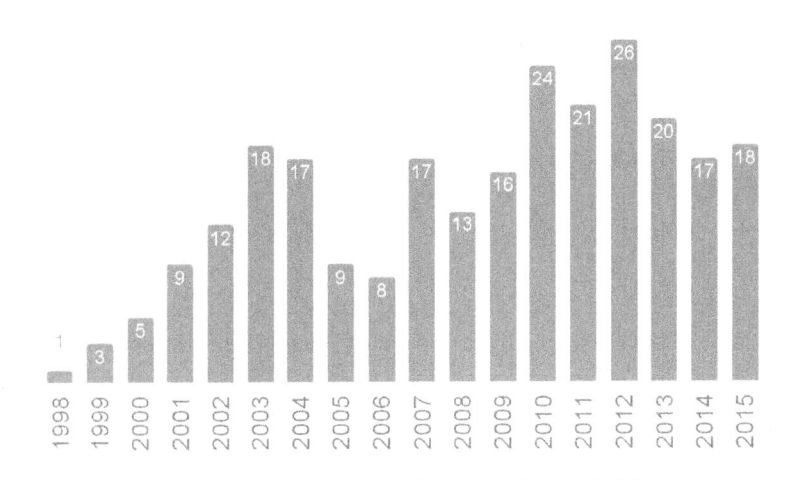

Figure 2. Number of commanders removed between 1998 and 2015

If two official studies were incapable of meaningful results, how might one address command reliefs? How might we look at reliefs beyond the singular or the sensational? One way is by expanding the examination of U.S. Navy incidents and accidents beyond the small sample of five years. While an examination of 240 years of naval history is valuable, there are clear and defined epochs within the U.S. Navy, and any comparison between commanding officers in 1805, or even 1905, with those in 2005 is frankly, moot. Modern military and naval history, especially since World War II is far more holistically consistent. Even with the immense technological changes of nuclear weapons, nuclear power, guided missiles, jet aircraft, and satellite communications the complexities of operations at sea remain surprising consistent over these seventy

---

[37] Naval Inspector General (2010).

years. In fact, no change comparable to the move from sail to steam or the introduction of naval aviation occurred in the seventy years after World War II. Even nuclear power, with its inherent technological danger, is just another way to heat steam. The legal regime under which the Navy operates is largely the same today as it was in 1950. The administrative procedures are more codified and regulated, but also remain comparable enough that an officer from 1950 would understand the processes of 1980, or 2010.

Prosopography provides one format for study. By looking at varying cases over a specified time period one can establish trends not otherwise identifiable through specific individuals. This is even more ideal for individuals who fell short of Navy standards and are at best infamous, and more likely simply lost to history. However, by combining prosopography with basic textual analysis, a chronological cultural trend establishes itself.

As the Navy had no central repository for command removal to support the 2004 study the first step is building such a list through archival research. Contemporary removals are easiest to catalog as the Navy notifies the press of each commanding officer, executive officer, and command master chief removal. Identifying incidents prior to 1990 is more challenging, with some actively hidden by Navy leaders.[38] Some removals can be identified from general Internet or newspaper database searches. Some come from stories told by other officers. The closest to a single repository lies in William Arkin's *Naval Accidents, 1945-1988* which catalogs almost a thousand incidents and accidents. However, what happened to the commanding officer is not the focus of *"Naval Accidents"* and Arkin rarely provides information on the aftermath of the accidents he catalogued. Naval Safety Center "Class 'A'" incidents, made available via the Freedom of Information Act, provided 1,088 individual incidents, however up to a third

---

[38] Vistica, 26.

duplicated *Naval Accidents* and another 446 provide no narrative information for the corresponding casualty. Class 'A' incidents are those involving a fatality, permanent disability, damage exceeding $2 million or destruction of an aircraft. Therefore, neither list is all-encompassing or exhaustive for crimes of command.

However, these incidents are almost solely focused on ships. Likewise, the lists of commanding officers for ships are more readily available than those for submarines or aircraft squadrons. In some cases, aviation squadron commanders were removed for operational incidents, but they were rare and public acknowledgement of those removals was, and is, also very rare. Submarine incidents, many of which are cataloged in *Naval Accidents*, are also rare, their reporting rare, and the names of their commanders not as well publicized. Recognizing these limitations and focusing on surface ships, the traditional centrality of any navy, provides an acceptable limit of extant or gatherable data with sufficient sample size to draw conclusions.

The core of the research began with each incident in *Naval Accidents* and from the Naval Safety Center, and also includes those incidents identified in open press and via any search or research method possible. Each item, including those listed in "Naval Accidents" and from the Naval Safety Center, was then verified through any accessible and reputable reference. In all, the research identified and verified 1,557 incidents. However, even this list is not comprehensive or exhaustive. It is, however, sufficiently representative to draw conclusions.

After establishing that an incident occurred the next step was determining who commanded and then what happened to the commanding officer. For some of the more storied incidents there are well-researched books. In some cases, the incidents entered the public consciousness through film or television. In many of them only the direct participants and subsequent investigators recall the events and nothing official, or unofficial, remains outside of oral histories and newspaper articles.

For less well known or publicized events you can reasonably determine who commanded a ship in a particular period via an online database at www.navsource.org. Sometimes news articles name the subject commander, and later articles contain information about courts-martial or administrative proceedings against an officer. In others command histories, biographies, oral histories, or even obituaries provide insight. Some cases require a line of inductive reasoning. If an officer in command is relieved within weeks of an incident, and that relief is earlier than might reasonably be expected, then it is more than likely the officer was removed because of that incident. However, in some cases, an officer might be relieved early for some other wholly unrelated reason.

Another possible discriminator is determining whether an officer promotes to the next higher rank following an incident or possible removal. Once a commanding officer's name is linked to an incident Navy records were searched to determine whether that officer was ever promoted again and whether that officer went on to command again. Establishing whether an officer promotes requires identifying each commanding officer and then locating that officer's name in the *Register of Retired Commissioned Officers, Regular and Reserve, in the United States Navy.* Any subsequent command can be determined via biographies, obituaries, newspaper articles, or the database at www.navsource.org.

Of the 1,557 identified incidents, appropriate commands were linked to 1,292 specific commanding officers. Of the 1,292 identified officers, roughly one-third promoted, while two-thirds did not. It was then possible to generate a quantitative understanding of how many commanding officers remained in command after an incident, i.e. how many continued with a viable career and how many did not.

From here I selected fourteen representative cases. The candidate cases included available investigations and sufficient primary source information to compose a narrative and illustrate the subsequent changes to the Navy. Additionally, and to be as accurate as possible, I selected comparable incidents. Fires and their causes differ greatly from collisions, or groundings, and their respective causes. Therefore, a major fire from the 1950s is best compared to a major fire in the 1990s, a collision to a collision, a grounding to a grounding and so on. This grand story is of a system, administered by a set of rules and procedures governed by institutional culture. It is also the story of individuals and choices, some made on the spur of the moment, in fear, and sometimes solitude.[39]

Despite almost 1,300 possible incidents, there are fewer than two dozen potential case studies - cases with sufficient investigation material available, or even in existence. Most histories are linear narratives, following horizontal lines of famous battles or specific incidents in time or vertical lines of individuals across time. This narrative is diagonal in nature, looking at a number of specific incidents and tracking changes in technology, administration, and values across time. This book is not a narrative of failure, but an examination of command from historical, legal, philosophical and psychological perspectives which together provide a path for questioning, challenging, and examining[40] naval concepts of command. Using primary source material, including official Navy investigations and incident reports, this book shows how the Navy uses the same language of command and crimes of command over the seven decades, yet the actions related to that language are now different thus ultimately providing insight into the question: *Why does the Navy remove commanding officers and has the Navy always removed as many commanding officers as it does today?*

---

[39] Chris Bray, *Court-martial: How Military Justice Has Shaped America from the Revolution to 9/11 and Beyond* (New York: W.W. Norton & Company, 2016). 273.
[40] Gortner, 517.

2: 1945-1965

The truth depends on where you start and this truth starts in the final days of World War II. In August 1945 the United States Navy was the largest and most powerful navy in the world, arguably the most powerful navy ever. Not only was the fleet at its largest, but it was also multiple times larger than at any other time before or since, with 6,768 ships and 3.3 million sailors. By comparison in 1940, only five years earlier, the Navy was 478 ships and 161,000 sailors. Five years later, 634 ships and 381,000 sailors. Today, 277 ships and 324,000 sailors.

Within those 6,768 ships some officers were removed from command, but very few. In the final year of the war, 164 ships were lost; either missing in action, sunk or seriously damaged and never repaired. Of those 164 ships, only one commander faced courts-martial for his actions.

USS *Indianapolis* - 1945

Despite its size, this monstrous navy was combat experienced, accustomed to risk, and loss. Like today, captains in command were officers with twenty or more years of service, much of it pre-war and in many different ship types and with many commands. One such officer was Charles B. McVay, III, commanding officer of USS *Indianapolis* (CA 35).

McVay was the son of an admiral and a model captain. He graduated from the United States Naval Academy in 1920 and over the next twenty-four years served in twelve ships, commanding at every rank from lieutenant to captain. He commanded patrol craft USS *Sylph* (PC 5) as a lieutenant in 1927 and 1928. As a lieutenant commander, he commanded destroyer USS *Ellis* (DD 154) from 1935 to 1936 and Yangtze River gunboat USS *Luzon* (PG 47) from 1938 to 1939. In 1940 he recommissioned USS *Kaweah* (AO 15), a twenty-year old oiler, before transferring to the light cruiser USS *Cleveland* (CL

55) where he served as executive officer. He remained aboard *Cleveland* supporting the November 1942 landings in North Africa (Operation TORCH) and later earned the Silver Star for action off the Solomon Islands in March 1943. While aboard *Cleveland* he was promoted to Captain. Returning to Washington McVay led the Joint Intelligence Staff from May 1943 to October 1944. He took command of *Indianapolis* on November 18, 1944.[1]

McVay was handsome, dashing, and rumored to have dated Hollywood starlets before marrying a Hawaiian heiress. His crew saw him as confident and capable, but also approachable and human. He enjoyed shooting skeet at sea as well as throwing a fishing line over the side, sometimes alone, sometimes inviting his crew to join him.[2]

USS *Indianapolis* joined the fleet in 1930, one of a series of so-called "treaty cruisers" built within the constraints of the Washington Naval Treaty of 1922 that limited the overall size, number, and type of ships built by the major naval powers – something of a naval version of the modern salary cap in professional sports. She was big for the time, 10,000 tons and 610 feet long. Eight steam boilers provided 107,000 shaft horsepower and could move the ship at almost 33 knots. She carried nine eight-inch guns, eight five-inch guns, and four float planes. Her armor belt varied between three and five inches thick. While designed to carry 950 sailors, her complement exceeded 1,200 during the war.[3]

Under McVay's command, *Indianapolis* participated in attacks on Iwo Jima and Tokyo while also serving as Admiral Raymond Spruance's flagship for almost two years. Admiral

---

[1] All dates collected from Navsource.org
[2] Pete Nelson, *Left for Dead: A Young Man's Search for Justice for the USS Indianapolis* (Delacorte Press, 2002). 16.
[3] United States, Department of the Navy, *Ships' Data, U. S. Naval Vessels, 1911-* (Washington, DC: Government Printing Office, 1935).

Spruance saw McVay almost daily and was well acquainted with him as an individual and commanding officer. Unlike some flagships, McVay's crew and Spruance's staff got along well.[4] *Indianapolis* was badly damaged by a kamikaze attack off Okinawa on March 31, 1945 and steamed to San Francisco for repairs. While in San Francisco *Indianapolis* was selected for a secret mission: deliver atomic bomb parts to Tinian. On her return trip from Tinian, she called in Guam to take on newly reporting sailors before continuing to the Philippines for the anticipated invasion of Japan. She never made it. Many Americans know her story, not from history, but instead from popular film via an emotional monologue delivered by a grizzled and scarred shark hunter in Steven Spielberg's 1975 blockbuster "Jaws."

Robert Shaw played Quint, a hardened fisherman drafted to help coastal New England sheriff Brody (played by Roy Scheider) and shark scientist Matt Hooper (played by Richard Dreyfuss). While on their mission to find and kill a shark terrorizing their summer resort town, Hooper asks Quint about his various scars, now faded and dim from exposure to sun and salt. Hooper and Quint end up playing a game of one-upmanship over scars and the mood starts out light, with all three men laughing as the two tell their tales.

Hooper points to a scar on Quint's left arm. Learning it was the scar from a removed tattoo he jokes that the tattoo was likely "Mother." Quint is suddenly still and distant. "You know what that is? That's the USS *Indianapolis*."

Hooper is immediately silent, then incredulous. "You were on the *Indianapolis*?" he asks. Brody, now a clear outsider asks "What happened?" Over the next three minutes Quint tells the USS *Indianapolis*'s story.

Two days out of Guam and only a day from the Philippines, steaming in uneventful, seemingly pacified and

---

[4] Thomas B. Buell, *The Quiet Warrior: A Biography of Admiral Raymond A. Spruance* (Little, Brown and Company: Boston, 1974). 383.

calm seas, *Indianapolis* was struck by two torpedoes fired from the Japanese submarine I-58 shortly after midnight on July 30, 1945; she sank in less than 15 minutes. Quint summarizes the story of the next four days: "1100 men went in the water, 316 come out. The sharks took the rest." Their mission was so secret, and the Pacific theater so large, that no one noticed *Indianapolis* was late arriving in port; on August 3rd a passing seaplane chanced upon survivors and sent out the distress call. The rescue and recovery operations went on for five days.

Indianapolis' loss was the single greatest loss of life in U.S. Navy history. Her loss, and the tragic and fantastic circumstances threatened the joy and relief that came with Japan's surrender. The Navy intentionally released news of the sinking after Japan's surrender – on the same day, but an hour after President Harry Truman's press conference announcing the surrender – hoping the story would disappear.[5]

Unsurprisingly, early reports called the sinking and loss of life a disaster. The *New York Times* wrote, "Her loss just a month before the dawn of peace, with nearly nine hundred dead marks one of the darkest pages of our Naval history"[6] juxtaposed next to a story on the closing of the federal Officer of Censorship.[7] Unlike previous disasters this one made the papers while the incident was still fresh. The public could, and did, pressure the Navy on action and the Navy kept one eye on the papers as it determined the way forward. While not disputing the tragedy, some think that the greater disaster happened after the survivors were all ashore.

The survivors collected in Guam where they were hospitalized and given medical care for shock and severe dehydration. Spruance visited his former flagship captain and many of his staff visited their former shipmates.[8] Meanwhile, as

---

[5] Nelson, 114.
[6] Raymond B. Lech, *The Tragic Fate of the U.S.S. Indianapolis: The U.S. Navy's Worst Disaster at Sea* (New York: Cooper Square Press, 2001). 187
[7] Bray, 279.
[8] Buell, 383.

Navy leadership asked "how did this happen?" Pacific Fleet Commander Chester Nimitz appointed the commander of Pacific Fleet submarines, Admiral Charles A. Lockwood, to head an official Court of Inquiry. The court had three members: Vice Admiral Lockwood; Rear Admiral Francis E. M. Whiting, who commanded a Navy cruiser division in Iwo Jima, Okinawa and Leyte Gulf;[9] and Vice Admiral George D. Murray, Commander Marianas.[10] Admiral Murray commanded the very group charged with monitoring port arrivals and as such clearly had a conflict of interest.[11] Rarely does a commander with a conflict of interest in an investigatory or fact-finding body recuse himself. In fact, most investigations are ordered by, made by, or approved by officers who have a very clear and undeniable conflict of interest.

A Navy Court of Inquiry is a fact-finding body which, unsurprisingly, primarily seeks out facts. The court should not express any opinions or make any recommendations unless directed so by the convening authority. The rules for Courts of Inquiry are the same now as they were in 1945.[12] Courts of Inquiry are formal and open investigative tools for the convening authority[13] and should not be confused with courts-

---

[9] "Vice Adm. F. E. M. Whiting, 87, Dies," *The New York Times*, June 7, 1978.

[10] United States, Department of the Navy, Commander Marianas, *Record of Proceedings of a Court of Inquiry Convened at Headquarters, Commander Marianas, Guam by Order of Commander in Chief, United States Pacific Fleet and Pacific Ocean Areas to Inquire into all Circumstances Connected with the Sinking of the USS Indianapolis (CA-35), and the Delay in Reporting the Loss of that Ship August 13, 1945.* (Washington, DC: United States Navy, 1945). First Day. CINPAC #5083, CINPAC 1945, Flag Files Screening Documents RG 38/370/13/05/06, Box 45

[11] Nelson, 111.

[12] Roger D. Scott, "Kimmel, Short, McVay: Case Studies in Executive Authority, Law and the Individual Rights of Military Commanders," *Military Law Review* 156 (June 1998).

[13] Scott

martial or any other investigative procedure. Courts of Inquiry are something in between – more structured and open than a formal investigation but less juridical than a court-martial.

On August 13, 1945, the Court of Inquiry convened and questioned Captain McVay. The transcript provides short statements absent any emotional language but filled with specificity. His testimony detailed the condition of the ship, the number and location of lookouts, his actions and those of the officers and crew he observed immediately before and after the ship was struck by the two torpedoes. In that testimony, he is clear that he believed the ship's speed was sufficient to avoid a submarine attack, especially in the partially moonlit night.[14]

The members disagreed and in their findings published on August 20, 1945, wrote: "The court is of the opinion that a contributory responsibility for loss *Indianapolis* rests upon Captain Charles B. McVay, III, U. S. Navy, for failure to order zigzag courses to be steered… [and that he] incurred serious blame for failure to order zigzag courses to be steered on the night in question.[15]" They went further and placed additional "contributory responsibility…upon Captain Charles B. McVay, III, U. S. Navy, for…failure to send out a distress message."[16] Finally, the Court of Inquiry recommended:

> 1. That Captain Charles B. McVay, III, U. S. Navy, be brought to trial by general court-martial on the following charges:
> 1. CULPABLE INEFFICIENCY IN THE PERFORMANCE OF HIS DUTY under Article 8, Section 10, Articles for the Government of the Navy. and
> 2. NEGLIGENTLY ENDANGERING LIVES OF OTHERS under Article 22, Articles for the Government

---

[14] *Record of Proceedings of a Court of Inquiry…Connected with the Sinking of the USS Indianapolis (CA-35), and the Delay in Reporting the Loss of that Ship August 13, 1945*
[15] Ibid, Opinion 42
[16] Ibid, Opinion 40

of the Navy.

2. That a letter of admonition be addressed to Lieutenant Stewart B. Gibson, U. S. Naval Reserve, based on Opinion 38(a) of this record of proceedings.

3. That CTG 95.7, Rear Admiral Lynde D. McCormick, U. S. Navy, be directed to take necessary disciplinary action with regard to blame incurred by his communications staff.[17]

Admiral Nimitz disagreed with the findings and instead issued Captain McVay a letter of reprimand: "The Commander in Chief, U.S. Pacific Fleet, does not agree with the court in its recommendation that Captain Charles B. McVay III, U.S. Navy, be brought to trial by general court-martial . . . His failure to order a zigzag course was an error in judgment, but not of such nature as to constitute gross negligence."[18] Nimitz accepted McVay's judgment and also accepted the Navy's own failing in launching a search for *Indianapolis*. McVay and his remaining crew left Guam in early September via the aircraft carrier USS *Hollandia* (CVE 97)[19] and arrived in San Diego on September 26, 1945.[20]

The issue for others was not McVay's decision or judgment, but the consequences of his decision and judgment. Accordingly, Chief of Naval Operations, Admiral Ernest King, sided with the Court of Inquiry and recommended to Secretary of the Navy James Forrestal that McVay face a court-martial. The Chief of Naval Personnel, Vice Admiral Louis Denfeld, was unsure of either conclusion and repeatedly asked King and

---

[17] Ibid, Recommendation 1.
[18] Cong. Senate, Committee on Armed Services., *The Sinking of the U.S.S. Indianapolis and the Subsequent Court-martial of Rear Adm. Charles B. McVay III, USN: hearing before the Committee on Armed Services, United States Senate, One Hundred Sixth Congress*, First session, September 14, 1999, 106 Cong., Rept. (Washington: U.S. G.P.O., 2000). 49.
[19] Nelson, 114.
[20] Ibid, 117.

Forrestal to further investigate the disaster before proceeding to trial. King ultimately agreed that the court of inquiry was insufficient. On October 8, 1945, Forrestal ordered the Naval Inspector General to conduct an independent investigation, anticipating its completion within a month.[21]

Through early November, King vacillated between waiting for the Inspector General to finish and an immediate trial. Denfeld repeatedly recommended waiting for the Inspector General and on November 8th sent a memo to King and Forrestal advising that any trial should wait until after the supplemental investigation finished.[22]

On November 10th King agreed with Denfeld, however, that same day he also asked the Navy Inspector General to "comment on the feasibility of bringing C.O. *Indianapolis* to trial *now*."[23] The Inspector General, Admiral Charles P. Snyder, likely less politically minded, generally saw no objection to a trial before his investigation was complete. His exact words, however, are curious: "Captain McVay feels that due to the exhaustive manner in which this office is conducting its investigation, additional facts favorable to his case may be developed [however] Should you desire to bring Captain McVay to trial before my investigation is completed, it is, in my opinion, entirely feasible to do so."[24]

On November 12, 1945, only slightly more than three months after *Indianapolis* sank, Secretary of the Navy Forrestal ordered the General Court Martial of Captain Charles B. McVay, III.[25] The order did not include the charges.

Prosecutors select charges they can prove, and Navy

---

[21] Lech, 177.
[22] Ibid, 178.
[23] Ibid
[24] Ibid
[25] Cong. Senate, Committee on Armed Services. First session, September 14, 1999, 106 Cong., Rept. (Washington: U.S. G.P.O., 2000). 49.

leaders believed the recommended charge that McVay failed to zig-zag was the strongest and most easily proved.[26] Deciding on other charges took almost two weeks.

Rear Admiral O. S. Colclough, the Navy Judge Advocate General (JAG),[27] also recommended a second charge on McVay's delay in ordering abandon ship. The JAG reasoned the abandon ship charge provided McVay a chance "to clear himself of criticisms made in the press....[and] Full justification for ordering a trial on Charge II springs from the fact that this case is of vital interest not only to the families of those who lost their lives but also to the public at large."[28] With this official statement the Navy's senior lawyer recognizes that the court-martial was less about culpability or accountability and more about placating the American public and placing blame - ideally at a level that did not affect leaders in Washington, DC. The consequences of McVay's decision not to zig-zag moved to the forefront. The Japanese submarine's actions, the delay in sending search parties, and the failure to provide a destroyer escort fell to the wayside.

The charges were finally published November 29, 1945, a Thursday, a week after Thanksgiving. Navy leadership scheduled the trial for the following Monday giving McVay four days to prepare his defense.[29]

Monday morning the trial judge asked McVay if he was ready for trial, and McVay said no. With only four days' notice and denied his choice of counsel[30] a delay was reasonable. McVay requested, and was granted, an adjournment until the next day and on Tuesday, December 4, five days after the

---

[26] Lech, 180, 182.
[27] Nelson, 133.
[28] Lech, 183.
[29] Ibid, 186.
[30] Nelson, 161.

charges were published, the trial started.[31] The trial lasted just under two and a half weeks and featured thirty-nine prosecution witnesses and eighteen for the defense.[32] The most controversial witness at the trial was none other than the commander of *I-58*, the very man credited with sinking *Indianapolis*.

Commander Iko Hashimoto testified he had sufficient visibility to track *Indianapolis* for almost half an hour before he closed his range to three-quarters of a mile and fired his torpedoes.[33] Both Hashimoto and U.S. Navy submarine Captain Glynn Donaho testified that zigzagging alone would not defeat an attack by a proficient submarine commander. On cross-examination, Captain Donaho admitted that zigzagging made targeting more difficult and might increase the chance of evading torpedoes after launch.[34] This testimony allowed the court to convict McVay on the charge of failing to zig-zag. The court acquitted McVay of the second charge. McVay's sentence was to "lose one hundred (100) numbers in his temporary grade of Captain and to lose one hundred (100) numbers in his permanent grade of Commander."[35] With promotion largely based on seniority and longevity, a loss of numbers was a common sentence for crimes of command that allowed both a guilty verdict at court-martial as well as a punishment that could, with time, be overcome. Movement down the list did not immediately preclude promotion, only delayed it so long as the officer had enough time remaining on active duty to overcome the decrement. More importantly, since crimes of command were not linked to modern criminal culpability, the World War II-era court-martial was not faced with an issue of choosing between guilt under criminal statute or a finding of not guilty.

---

[31] Lech, 188.
[32] Lech, 193.
[33] Scott, 165.
[34] Ibid, 166.
[35] Lech, 200.

Loss of numbers remained in effect under the Uniform Code of Military Justice until 1999 when President William J. Clinton signed legislation ending its use.[36] By that time the Navy had long since moved away from courts-martial for crimes of command and the sentence went the way of warships with sails, but, as the cases in this study show, this seemingly trivial punishment's absence also negates courts-martial for crimes of command.

Four days after McVay's trial concluded, Admiral Snyder finished his investigation. Edward Hidalgo, Special Assistant to Secretary of the Navy, forwarded the report to Secretary Forrestal with a memorandum that now looked at McVay and the trial in a different light, writing:

> ...you have it in your power to reverse the conviction without advancing any particular reason. Therefore, I consider this to be strictly a legal problem in which the Secretary of the Navy acts in a capacity comparable with that of an appellate court. Measured by this test there seems to have been sufficient evidence to support the court's finding: 1. That McVay was responsible for the safety of his ship. 2. That the ship was not zigzagging; 3. That in accordance with the U.S. Fleet Orders it should have been zigzagging...It is true that the causal nexus between the failure to zigzag and the loss of the ship appears not to have a solid foundation. In fact, a good percentage of the testimony on this issue was given by a witness for the defense (Captain Donaho, a submarine commander) who, in effect, stated that zigzagging merely increased the difficulty of an attack. The fact remains, however, that the technical charge on which McVay was convicted was that of 'hazarding' his ship not of causing its loss or sinking.

In a February 23, 1946 press release the Navy publicized the court's verdict:

---

[36] Fidell and Fidell

The following disciplinary action has been taken in connection with the loss of the *Indianapolis*: Captain Charles B. McVay, III, U.S.N., has been brought to trial by General Court Martial. He was acquitted of failure to give timely orders to abandon ship. He was found guilty of negligence in not causing a zigzag to be steered. He was sentenced to lose one hundred numbers in his temporary grade of Captain and also in his permanent grade of Commander. The Court and also the Commander in Chief, United States Fleet recommended clemency. The Secretary of the Navy has approved these recommendations, remitted the sentence, and restored Captain McVay to duty.[37]

Four other officers received letters of reprimand, letters which they never saw and apparently were never issued.[38] That same press release also said:

The conduct of Captain McVay and of the other officers and men of the ship was, in the face of this emergency, satisfactory. Captain McVay did not order abandon ship when it was first suggested by the First Lieutenant. Shortly thereafter, the Executive Officer recommended abandoning ship. The Captain, approving this recommendation, ordered the word to be passed to all hands to abandon ship.[39]

In its press release, the Navy showed why the court acquitted McVay of the charge of negligence for failing to order abandon ship – his performance was satisfactory. The release

---

[37] United States, Department of the Navy, Naval History and Heritage Command, The Sinking of USS Indianapolis: Navy Department Press Release, *Narrative of the Circumstances of the Loss of USS Indianapolis, 23 February 1946* (Washington, DC, 1946), , July 8, 2016, accessed June 1, 2017, https://www.history.navy.mil/research/histories/ship-histories/loss-of-uss-Indianapolis-ca-35/investigation-and-court-martial.html.
[38] Ibid
[39] Ibid

also indicated that no enemy vessels were "sighted either before the explosions occurred or afterward. Watches were properly stood and good lookout was kept, both visual and radar. Normal precautions were being taken against enemy submarines."[40] Those same "normal precautions" included zig-zagging, which wasn't, by McVay's admission, done.

By the time the court-martial results were released, Admiral King was no longer Chief of Naval Operations; Admiral Nimitz, who recommended against court-martial, assumed the office two days after McVay was found guilty. Nimitz later told a survivor that the court-martial was a mistake and should not have happened.[41] He also told the family member of one of the lost sailors:

> As Commander in Chief of the Pacific Fleet and Pacific Ocean Areas, I carried the broad responsibility for all operations of the Pacific Fleet in the areas under my command. This included, of course, responsibility for both successes and failures. To the extent that a commander in chief should be held responsible for failures or errors of judgment on the part of subordinates, I must bear my share of responsibility for the loss of *Indianapolis*.[42]

McVay, however, was personally and publicly held responsible for *Indianapolis*' loss. After the trial McVay served as chief of staff for the Eighth Naval District Commandant in New Orleans before retiring on June 30, 1949,[43] having reached thirty years of service. Of the nearly 700 classmates who graduated from the U.S. Naval Academy thirty years earlier, 22

---

[40] Ibid
[41] William J. Toti, "The Sinking of the Indy & Responsibility of Command," *United States Naval Institute Proceedings Magazine*, 1160th ser., 125, no. 10 (October 1999):
[42] Lech, 202.
[43] Lech, 205.

rose to three or four-star rank - including most of McVay's fellow cruiser and battleship commanders.[44] Absent the very public court-martial McVay was likely to promote and wear admiral's rank on active duty; his court-martial ended that possibility.

McVay never spoke publicly of the sinking or his court-martial. Instead, for over thirty years McVay routinely received hate mail from relatives of sailors killed on *Indianapolis*.[45] While he accepted the verdict and never challenged it, he also carried intense feelings of shame and guilt - largely because he was publicly found culpable in the loss of the ship and over 900 lives.[46] On the morning of November 6, 1968, he walked into his front yard, placed his pistol against his head and committed suicide.

USS *Queenfish* and *Awa Maru*

Four months before USS *Indianapolis* went to the bottom, a different submarine sank a different large ship and a different American captain was court-martialed for his actions in command. The eventual results, however, differed significantly.

Japan's rapid thrust into the Pacific left thousands of American, British, and Australian citizens behind enemy lines. Allied forces worked through neutral Switzerland and transferred thousands of tons of relief supplies behind Japanese lines to assist the detainees. This practice continued through 1943 but halted in 1944, and there were no exchanges for over twelve months.[47]

---

[44] List provided by U.S. Naval Academy Institutional Research Division
[45] Nelson, 147.
[46] Toti
[47] Payson Sibley Wild, *International Law Documents: 1944-45* (Washington, DC: U.S. Government Print. Office, 1946).

In early 1945 the Japanese, perhaps recognizing the impending end, agreed to restart relief deliveries. 2,000 tons of Red Cross packages were delivered to Soviet Siberia and loaded on two Japanese merchant ships: *Hoshu Maru* and *Awa Maru*. The Japanese freighter *Hoshu Maru* safely transported 275 tons to Shanghai.[48] The second ship, *Awa Maru*, carried the remaining 1,725 tons of supplies and took a more circuitous route leaving Japan in mid-February, traveling to Singapore, then returning via Hong Kong, Taiwan, Saigon, Indonesia before sailing for Japan.[49] The ship had special markings identifying her as a non-combatant[50] and her route was provided to the Allies — detailed with expected positions, port call times, and speed of travel. The Allies, in turn, guaranteed *Awa Maru*'s safety. Pacific Fleet command sent orders to all ships and submarines in the Pacific Theater detailing *Awa Maru*'s intended transit times and locations, admonishing that anyone attacking her violated the laws of warfare. But, not all guarantees are infallible, and this was the case for *Awa Maru*.

When *Awa Maru* departed Singapore on March 28, 1945, she carried 2,071 passengers and crew in addition to the relief supplies. By April 1, she was well on her way to Japan but entered dense fog in the Formosa (now Taiwan) Strait. Also in that fog was USS *Queenfish* (SS 393) under command of Lieutenant Commander Charles Eliot Loughlin, U.S. Navy. Originally from Wilmington, North Carolina, Loughlin's father was killed in the final days of World War I when Loughlin was only eight-years old. A 1933 Naval Academy graduate and All-American basketball player, *Queenfish* was Loughlin's second

---

[48] Daniel F. Gilmore, "Full Story Told of sinking of the *Awa Maru*," *United Press International*, September 18, 1982, http://www.upi.com/Archives/1982/09/19/Full-story-told-of-WWIINEWLNsinking-of-the-Ava-MaruNEWLNMistakenly-torpedoed-by-U.S.-sub-Mistakenly-sought-by-treasure-hunter/4980401256000/.
[49] Clay Blair, Jr., *Silent Victory* (New York: Bantam Books, 1975). 836-7.
[50] Ibid

command and third submarine assignment. At 35, Loughlin was an aggressive commander on his third war patrol with two Navy Crosses, a Silver Star[51] and 11 sunken enemy ships to his credit.

Queenfish surfaced and located a target by radar. The target was moving relatively fast, at 17 knots, and was not zigzagging.[52] Loughlin, never seeing the other ship, decided it was a destroyer.

Queenfish closed to 1,200 yards and fired four torpedoes. All four struck *Awa Maru*, and the ship sank within two minutes. *Queenfish* rescued the sole survivor. Loughlin eventually learned that he attacked a protected aid ship[53] and notified his commanders.[54] When Chief of Naval Operations Ernest King learned of the sinking, he directed Pacific Fleet Commander Chester Nimitz to order *Queenfish* back to Guam, remove Lieutenant Commander Loughlin from command and try him by a General Court-Martial.[55]

Loughlin was not told of his relief until *Queenfish* returned to Guam, arriving on April 12, the same day President Roosevelt died in Washington, DC.[56] Loughlin's boss, Admiral Charles Lockwood — the same Lockwood who later presided over Captain McVay's Court of Inquiry — met the returning *Queenfish* and gave Loughlin the news. Lockwood recalled Loughlin as "dispirited and remorseful over what had occurred but lacking any feeling of guilt of having violated any orders,

---

[51] Charles Elliott Loughlin, *The Reminiscences of Rear Admiral Charles Elliott Loughlin, U.S. Navy (Retired)* (Annapolis: U.S. Naval Institute, 1982). 1-3.
[52] "Sinking of Japanese Ship *AWA MARU*; Report of," C. E. Loughlin to Commander Submarine Force, Pacific Fleet, April 8, 1945. 1.
[53] Ibid, 4.
[54] Chester W. Nimitz and James M. Steele, *The Nimitz Graybook: the CINCPAC-CINCPOA Running Estimate of the Situation, 1941-1945* (Newport, RI: United States Naval War College, 2014). 2812.
[55] Ibid, 2595.
[56] Blair, 836-7.

and he was stunned to learn that he was to be relieved of his command and court-martialed."[57] Loughlin had dinner with Lockwood that night[58] where he told his boss his side of the story. Loughlin later recalled telling Lockwood:

> Well, Admiral Lockwood I just feel that we ain't been done right. The only thing I knew about the *AWA MARU* was the message we got the night before which said, "let it pass clear and it's going to pass through your area." And, I said to myself and my officers, what area? What are you talking about? It ranged from Australia to the Aleutian Islands. Every submarine in the Western Pacific was given this dispatch.[59]

That message, sent in code, read:
LET PASS SAFELY THE *AWA MARU* CARRYING PRISONER OF WAR SUPPLIES X SHE WILL BE PASSING THROUGH YOUR AREAS BETWEEN MARCH 30 AND APRIL 4 X SHE IS LIGHTED AT NIGHT AND PLASTERED WITH WHITE CROSSES.[60]

Presumably, over that same dinner, Loughlin learned this his boss was on his side. Lockwood was already well into plans for Loughlin's defense, sending memos to Nimitz taking the blame for the wording and routing of the messages regarding *Awa Maru*'s safety and arranging defense counsel. When the court convened, Lockwood submitted written support of Loughlin's actions, officially taking the blame for the wording of the messages.[61]

Lockwood arranging defense counsel weighed heavily in

---

[57] Richard G. Voge, "Too Much Accuracy," *Proceedings*, 565th ser., 76, no. 3 (March 1950): 259.
[58] Loughlin (1982), 133.
[59] Ibid, 126.
[60] Gilmore
[61] Blair. 836-7 and Loughlin (1982)

Loughlin's favor. Lockwood selected Captain Henry C. Bruton, U. S. Navy, and Lieutenant Colonel John H. Coffman, U. S. Marine Corps and both officers were flown to Guam to defend Loughlin.[62]

During the trip back to Guam, and before he knew of his ordered removal from command, Loughlin wrote in his April 8, 1945, post-patrol report that he and his crew "regret the sinking" but also wrote that:

> ...the attack was made in the sincere belief that this ship was a legitimate target...It seems incredible that a ship protected by lights, marking, and advance notice guaranteeing safe passage, would proceed through an area, known to be patrolled by hostile submarines, at a speed in the existing weather conditions which would obviously preclude close observation of such protective markings without placing the submarine in an untenable and dangerous position. The U.S. submarine force has been thoroughly indoctrinated in aggressive tactics and this ship during four patrols has endeavored to carry out this policy in submarine patrol areas where, normally, any contact is a legitimate target. Considering the circumstances surrounding this attack, the Commanding Officer would find it most difficult to justify and explain any other action which would have permitted this unidentified ship to proceed unmolested.[63]

Lockwood was even more direct in his endorsement of April 17, 1945:

> It is desired to invite attention to two salient features: (a) That the Commanding Officer, *QUEENFISH*, Commander C. E. Loughlin, was operating under orders to conduct unrestricted submarine warfare against all enemy ships, except hospital ships and those granted safe conduct by proper authority; (b) That the safety of

---

[62] Voge, 259.
[63] Loughlin to Commander Submarine Force, 6-7.

the *AWA MARU* depended upon two things: First her markings and illumination; second, pre-knowledge of her course, speed, and position. The first factor of safety was nullified by the fog in which she was navigating through in what she must have known were submarine infested waters...The Commander Submarine Force considers that the sinking of the *AWA MARU* was due primarily to her own negligence...The Commander Submarine Force deeply regrets this tragic incident but considers that it is an unavoidable accident of war.[64]

These two documents laid out the basis for Loughlin's defense. The trial began less than a week after *Queenfish* arrived in Guam. Through two days of testimony, with all involved feeling pressure from the Commander in Chief of the Pacific and the Chief of Naval Operations,[65] Loughlin was tried on three counts:

>Charge I. Culpable inefficiency in the performance of duty.
>Charge II. Disobeying the lawful order of his superior officer.
>Charge III. Negligence in obeying orders.[66]

Loughlin's counsel convinced him to not take the stand,[67] believing if Loughlin truthfully testified he had not seen the applicable messages he would implicitly convict himself of the inefficiency charge.[68] Rather, the defense began with placing the blame elsewhere — on *Awa Maru,* citing a claim she was transporting munitions and contraband, thereby sacrificing her

---

[64] Commander Submarine Force Pacific Fleet endorsement on "Sinking of Japanese Ship *AWA MARU*; Report Of," C. E. Loughlin to Commander Submarine Force, Pacific Fleet, April 8, 1945. 17 April 1945. 10.
[65] Loughlin (1982).
[66] Voge, 259.
[67] Loughlin (1982), 128.
[68] Voge, 259.

right of safe passage.[69]

The court quickly rejected this line of thinking, recognizing that not only did Loughlin not know what *Awa Maru* carried, but also that if he had it was not his place to disregard a guarantee of safe passage.[70] Finally, the idea that Loughlin sank *Awa Maru* intentionally because she carried contraband would require that he first identify the ship — which he only did after questioning the sole survivor.

Unable to shift blame to *Awa Maru*, Benton and Loughlin tried instead to prove lack of intent,[71] presenting evidence that Loughlin did not know *Awa Maru*'s status or even her existence. Of the three messages regarding *Awa Maru*, *Queenfish* did not receive one message, the second was seen, filed, and forgotten;[72] and the third did not make sense without information from the previous two. This argument also failed.

Ultimately Lockwood's support did not alter the outcome of the trial and Loughlin was found guilty of negligence and awarded a letter of admonition,[73] one of the lowest punishments possible following a guilty verdict. When Nimitz learned of the punishments, he was so irate that he ordered letters of reprimand for the court-martial members — punishments greater than what they gave the guilty Loughlin.[74] One of Loughlin's defenders, fellow submariner Richard "Dick" Voge, wrote in 1949 that:

> The convening authority, Fleet Admiral Nimitz, severely criticized the members of the court for the total inadequacy of the sentence, and rightfully so. By choosing a middle course the court had decided

---

[69] Ibid
[70] Ibid, 260.
[71] Ibid
[72] Loughlin (1982). 127.
[73] Voge, 261.
[74] United States, National Security Agency, *The Sinking and the Salvage of the Awa Maru* (Washington, DC, 1977).

nothing. By finding Loughlin guilty, they had cast a stigma not only on him but on the entire Submarine Force, Whereas, by the lightness of the sentence they had nullified their own finding.[75]

Loughlin, however, believed that both King and Nimitz wanted him found guilty and severely punished and their anger at being stymied led to the letters of reprimand and later actions against his career.[76]

With the court-martial over, Loughlin needed a place to go. He asked Admiral Lockwood to go back into the queue for command of a new submarine, and Lockwood agreed.[77] Loughlin transferred to the Pearl Harbor training command and served under Admiral John Herbert 'Babe' Brown; Brown was also a member of the court-martial that convicted Loughlin. Leaving a court-martial to serve under one of the members is unheard of as one would expect a member of a court-martial to be ill-disposed towards an officer the same court found guilty. Babe Brown, however, was one of only two submariners on the court and was well known for giving submarine officers a second chance, especially Naval Academy varsity athletes.[78]

Within a month, however, the situation didn't matter as word filtered down that Admiral King banned Loughlin from ever commanding a submarine again.[79] Downtrodden and with the war ending, Loughlin contacted Washington, DC to see what lay in store. Once again his fellow submariners went to bat for him as the Vice Chief of Naval Operations, Admiral Richard S. Edwards, prevailed upon the Chief of Naval Personnel to ensure that Loughlin got a "good job."[80]

Unlike Captain McVay and *Indianapolis*, there was more to the case of *Awa Maru* and Charles Elliott Loughlin.

---

[75] Voge, 261.
[76] Loughlin (1982), 130.
[77] Ibid, 131.
[78] Blair, 836-7 and Loughlin (1982).
[79] Loughlin (1982), 130.
[80] Loughlin (1982), 131.

While the war was winding down when Loughlin sank *Awa Maru,* the end was far from certain, and thousands of Allied nationals remained in Japanese hands. There were significant and legitimate concerns that *Awa Maru*'s sinking might lead to reprisals. Communications between Japan and the U.S. lifted above the normal fever pitch of war into hyperbolic levels.

Japan was first informed of the sinking on April 11th — 10 days after the fact. During the communications, the United States government informed the Japanese that "no lights or special illumination were visible at any time." [81] In their first response, the "Japanese Government most emphatically demand that United States Government bear the whole responsibility for this disgraceful act committed in violation of the fundamental principles of humanity and international law"[82] and that "This is the most outrageous act of treachery unparalleled in the world history of war."[83] The Japanese further stated that "Therefore, it cannot but be concluded that she was deliberately and willfully attacked and sunk by United States submarine, responsibility for disaster, therefore, unmistakably lies with United States Government."[84] Most distressing, beyond the hyperbole, was this statement:

> United States Government are to be deemed to have abandoned their former desire relating to the treatment of United States prisoners of war and civilian internees in Japanese hands...Japanese Government as well as Japanese people, are most profoundly indignant at occurrence of this extremely outrageous incident. They will watch United States Government's attitude concerning this matter with most serious concern.[85]

---

[81] Wild, 126.
[82] Ibid, 128.
[83] Ibid
[84] Ibid
[85] Ibid

Working through Switzerland, U.S. diplomats communicated with Japan through May, June, and July of 1945. In May, Japan was informed that an investigation was underway and the United States "categorically denie[d] the Japanese Government's charge that the ship was deliberately and willfully attacked and sunk."[86] In July, the Japanese were told that "*Awa Maru* was substantially complying with all conditions of the safe-conduct agreement. In the circumstances the burden of making positive identification was placed upon the United States submarine"[87] – a clear change from April's claim she was not showing lights. The U.S. government also said that "There is no valid connection between this disaster and the matter of treatment to be accorded prisoners of war and civilian internees in Japanese custody."[88]

Finally, the U.S. government accepted responsibility and stated that the "Commanding Officer of the submarine did not see the *Awa Maru* prior to or after she had been torpedoed, [and the] burden of establishing identity was that of the commander of the American submarine and in view of his failure to do so, the United States Government acknowledges responsibility for the sinking of the vessel."[89] Japan requested indemnification and replacement of the vessel; the U.S. government agreed. However, the U.S. government also recommended that final resolution should wait until after the war.[90]

The astute reader will have noticed that the timelines do not match. Loughlin returned to Guam and was removed from command on April 12th. His court-martial was roughly a week later. By the end of April, his sentence was pronounced, and he'd moved to work under Babe Brown in Pearl Harbor. The facts known to the U.S. government were different from those communicated to Japan. Given the state of war, this might be

---

[86] Ibid, 129.
[87] Ibid, 130.
[88] Ibid, 129.
[89] Ibid, 132.
[90] Ibid, 132.

expected. However, the issues under discussion were not secrets, or operational, or even related to Loughlin and *Awa Maru*. Rather, the concerns were strategic and humanitarian, namely the care and well-being of the detainees.

However, as late as July, Japan was told "Disciplinary action is being taken with respect to the commander of the American submarine concerned"[91] rather than explaining that action was long complete. July news reports had Secretary of the Navy Forrestal saying that it was difficult to decide what to do with the commander who sank the *Awa Maru* — a full three months after the court-martial was complete. The Bureau of Naval Personnel admitted that Loughlin, still not named, was removed from command and court-martialed, but were uncertain if the sentence was approved.[92]

In the end, any legal issues between Japan and the U.S. ended on September 2, 1945, with Japan's formal surrender to Allied forces in Tokyo Bay aboard USS *Missouri* (BB 63). Some short time later press reports acknowledged "that the *Awa Maru* had been sunk by the U.S.S. *Queenfish*, commanded by Commander Charles Elliot Loughlin, U.S. Navy, of North Wales, Pennsylvania."[93]

In 1949 the final discussion of reparations was laid to rest, and those were the last words the Navy or U.S. government made about *Awa Maru*. They were not the final words from Loughlin or his supporters. As indemnification discussions resurfaced, retired Admiral Richard 'Dick' Voge penned an article for the U.S. Naval Institute *Proceedings* magazine. "In justification of the Submarine Service, and of Loughlin, a most honorable, efficient, and outstanding naval officer, the chain of circumstances which led up to his fatal mistake should be brought to light."[94]

---

[91] Ibid, 132.
[92] "Hard to Fix Blame in Awa Maru Sinking," *The New York Times*, July 15, 1945, accessed March 23, 2017, Historical Newspapers.
[93] Voge, 257.
[94] Ibid

Here Voge repeated much of Loughlin's defense at the court-martial including the ideas that *Awa Maru* intentionally violated the spirit of the agreement for safe conduct, that *Awa Maru* contributed to her sinking by not sounding fog signals, and that the firing pattern for the torpedoes showed Loughlin believed he was firing at a destroyer, those tactics being clearly the wrong choice for a cargo ship *Awa Maru*'s size. Voge, also a submarine officer, wrote: "Loughlin, one of the most capable and outstanding of our submarine commanders with many previous sinkings to his credit, was not the type to make such elementary mistakes."[95] Apparently, choosing the wrong tactic was an elementary mistake but Loughlin sank *Awa Maru* because he hadn't seen the messages giving her safe passage and didn't visually identify his target. Voge wrote that "blame lay with the *Queenfish* but not necessarily with her captain"[96] and that a "search through the communication files of the *Queenfish* revealed the answer. Not only one but several copies of the despatches [sic] in question were found, but strangely these despatches[sic] had never left the radio room and Loughlin himself had never seen them."[97] While Loughlin hadn't seen the messages, it wasn't his fault, but that of his communications officer.

> The hagiographic defense concluded that Loughlin:
> remains today, as he was before the *Awa Maru* incident,
> a highly honored and respected member of our
> Submarine Service, in which he has continued to serve
> in various capacities other than submarine commander.
> His contemporaries and associates, while regretting the
> incident which led to his difficulties, can hardly help
> but admire and envy his uncanny ability – there were
> but a mighty thin few of our submarine captains that

---

[95] Ibid, 260.
[96] Ibid
[97] Ibid, 259.

could have accomplished what he did – to hit, with all torpedoes of a four-torpedo salvo, a ship which he had never seen. Loughlin was an innocent victim of his own fighting spirit, coupled with too much accuracy. [98]

In 1955, Admiral Charles Lockwood wrote his version of the Pacific War, *Hellcats of the Sea*, in which he touches on Loughlin, *Queenfish*, and *Awa Maru*. He reiterated the idea that *Awa Maru* was not sounding fog signals and repeated the charge that *Awa Maru* carried contraband. Lockwood's determination? "It is my humble opinion that Loughlin deserved a medal for ending [*Awa Maru*'s] hypocritical career." His thoughts on the letter of admonition? That it was "a sentence which I am confident James V. Forrestal carried out with deep regret."[99]

Loughlin got that "good job" the Vice Chief lobbied for and over time moved to jobs in Annapolis, Maryland as naval station executive officer, commanding officer, and Naval Academy athletic director. At sea, he served as executive officer of USS *Orion* (AS 18) and commanded USS *Mississineawa* (AO 144) and USS *Toledo* (CA 133) though he never commanded a submarine again. In 1961, he was selected to flag rank — something everyone thought his court-martial precluded. Reaching out to a board member he asked: "What happened? How was the S S *AWA MARU* handled in the deliberation?"... "Elliott, it never came up. Somebody did mention it once and then somebody else said, 'Well he sank a lot of Japs didn't he?' That was the only mention of the *AWA MARU*."[100]

As a Flag Officer, Loughlin commanded Submarine Flotilla Six and the Washington Naval District.[101] After retiring from the Navy in 1968, he returned to Annapolis and served as

---

[98] Ibid, 263.
[99] Charles A. Lockwood and Hans Christian Adamson, *Hellcats of the Sea* (New York: Bantam Books, 1988).
[100] Loughlin (1982), 271.
[101] Ibid, 3.

president and executive director of the U.S. Naval Academy Foundation Inc.[102]

In 1975, journalist Clay Blair published *Silent Victory*, considered the definitive account of the Pacific War's submarine campaign. Blair asserted that while Loughlin's "communications officer [never] bothered to show him any of the many plain-language broadcasts regarding her that had been received on *Queenfish*," that during his court-martial Loughlin "steadfastly refused to put any blame"[103] on that officer. Neither Voge's or Lockwood's accounts support this assertion. Loughlin's recollections on the communications officer are conflicted.

In 1982 Loughlin sat down with the U.S. Naval Institute and in a series of interviews provided his oral history. Loughlin was 72 at the time, but his recall of events is consistent with his patrol reports and all available sources contemporary to the sinking, making his recollections, and rationalizations, all the more interesting.

Across a half dozen pages, Loughlin tells the story maintaining that he was held accountable, but also subtly laying the blame at many other feet. He repeatedly mentions that "no one paid any attention to plain language dispatches during World War II."[104] He asserts that before leaving Saipan on patrol the Commander Submarines Pacific Operations Officer briefed him, and that he never mentioned *Awa Maru*. Louglin's summation: "It was missing. It should have been one of the main purposes of the briefing."[105]

Loughlin sank *Awa Maru* during wolf pack operations – a tactic pioneered by the Germans in the Atlantic and used with some success by the Americans in the Pacific. In a wolf pack, a group of submarines operate in concert and under the leadership of the senior commander. Contrary to common wolf pack

---

[102] Gilmore
[103] Blair, 836-7.
[104] Loughlin (1982), 121.
[105] Ibid, 122.

procedures, the other commanding officer in the wolf pack, Commander William Post in USS *Sea Fox*, was operating hundreds of miles away and did not tell Loughlin of a convoy – something Loughlin saw as a clear dereliction of Post's duties. Loughlin said, "had we gotten that, or had he sent us a contact report we very easy could have been a hundred miles away from where we actually did pick up the *AWA MARU* the next night."[106]

Other rationalizations? "If we hadn't told [Commander Submarines, Pacific] that we had sunk the *AWA MARU* the Japanese to this day would never know what happened. If we hadn't picked up the survivor I would have gone to my death bed insisting that we sank a destroyer."[107]

As for the communications officer who Clay Blair claims Loughlin protected or at least didn't blame? "He was derelict in his duty and as much as I liked him I had to give him an unsat fitness report for failing to bring to the attention of the proper authority a dispatch which he himself had seen."[108]

In the final calculus, Loughlin maintained that "Based upon the information that I had I felt that I was justified in making the attack. Based upon the information that I had I would do the same thing over again...The only thing is I never had a guilty conscience."[109] Loughlin died in 1989 after a stroke. His obituary did not mention *Awa Maru*, or even command of USS *Queenfish*.[110] There is a clear and stark contrast between Admiral Loughlin, who felt no guilt and placed blame on everyone but himself, and Captain McVay whose guilt and tortured acceptance of blame led him to suicide. In both cases, however, the officers were called to account, tried, found guilty,

---

[106] Ibid, 123.
[107] Ibid, 125.
[108] Ibid, 127.
[109] Ibid, 137.
[110] Bart Barnes, Charles E. Loughlin Obituary, *The Washington Post*, November 1, 1989, accessed September 11, 2017, http://www.highbeam.com/doc/1P2-1220528.html?refid=easy_hf.

and punished for their own personal and professional actions executed in the normal course of command. Personal accountability for personal action was the standard from the beginning of the Republic through the World Wars and into the second half of the twentieth century. It did not stay that way.

When World War II ended, American focus shifted from the horrors of war to homecomings and a positive future. In just one year the U.S. Navy decommissioned over 5,000 ships and demobilized 1.3 million officers and sailors. By 1947 another 800 ships and 1.5 million officers and sailors. The five years after the war show very few documented incidents. Ship accidents were common, as were aircraft accidents. Between 1946 and 1949 accidents destroyed over seven thousand Navy and Marine aircraft and killed almost a thousand people.[111] There was a lot going on, but the Navy, press, and American citizens were focused elsewhere.

Of those known incidents, recoveries ranged between a third and half of affected commanders. 8 groundings, 26 collisions, 9 major fires or explosions. In January 1946, USS *Honolulu* (CL 48) struck USS *Argonaut* (SS 475), badly damaging the submarine as both operated in the Atlantic Ocean. Both ships made port on their own power. The ensuing board of inquiry recommended a court-martial for *Honolulu*'s commander, Commander William J. Lederer, Jr.. This surprised both Lederer and his defense counsel. The counsel sought out the board members and eventually told Lederer that "They had orders to make an example of you to stop collisions in the future."[112] Commander Lederer was court-martialed for the accident, found guilty, and lost fifty numbers in seniority. The court martial was later overturned on review and struck from Lederer's record.

Lederer was not removed from command, and when

---

[111] Dunn, 8.
[112] William J. Lederer, *All the Ship's at Sea* (New York: Sloane, 1950) 232-255 and Alex Arthur Kerr, *The Reminiscences of Captain Alex A. Kerr*, U.S. Navy (Retired) (Annapolis: U.S. Naval Institute, 1984). 98-111.

Honolulu decommissioned a few months later, transferred to the public affairs community where he served with distinction and promoted to Captain. While on active duty he was an avid writer publishing four books and continued writing after retirement. Shortly after his retirement in 1958 he, with co-author Eugene Burdick, published *The Ugly American* – originating a phrase that lives on. Lederer died of respiratory failure in 2009 at the age of 97.[113]

Despite the counsel's claim that Lederer was court-martialed to "stop collisions in the future," few collisions were documented in 1945 and 1946 and only 26 collisions between 1945 and 1950 among 800 ships, many without radar. There are no records that any of those commanders were removed from command, and a third of them continued with upward progress in their careers.

In 1949 another incident marked a change in command removal — the Revolt of the Admirals. As part of the continuing post-war drawdown every service was under scrutiny for budget reductions. At the same time many World War II leaders looked towards unifying the military into a single service to reduce duplication and save costs. New long-range bombers and the nuclear bomb signaled a technological change for war and many expected the Army and Navy to fall behind the new Air Force in importance and capability.

In 1949, Secretary of Defense Louis A. Johnson cancelled the planned and under construction supercarrier USS *United States*. Secretary of the Navy John L. Sullivan resigned in protest and Johnson selected Francis P. Matthews to replace Sullivan. With Matthews beholden to Johnson, Johnson moved to transfer Marine Corps aviation assets to the Air Force and Congress stepped in to halt the move. A series of papers leaked to the press alluded to a conflict of interest between aviation contractors and Johnson. Rear Admiral Daniel V. Gallery

---

[113] Bruce Weber, "William J. Lederer, Co-Author of 'The Ugly American,' Dies at 97," *The New York Times*, January 14, 2010.

published a series of articles critical of Johnson's decisions. Johnson wanted Gallery court-martialed for insubordination but had to settle for ending Gallery's career by not promoting him to Vice Admiral.

During Congressional hearings in October 1949 a number of retired and active duty Navy officers testified for continued naval power. After the hearings Matthews moved against the active duty officers and either removed or hastened retirement for a number of officers, including Chief of Naval Operations Louis E. Denfeld – the same Denfeld who recommended against rushing McVay's court-martial in 1945. While some saw the Revolt of the Admirals as a principled stand by naval officers, others saw a threat to civilian control of the military.

Denfeld's removal presaged future and contemporary action. While Denfeld testified, Matthews called President Truman, informed him of the testimony and was directed to fire Denfeld. Denfeld learned of his firing from a radio report later that day.[114]

President Truman's naval aide, Rear Admiral Robert L. Dennison was a longtime friend of Denfeld. Dennison received Truman's permission to visit Denfeld that night, but Secretary Matthews was furious when he learned Dennison had visited the fired CNO. Reportedly Matthews told Dennison "That's the most disloyal act that I can possibly imagine. Here an officer's been fired and you go up to see him."[115] Matthews did not know that his attitude towards an officer removed from command would become the standard attitude as time went on, and Dennison's kind visit would become less and less the norm.

In 1949, Charles B. McVay retired and immediately

---

[114] David Bruce Dittmer, *The Firing of Admiral Denfeld: An Early Casualty of the Military Unification Process*, PhD diss., University of Nebraska at Omaha, 1995. 162.
[115] Ibid, 162-3.

received an honorary promotion to Rear Admiral. This honor, known colloquially as a "tombstone promotion" provided officers increase title, but no increased pay, as recognition of valorous acts during the war. Congress ended the practice in 1959.[116] Charles Loughlin spent two years on the Staff of Commander Submarine Force, U.S. Atlantic Fleet, a year as Executive Officer in USS *Orion* (AS 18) before taking command of Submarine Division Sixty-two in 1948 as a Commander.

Despite the Korean War force level increases, the rapid technological advancements of 1941-1945 ground to a crawl as the entire United States' military shrank to almost pre-war levels. Even the most technologically advanced ships of this time were extremely labor intensive. The crews were all male, and largely all white. The most common ship in the Navy, the destroyer, averaged 375 feet long, displaced 2000 tons, and had a crew of 329 officers and men. Submarines were diesel powered, 311 feet long, displaced 1,525 tons and had a crew of 60 officers and men. Surface navigation technology consisted of using radar and optical devices to determine lines of position, then transferring those lines to a chart and fixing the ship's position, or dead reckoning (a form of scientific guesswork), and celestial navigation on inexact charts. In coastal waters, an experienced team can calculate a fix every three minutes, which effectively means they knew where the ship was two minutes earlier. Computers existed but were in their infancy and had limited shipboard utility. Naval operations remained much as they had during the war, which in turn were not dissimilar to pre-war operations. North Korea's attack on the South brought a renewed emphasis on wartime equipment, manning and operations, an emphasis that carried risk even away from the battlefield.

---

[116] "14 United States Code 239 (Repealed)". U.S. Govt. Printing Office. Retrieved 15 September 2016. Section 10(b) of Pub. L. 86–155 provided that repeal of this section and section 309 of this title shall become effective on Nov. 1, 1959.

USS *Brownson* and USS *Charles H. Roan* - 1950

In the early morning of November 8, 1950, during Atlantic Ocean night operations, someplace between the United States and Bermuda, the U.S. destroyers USS *Charles H. Roan* (DD 853) and USS *Brownson* (DD 868) collided. Both ships suffered significant damage, and five sailors died.

The two ships were *Gearing*-class destroyers, 390 feet and six inches long drawing 3,479 tons fully loaded. They each carried approximately 325 sailors and 20 officers. The *Gearing*-class was a subtly upgraded version of the *Allen M. Sumner*-class which in turn were upgraded *Fletcher*-class destroyers. All told, there were almost three hundred ships of these three classes and their memory forms the core legend of a U.S. Navy destroyer; lean, quick, lightly armed, multi-task, small crews – commonly called 'tincans' or 'greyhounds of the fleet.' Built between 1942 and 1946, these ships served in the U.S. Navy into the 1980s and many continued in foreign service for decades longer. They were at the same time hardy, and fragile. The last active *Gearing*-class destroyer decommissioned in 2014 after almost 70 years of service in the U.S. and Mexican Navies. Destroyers, in the World War II vintage, were plentiful, relatively inexpensive, and surprisingly hardy.[117]

Another feature prevalent in World War II destroyers was the ease of upgrades. While both *Brownson* and *Charles H. Roan* were only a few years old at the time of their collision, both were improved over original construction and *Brownson* was fresh from a major upgrade, some of which received credit for lessening her damage in the collision.

The operations included other destroyers, a repair ship, and an anti-submarine aircraft carrier, USS *Palau* (CVE 122). Operating at night is always challenging and wartime operations

---

[117] Norman Friedman, *U.S. Destroyers: an illustrated design history* (Annapolis, MD: Naval Institute Press, 2004). 129-31.

are even more so. *Brownson* and *Charles H. Roan* were in position protecting the carrier which included turning off their navigation lights.[118] At around 1 a.m. on November 8th, *Palau* radioed that she was changing course, a signal each ship interpreted differently.[119] As the two destroyers adjusted their positions in the protective screen around the carrier, they essentially turned into one another.

At high speed, at night, in the open ocean, *Brownson*'s Executive Officer, Lieutenant Commander Francesco Costagliola, said the initial impact was like striking a large wave.[120] The results, however, were very different. In *Charles H. Roan* the impact punched a hole that flooded her after engine room, crushed the amidships deckhouse, and nearly tore off a five-inch gun mount. The collision also demolished the aft officers' quarters, aft chief's quarters, machine shop and washroom facilities.[121] Five sailors aboard *Charles H. Roan* died.

Aboard *Brownson*, the damage was less critical, and less deadly, but visually more noticeable. Almost fifty feet of her forward bow, directly under her large painted ships numbers, were gone.[122] The collision was a classic t-bone strike - *Brownson* drove perpendicularly headfirst into *Charles H. Roan*'s midsection. *Brownson*'s bow looked like the open mouth of a large sea monster.

Both crews worked through the night to stabilize damage

---

[118] Francesco Costagliola, "Oral History Interview Capt. Francesco Costagliola USNA Class of 1941," interview by Donald R. Lennon, *East Carolina Manuscript Collection*, March 30, 1990. 23.
[119] Commander Destroyer Force U.S. Atlantic Fleet, letter of January 3, 1951. Author's personal file.
[120] Costagliola, 23.
[121] "Two Damaged Destroyers Here After Collision in "High Speed Manoeuvres," *The Royal Gazette* (Hamilton, Bermuda), November 13, 1950.
[122] ibid

and *Brownson* limped while a repair ship towed *Charles H. Roan* into Bermuda. *Brownson*'s damaged bow was removed and sealed over.[123] She steamed home fifty feet shorter than she left. That winter she underwent another upgrade period and received a transplanted bow from a decommissioned sister ship. *Charles H. Roan* spent a little more time in Bermuda before heading back to the states for permanent repairs.

The Navy conducted a Court of Inquiry, just as it did for the *Indianapolis* sinking. While *Brownson* was faulted, only her Officer of the Deck, the officer charged with operating the ship, was charged. Her captain was not on the bridge and not deemed legally culpable. *Charles H. Roan*'s commanding officer, Commander David L. Martineau, who was on the bridge, was recommended for court-martial. He left the ship on her return to the states, was tried and acquitted that spring. [124] Because of his acquittal there is no record of trial, no recorded testimony, not even a recorded charge sheet. *Brownson*'s Officer of the Deck, Lieutenant Robert G. Light, was tried, found guilty and, like Captain McVay, was moved down the seniority list.[125]

While *Brownson*'s captain was not legally culpable, the Board of Inquiry did recommend administrative action. On December 29, 1950, Commander Eugene B. Henry received notification from Commander Destroyer Force, U.S. Atlantic Fleet Admiral Frank G Fahrion that he intended "in the near future, to issue [him] a letter of censure" based on the findings and opinions of the Court of Inquiry. Fahrion closed the letter with "the necessity of taking this action is regretted."[126] This letter was an advance warning that a formal notice was coming - which it did on January 3, 1951. The subsequent exchange between Henry and Fahrion is fascinating.

---

[123] Costagliola, 27.
[124] "General Court-martial in Your Case," G. L. Russell to Commander David L. Martineau, U.S. Navy, May 2, 1951. Author's personal file.
[125] Costagliola, 27.
[126] "Proposed Disciplinary Action," F. G. Fahrion to Commander Eugene B. Henry, Jr. U.S. Navy, December 29, 1950. Author's personal file.

Admiral Fahrion's letter detailed the issues identified by the Court of Inquiry and his own staff's review. Critical to this review were the facts that the International Rules of the Road required *Brownson* to avoid *Charles H. Roan*, that *Brownson* should have slowed, and should have turned on emergency lighting. The letter recognized that Henry was not on the bridge, did not know of the course changes, and that Lieutenant Light was required to notify Commander Henry of any course changes.[127] In other words, while Henry was in command, he was potentially liable for actions by his command and not merely his own actions.

Fahrion's letter laid out three specific charges against Henry: that he failed to prepare and promulgate adequate night orders, that he failed to "indoctrinate and impress upon the officers of [his] command standing watches underway...with the necessity of keeping [him] fully informed," and that he failed to properly train his officers in the Rules of the Road and use of emergency lighting.[128]

With clear understanding of what Admiral Fahrion believed, Commander Henry provided a reply refuting each charge. In three and a half single-spaced pages Henry defends himself, and Lieutenant Light, against each of the charges. Commander Henry submitted detailed training schedules for formal instruction held with his officers before the exercise, including the Rules of the Road, and that this formal instruction was repeatedly reinforced via watch instruction.

Henry detailed that over three months in command he was unaware of any instance where he was not properly notified. At the time of the collision, the ship had been underway for a week with clear and correct information passed to him by all his

---

[127] "Letter of censure, proposed action concerning," F. G. Fahrion to Commander Eugene B. Henry, Jr. U.S. Navy, January 3, 1951. Author's personal file.
[128] "Statement in regard to proposed letter of censure; submission of," Eugene B. Henry, Jr. to Commander Destroyer Force, U.S. Atlantic Fleet, January 18, 1951. Author's personal file.

watchstanders. After seven consecutive days, he saw no need to reiterate what was, by then, obvious to all.

Henry dedicated almost a page to Lieutenant Light's defense — partly in support of his own actions and also supporting Light's. Light not only knew the Rules of the Road, he was one of the ship's trainers. Light knew to steer clear of *Charles H. Roan*, but because of the operations with darkened ship and reduced radio signals, he did not contact his opposite number and instead assumed action on *Charles H. Roan*'s part. Light did not turn on lights, not because of oversight, but because he did not have time and chose instead to order the engines back full and warn the crew of impending collision.

While Henry closed with his defense of Light, his opening statement is also important and contains the only use of responsibility, accountability, or culpability in the files.

> I have no desire whatsoever to attempt to evade or belittle my responsibilities as Commanding Officer of the U.S.S. *BROWNSON* (DD868) either as to general duties and responsibilities or in regard to the adequacy of specific night orders for the night of 7-8 November 1950, the indoctrination and training of my officers in the use of emergency lighting and in the Rules of the Road and with respect to the officer of the deck keeping me fully informed of all emergencies for radical changes in course or 'speed actual or proposed.[129]

Fahrion's response? "You are informed that the explanation submitted by you...concerning the deficiencies alleged against you...is satisfactory, and Commander Destroyer Force, U.S. Atlantic Fleet, considers that you are fully exonerated."[130] Farhion recognized that Henry's actions prior to

---

[129] "Letter of censure, proposed action concerning," F. G. Fahrion to Commander Eugene B. Henry, Jr. U.S. Navy, January 3, 1951. Author's personal file.

[130] "Letter of censure, reconsideration of action concerning," F. G. Fahrion to Commander Eugene B. Henry, Jr. U.S. Navy, January 25, 1951. Author's personal file.

the collision were appropriate – he trained his officers, he advised them on ship operations, and he had clear and promulgated standards. While Lieutenant Light's actions might have prevented the collision, Light did not act negligently or recklessly; those actions occurred aboard *Charles H. Roan*. Of note, the letters between Henry and Fahrion concluded at least three months before Martineau's trial and acquittal.

Commander Henry completed command of *Brownson* and continued with command of destroyer tender USS *Arcadia* (AD 23), Commander Destroyer Flotilla FIVE, and service with the Joint Chiefs of Staff. He retired in 1969 after 30 years of service and died in Newport, RI in 1995.

While Henry's career bounced back, the court-martialed and acquitted captain of *Charles H. Roan* bounced farther. After command of *Charles H. Roan*, and subsequent acquittal at court-martial, Commander Martineau promoted to Captain in 1952, and at sea commanded the destroyer tender USS *Everglades* (AD 24, 1957-1958), and the heavy cruiser USS *Los Angeles* (CA 135, 1958-1959). Ashore, before commanding *Charles H. Roan*, he served as the Chief of Naval Personnel's legislative assistant where he was instrumental in developing the Officer Personnel Act of 1947. These laws governed commissioned officer selection, promotion, and retirement for almost 40 years. Based on this experience he later served as Assistant Chief of Special Projects where he helped create legislation providing Social Security, Survivor Benefits and Civilian Medical Care to military personnel and their dependents. He retired in 1959 as a Rear Admiral and also served as a military consultant to the House Armed Services Committee on Vietnam.[131]

After his death in 1994, Admiral Martineau's daughter donated his records, papers, correspondence, and orders to Eastern Carolina University. There are detailed records of his work with Congress, his service aboard *Los Angeles*,

---

[131] Joe Lambert, "Rear Admiral David L. Martineau," *The Jolly Cholly* 18 (Spring 2015):10-11.

Everglades, war diaries, and even videotapes. There is scant mention of his time in command of *Charles H. Roan* — and not a single mention of the court-martial. In fact, it is almost as if the years 1950 to 1953 were erased from his legacy. While the collision was avoidable, as almost all are, neither commander was deemed culpable for the actions of others. Each was called to account, the account was given, the officer was held accountable. In 1952 the glimmer of a coming change appeared on the horizon.

USS *Wasp* and USS *Hobson* - 1952

World War II aircraft carriers were smaller than today's behemoths but were still exceptionally large ships. Almost 900-feet long, 40,000-tons displacement at full load, 150-feet wide, and manned with 2,500 officers and crew the ships were, and are, floating cities living under an active airport. These ships were powered by steam boilers: pressurized and superheated steam driving turbines to move their massive bulk at over 30 knots. With limited local self-defense capability, and mindful that any aircraft failing to launch or land needed rescue, these monsters used smaller ships as escorts, normally destroyers or destroyer escorts. From World War II into the Vietnam War these escorts ranged from between 2,000 to 6,000 tons. When two identical ships collide the relative size disparity is unnoticed, as with *Brownson* and *Charles H. Roan*; the resulting damage was comparable between them. When a 40,000-ton ship strikes a ship 1/20th her size, the result is significantly, and horrifically, different.

On April 26, 1952, the World War II-era *Essex*-class aircraft carrier USS *Wasp* (CV 18) launched a flight of aircraft on a simulated strike as she steamed toward the Mediterranean Sea. Two destroyers, USS *Rodman* (DMS 21) and USS *Hobson* (DMS 26) acted as plane guards, standing by to recover any pilot or crew from crashed aircraft. All three ships were dark — no running lights, in fact, no visible lights other than red aircraft warning lights on the top of each ship's mast.

Shortly after 10 p.m., *Wasp* informed the destroyers that the simulated strike mission was returning and she was altering course and speed to recover the aircraft. *Wasp* and *Rodman* needed to simply turn and change speed. However, *Hobson's* maneuver was more complicated, but not unusual, as she closed from a mile and a half away from *Wasp* to within a half mile. *Hobson*'s captain, Lieutenant Commander William J. Tierney, on his seventh day underway after only five weeks in command, decided to change course, speed up and then turn left towards the carrier as he arrived in his assigned position. His officer of the deck advised an alternate course of action. However, Tierney believed his plan was best, and fastest, and took control of the ship's movements.

> *Hobson* first turned right to 130° true and increased speed to 27 knots. After about two minutes or at 2223 [10:23 pm] as noted on the chart and well before the *Wasp* bore 010°T, the *Hobson* came left to an average course of about 090° true which she held until the distance to the *Wasp* was closed to about 1240 yards. The next move of the *Hobson* at 2224, directed by her commanding officer, was an inexplicable turn to the left using standard rudder. The commanding officer apparently soon realized that he was crossing about the bow of the *Wasp* and was in an extremely dangerous position, so he attempted to extricate his ship by increasing his rudder to full left, followed by hard and emergency flank speed ahead.[132]

At roughly the same time *Hobson* turned left, *Wasp* also

---

[132] United States, Department of the Navy, The Atlantic Command and United States Atlantic Fleet Headquarters of the Commander In Chief, *Record of Proceedings of a Court of Inquiry to inquire into all of the circumstances surrounding the collision between the USS Wasp (CV-18) and the USS Hobson (DMS-26) which occurred at or near Latitude 42-21 North Longitude 44-15 West on or about 27 April 1952* (Washington, DC, 1952). 2.

came left to the recovery course and *Wasp*'s commanding officer, Captain Burnham C. McCaffrey, saw *Hobson* coming towards his ship. McCaffrey took control of *Wasp*'s movements, and ordered the engines "back emergency full." A minute after Tierney turned *Hobson* left, in front of the speeding carrier, *Wasp* sliced into the much smaller destroyer at a nearly perpendicular angle, cutting *Hobson* in half.

Hobson, a *Gleaves*-class destroyer smaller than *Brownson* and *Charles H. Roan*, carried 237 officers and men. 176 lost their lives that night, 61 survived. Lieutenant Commander Tierney was one of those who died. Both halves of the ship sank within five minutes, and all records were lost. The resulting Court of Inquiry relied on *Wasp's* records and survivor testimony in recreating the accident. The Court opined that sole fault for the collision lay with Tierney even though they could not determine why he turned left when he did.[133]

The accident itself, tragic as it was, at first glance provides little direct insight into crimes of command. The aftermath, however, both exemplified and hyperbolized the mystique of command. Less than three weeks after the collision, and a month before the Court of Inquiry was complete, the *Wall Street Journal* published an editorial which became part of modern naval lore:

> One night past some thirty thousand tons of ships went hurtling at each other through the darkness. When they had met, two thousand tons of ship and a hundred and seventy-six men lay at the bottom of the sea in a far off place.
> Now comes the cruel business of accountability. Those who were there must answer how it happened and whose was the error that made it happen.
> It is a cruel business because it was no wish of destruction that killed this ship and its hundred and seventy-six men; the accountability lies with good men

---

[133] Ibid, 3-4.

who erred in judgment under stress so great that it is almost its own excuse. Cruel, because no matter how deep the probe, it cannot change the dead, because it cannot probe deeper than remorse.

And it seems more cruel still, because all around us in other places we see the plea accepted that what is done is beyond discussion, and that for good men in their human errors there should be afterwards no accountability.

We are told it is all to no avail to review so late the courses that led to the crash of Pearl Harbor, to debate the courses set a Yalta and Potsdam, to inquire how it is that one war won leaves us only with wreckage and with two worlds still hurtling at each other through the darkness. To inquire into these things, now, we are reminded, will not change the dead in Schofield Barracks or on Heartbreak Ridge, nor will it change the dying that will come after the wrong courses.

We are told, too, how slanderous it is to probe into the doings of a Captain now dead who cannot answer for himself, to hold him responsible for what he did when he was old and tired and when he did what he did under terrible stress and from the best of intentions. How useless to debate the wrong courses of his successor caught up in a storm not of his own devising. How futile to talk of what is past when the pressing question is how to keep from sinking.

Everywhere else we are told how inhuman it is to submit men to the ordeal of answering for themselves. To have them before committees and badger them with questions as to where they were and what they were doing while the ship of state careened from one course to another. This probing into the sea seems more merciless because almost everywhere we have abandoned accountability. What is done is done and why torture men with asking them afterward, why?

Whom do we hold answerable for the sufferance of dishonesty in government, for the reckless waste of public monies, for the incompetence that wrecks the currency, for the blunders that killed and still kill many times a hundred and seventy-six men in Korea? We can bring to bar the dishonest men, yes. But we are told men should no longer be held accountable for what they do as well as for what they intend. To err is not only human; it absolves responsibility.

Everywhere, that is, except on the sea. On the sea there is a tradition older even than the traditions of the country itself and wiser in its age than this new custom. It is the tradition that with responsibility goes authority and with them goes accountability.

This accountability is not for the intentions but for the deed. The Captain of a ship, like the Captain of a state, is given honor and privileges and trust beyond other men. But let him set the wrong course, let him touch ground, let him bring disaster to his ship or to his men, and he must answer for what he has done. No matter what, he cannot escape.

No one knows yet what happened on the sea after that crash in the night. But nine men left the bridge of the sinking ship and went into the darkness. Eight men came back to tell what happened there. The ninth, whatever happened, will not answer now because he has already answered for his accountability.

It is cruel this accountability of good and well-intentioned men. But the choice is that or an end to responsibility and finally, as the cruel sea has taught, and end to the confidence and trust in the men who lead, for men will not long trust leaders who feel themselves beyond accountability for what they do. And when men lose confidence and trust in those who lead, order disintegrates into chaos and purposeful ships into floating derelicts.[134]

While unsigned, Vermont C. Royster is widely accepted as the editorial's primary author. Royster served in the Navy during World War II and his service exemplified *The Naval Officer's Guide* when it recognized that wartime commanding officers might not have the same level of experience as in peacetime. Royster joined the Naval Reserve in 1940, rose to lieutenant commander by 1944 and commanded destroyer escort USS *Jack Miller* (DE 410) in 1944 and 1945. Royster was the subject of an inquiry when he ran his training patrol boat, PC-1262, aground on the Miami Beach causeway in 1942 or 1943. Royster was found blameless and a mechanical failure faulted for the accident.[135] He left the Navy when the war ended and returned to journalism at the *Wall Street Journal*. By contrast, Tierney was commissioned in 1941, and at the time of the collision had eleven years' experience as a commissioned officer and was in his second command in *Hobson*.

Where the court placed blame with Tierney, citing reports of Tierney's personal action in command, it absolved Captain McCaffrey of any culpability. In August 1953, he took command of Naval Air Station Jacksonville and two years later served as the Vice Deputy Commandant of the Industrial College of the Armed Forces before retiring in 1956 as a Captain. McCaffrey was *Wasp*'s seventh captain. Her first four all promoted to Flag rank, and her next two were caretaker commanders after World War II. Four of the five captains after McCaffrey promoted to Flag rank. Given McCaffrey's otherwise unblemished record the collision and press coverage are the most likely reasons he did not promote. He died in 1966 and is buried in Arlington National Cemetery.

One commanding officer lost his life, another likely lost promotion, however, the lasting legacy of the collision lies not in the commander's legacy, but in Vermont Royster's words via

---

[134] "*Hobson*'s Choice," *The Wall Street Journal* (New York), May 14, 1952.
[135] Vermont Royster, *My Own, My Country's Time: A Journalist's Journey* (Chapel Hill, NC: Algonquin Books, 1983). 107.

the *Wall Street Journal* editorial board. Royster was familiar with the "tradition older even than the traditions of the country itself" and the idea that "with responsibility goes authority and with them goes accountability." Royster, in citing accountability, clearly recognized that "those who were there must answer how it happened and whose was the error that made it happen." This accountability is far, far different from assigning blame or finding culpability. Blame however, was determined and placed with Lieutenant Commander Tierney. This action, of finding fault with a dead captain unable to defend or explain himself, had long and far reaching implications as the editorial now underpins the modern concept of naval accountability and its conflation with blame and culpability. Royster's words are still used today when naval officers discuss the burdens of command. However, at least in 1952, blame remained fixed on a commander's individual and personal actions in command, rather than the actions of others within the command. This too was to change, but not right away.

USS *Bennington* - 1954

Like *Wasp*, USS *Bennington* (CV 20) was part of the World War II-era *Essex*-class of aircraft carriers. Ordered in the initial buildup after Pearl Harbor she was commissioned in 1944 and served in the Pacific Theater conducting air strikes on the Japanese home islands, supporting the Okinawa invasion and later occupation of Japan. She decommissioned in 1946 as part of the post-war drawdown. During the Korean War buildup, *Bennington* spent two years undergoing modernization to support launching and recovering larger and heavier jet aircraft. This upgrade included new launch catapults, new arresting gear to recover faster and heavier aircraft, lengthening her hull, and completely redesigning her control island. When she recommissioned on November 13, 1952, she was the most modern aircraft carrier in the world.

The sea is already a dangerous place, but adding

pressurized steam, hydraulic catapults, almost a hundred jet aircraft, over 600 tons of bombs, rockets, missiles, 231,000 gallons of aviation fuel and 1.8 million gallons of diesel fuel-oil make these ships some of the most dangerous workplaces in the world. On April 27, 1953, a boiler explosion aboard *Bennington* killed eleven sailors, but a 1954 accident with one of her catapults became one of the worst shipboard accidents of the modern era.

On May 26, 1954, USS *Bennington* was operating 80 miles south-southeast of Brenton Reef transiting between Norfolk and Narragansett Bay. She began flight operations at 0600 and in thirteen minutes launched thirteen aircraft. Shortly after the thirteenth launch, bridge personnel saw smoke billowing from under the flight deck. Smoke also filled the forward hangar bay and many of the ship's forward spaces. The bridge sounded the general and fire alarms. Within minutes at least three explosions rocked the ship. Within seconds over 100 sailors were dead and by the time the fires were out over 200 were injured. Damage was localized, but in the catapult room and on the flight deck it was extensive. Investigators estimated repairs to *Bennington* would take three months and cost $2 million ($18 million in 2017).[136]

The ensuing Court of Inquiry determined that flammable hydraulic fluid used to pressurize the catapult system ignited and exploded. There was no major fire, but the explosions caused some smaller fires. The immediate impact of the explosion and later asphyxiation by smoke and gaseous fumes caused most of the deaths. Everyone in the catapult machinery and pump rooms died, leaving no witnesses to the actual cause of the accident. Forensics ultimately located a ruptured pipe that likely leaked hydraulic fluid, but no specific cause of fire or explosion was ever determined. Diesel ignition, the spontaneous combustion of

---

[136] United States, Department of the Navy, Commander Air Force, U.S. Atlantic Fleet, *Court of Inquiry to Inquire into an Explosion and Fire Aboard the U.S.S. BENNINGTON which occurred 26 May 1954* (Washington, DC, 1954).

oil under pressure, was opined as the most likely cause and sabotage was completely ruled out. The court also specifically opined that "no fault or blame should accrue" to the commanding or executive officer and the explosions were "not due to the intent, fault, negligence, or inefficiency of any person in the naval service."[137]

The court's recommendations were mostly related to engineering changes or improvements in carrier catapult systems. The court also recommended an emphasis on realistic damage control drills as well as clearly recommending against legal or disciplinary action for *Bennington*'s leadership. After eight endorsements and a year of administrative travel, the Chief of Naval Operations approved the court's recommendations.[138]

Ultimately, 178 members of the crew received medals for their actions that day. Over 300 dead and injured and the commanding officer was judged blameless. Naval leadership was aware of problems in catapult systems; a previous accident on board USS *Leyte* (CVA 32) which killed 37 was mentioned throughout the court's report. However, the Navy did not foresee an accident of this magnitude.[139]

Captain William F. Raborn took command of *Bennington* only three weeks before the explosion. He remained in command another year before selecting for promotion to Rear Admiral and transferring ashore. He spent the remainder of his career first leading the Polaris submarine-launched ballistic missile program and then serving as the Deputy Chief of Naval Operations for Development. He retired from the Navy in 1965 before appointment as the Director of Central Intelligence, where he served a little over a year apparently more interested in intelligence technology than working with foreign governments. At no point were there serious considerations of placing blame for 100 deaths on Captain Raborn.

Between 1945 and 1965 there were at least 309 incidents

---

[137] Ibid
[138] Ibid
[139] Ibid

that can be characterized as crimes of command — 74 major explosions or fires, 131 collisions, and 40 groundings. Among those incidents only 12 officers were removed from command; of those, at least five promoted afterwards. Of the 309 incidents, 105 officers promoted at least one rank afterwards.

While the two post-war decades saw little substantive or pervasive change in technology or operations, some administrative changes portended major changes. Nuclear ships and submarines were on the way, and with them a technocratic focus formerly anathema to the Navy. Personnel assignment procedures also changed. Prior to 1957 Pentagon-based staffs made all personnel decisions, even, or especially, for command. Without formal command selection boards a practice known as "cousin detailing" benefited known officers over other, possibly more talented but unknown officers. In 1957, responsibility for officer assignments moved from various offices within the Chief of Naval Operations staff (OPNAV) and consolidated into the Bureau of Personnel. With this consolidation came regular, and regulated, screening boards for command. This change is credited with slowing aviation mishaps,[140] but no records support similar changes on the surface or submarine side.

This era also lacked the later focus on the weight of command responsibility. In 1955 Captain Philip Gallery wrote of his command tour in USS *Pittsburgh* (CA 72).[141] He discusses practical matters of shipboard cleanliness and appearance, ship newspapers, and conduct ashore. Of the many lessons from the article come recognition that ship's crews had time for things other than work and watch keeping. While the weight of command is not mentioned, neither is Captain Gallery's removal from command after a collision on the Saint Lawrence River.[142]

---

[140] Dunn, 43.
[141] Philip D. Gallery, "A Few Ideas of a Cruiser Skipper," *Proceedings*, 81, no. 7 (July 1955)
[142] Daniel V. Gallery, *Eight Bells, and All's Well*, [1st ed. (New York:

While Gallery left command at sea, when his article was published he was in command ashore, as the Commander, Surface Anti-Submarine Development Detachment, Atlantic Fleet.[143] While Captain Gallery retired as a captain, his command experience remained important to the Navy. Admiral Dan Gallery who was involved in the Revolt of the Admirals was Captain Gallery's brother.

By the end of 1965 the United States Navy stood at 880 ships, many still of World War II vintage, and 668,000 personnel. The Cold War was warm, the war in Vietnam was violent and getting larger, and the country was on the precipice of significant social change.

Captain McVay felt the guilt of his decision for the rest of his life. Admiral Loughlin felt no guilt and promoted even though found guilty by court-martial. Lieutenant Commander Tierney lost his life while Captain McCaffree lost upward mobility in his career. Captain Henry and Admiral Martineau recovered, as did Admiral Raborn, and all three served their nation well after their crimes. The recoveries were contemporaneously normal but the change begun with Captain McVay was cemented into naval culture between 1965 and 1985.

Norton, 1965).
[143] Gallery (1955)

3: 1965-1985

The previous chapter showed how the Navy addressed crimes of command in the years following World War II. This chapter introduces the period of change where individual responsibility was replaced with an idea of culpability for the commanding officer, for simply being in command.

The middle of the twentieth century saw significant and far-reaching advancements in naval technology with the arrival of cruise missiles and nuclear-powered ships. USS *Nautilus* (SSN 571) in 1955, the nuclear-powered supercarrier, USS *Enterprise* (CVN 65) and USS *Long Beach* (CGN 9) in 1961 replaced oil-fired steam boilers with nuclear-heated steam creating virtually unlimited power levels. New technology in ship propulsion, missile guidance, and navigation complemented the major 'hot' conflicts of the Cold War, Vietnam and the Cuban Missile Crisis. The Baby Boom generation began service while the vast majority of World War II veterans retired.

The fleet continued shrinking in numbers while ship sizes grew. Destroyers were now over 400 feet long, displaced over 4000 tons, and had a crew of 350 officers and men; but oil-fired boilers still generated steam to turn turbines and rotate propeller shafts. *Long Beach* was 15,000-tons and over 700 feet long – larger and heavier than World War II armored heavy cruisers and the Navy's largest post-war surface combatant. Except for the new nuclear boats, submarines remained diesel powered and largely unchanged from their World War II counterparts at 300-feet long, displacing 1,500 tons and had a crew of 60 to 80 officers and men. The first two nuclear submarines, *Seawolf* and *Nautilus*, were respectively 350 and 320 feet long and both displaced over 3000 tons with crews of just over 100 officers and men. The first production class of nuclear submarine, *Skate*, displaced 2250 tons, was 267 feet long and manned by 84 officers and men. Ship navigation continued on inadequate and incomplete charts; however electronic navigation systems, (1944) and inertial navigation systems (1950), slowly replaced celestial navigation. By 1965 most ships had some means of electronic navigation for coastal, or even open ocean, positioning. Surface launched anti-air missiles debuted. Technological complexity in new ships rose while most of the force aged. The surface navy instituted a formal department head school in 1962[1] and a command school in 1969.[2] Both moves attempted to solve training, manning and experience problems in surface ships. Prior to 1962 department heads, the shipboard equivalent to middle managers, were sometimes newly commissioned officers with no experience,[3] or very limited experience. Creating the new department head course moved those middle management tours towards officers with at least five years of commissioned service – significantly increasing the experience and maturity of the officers in these positions.[4] This increase in experience and maturity made it to the fleet, unevenly and slowly, especially for smaller ships.

In between technological and training changes were collisions, groundings, and fires – at least 569 crimes of command removing 22 commanding officers, almost twice the number removed between 1945 and 1965. There were almost twice as many groundings (74 compared to 40), twice as many collisions (220 compared to 131) and twice as many explosions and fires (156 compared to 74). At the same time, ship numbers dropped, and by 1981, the Navy had 521 ships, the post-war low to that date. More importantly, the ideas of blame and culpability moved from one of individual responsibility of the commanding officer towards one of command culpability – the commander now responsible, even accountable and culpable, for the actions of the entire command.

---

[1] Raymond J. Hart, "Surface Warfare Officers: The Need for Professionalism," *Proceedings* 102, no. 6 (June 1976):40.
[2] Ibid, 41.
[3] H. H. Sacks, "Shoreside Checkout for Seagoing Destroyer Officers," *Proceedings 88*, no. 2 (February 1962).
[4] Hart, 40.

USS *Hartley* and *Blue Master* - 1965

At 4:30 a.m. on June 16, 1965, Norwegian motor vessel *Blue Master* struck USS *Hartley* (DE 1029) as they both steamed near the Chesapeake Bay entrance. *Blue Master* was on her way from Baltimore to the Atlantic Ocean and scheduled cargo delivery in New Orleans. *Hartley* was on her way from Newport, Rhode Island to a naval anchorage just inside the Chesapeake Bay. The weather was not unusual for a coastal mid-Atlantic early morning in the summer - intermittent rain showers causing reduced visibility, blustery winds followed by a rapid clearing of the weather and visibility up to 10 nautical miles, and then the cycle repeated.[5]

Blue Master's transit from Baltimore was uneventful. Following normal procedures, the 8,645 ton, 509-foot[6] break bulk freighter embarked a coastal pilot for assistance navigating the bay entrance and hove to and disembarked the pilot. The pilot testified that when he left the bridge, *Blue Master* was unaware that *Hartley* was in the area, and had neither seen her by eye nor by radar.[7]

Hartley's bridge team woke the captain, Lieutenant Commander Reo Beaulieu, at 3:45 a.m. as scheduled and within minutes he was on the bridge to supervise the inward passage. *Hartley*'s bridge team could see two ships and a pilot vessel.

---

[5] United States, Department of the Navy, Commander Cruiser-Destroyer Force, Atlantic Representative, *Formal Board of Investigation to Inquire into the Circumstances Surrounding the Collision of USS Hartley (DE-1029) and Motor Vessel Blue Master and Possible Subsequent Grounding of Hartley* (Washington, DC, 1965).
[6] Skip Lewis, "M/V Steel Engineer - USMM Cargo Ship," Isthmian Lines, May 10, 2010, accessed September 21, 2017, http://www.isthmianlines.com/ships/sm_steel_engineer.htm.
[7] *Formal board of investigation to inquire into the circumstances surrounding the collision of USS Hartley (DE-1029) and motor vessel Blue Master and possible subsequent grounding of Hartley.*

Shortly before 4 a.m., *Hartley* turned towards Thimble Shoals Channel, the main thoroughfare from the Atlantic Ocean to Norfolk, Virginia.[8]

Hartley, a 314-feet long and 1,270 tons *Dealey*-class destroyer escort commissioned in 1956, maneuvered past one of the ships at the same time *Blue Master* finished disembarking her pilot. *Blue Master* turned left and sped up, headed to sea. In doing so, she changed from passing down *Hartley*'s port side and instead turned across *Hartley*'s bow. Beaulieu immediately took control of *Hartley*'s engines and rudder, increased speed and turned his ship left. Inexplicably, *Blue Master* turned right, closing the distance between the two ships. As *Hartley* passed in front of *Blue Master*, Beaulieu ordered his ship to the right, attempting to swing the stern away from *Blue Master*'s bow. *Blue Master* was still accelerating and struck *Hartley* on the starboard quarter, piercing her almost to the middle. *Hartley* sustained damage more than $700,000 ($5.4 million in 2017) and underwent significant repairs in Norfolk.[9]

A subsequent Court of Inquiry found fault on both sides. By turning left in front of *Hartley*, *Blue Master* violated the nautical rules of the road and placed both ships in danger. Her second turn, to the right, exacerbated the situation. *Hartley*, however, also violated the rules with her left turn. The second turn, the right turn that swung *Hartley*'s stern, was credited as mitigating the resulting damage and was cited as the primary reason there were no fatalities and that *Hartley* was not cut in two like *Hobson*. The investigation praised *Hartley*'s bridge team for calm behavior, maintaining control before, during, and after the collision, though criticizing Beaulieu for an aloof manner towards training issues aboard *Hartley*.[10]

While the Court of Inquiry placed the greater blame on *Blue Master*, it also recommended Lieutenant Commander Beaulieu receive a non-punitive letter of instruction. However,

---

[8] Ibid
[9] Ibid
[10] Ibid

the opinions and recommendations changed as the court's report moved up the chain of command. Beaulieu's immediate superior, Captain W. S Mayer, rejected the opinion alluding to Beaulieu's aloofness, citing his observations even though he took command of Escort Squadron Ten after the collision. However, the Commander Cruiser-Destroyer Force, Atlantic, citing Beaulieu's error in judgment evidenced in the left turn, also rejected the recommended non-punitive letter, calling instead for the greater punishment of a Fleet Commander letter of censure. Where a non-punitive letter would remain between the recipient and issuer, a letter of censure would permanently enter into Beaulieu's service record and certainly be a subject of discussion in future promotion boards.[11]

Beaulieu learned of the impending letter on October 9, 1965. The letter included an additional admonition about the use, training, and manning of *Hartley*'s Combat Information Center (CIC) and some personnel decisions Beaulieu made before getting underway in Newport. The convening authority recognized that these additional items did not cause the collision, but believed that different actions in and towards the CIC might have prevented the accident.[12]

Beaulieu appealed the letter, citing his vision and recollections of *Blue Master*'s movements, the timing of both ship's actions, and refuting the idea that additional or different manning in CIC might have changed the outcome. Despite a strong endorsement from Captain Mayer, Commander in Chief, U.S. Atlantic Fleet denied Beaulieu's appeal, and in February 1966 the letter of reprimand was placed in his official record.[13] Beaulieu was passed over for commander that same year.

In January 1967, Beaulieu wrote the court of inquiry's senior member, recently promoted Rear Admiral Francis J. Fitzpatrick, seeking his advice. Fitzpatrick replied that he was unaware of the changes or outcome - neither he nor any other

---

[11] Ibid
[12] Ibid
[13] Ibid

board members were apprised of the changing recommendations as the report moved up the chain of command. He wrote:

> At the time we concluded the proceedings, the Board members agreed that the intricacies of the collision situation were so great that probably no two people evermore would agree as to the factors involved. What has transpired in the process of review seems to have borne that out. As my own personal opinion I confess to considerable surprise that you received a punitive letter from the Type Commander.[14]

Admiral Fitzpatrick, from the limited information Beaulieu sent him, inferred that the letter of reprimand covered two issues - first, the action with the rules of the road, and second matters of Navy administration. The board, Fitzpatrick recalled, believed that the Navy bore some culpability in the second instance,[15] an opinion Commander Cruiser-Destroyer Force, Atlantic certainly did not share, instead placing all administrative actions squarely with Beaulieu.

In the end, Fitzpatrick recommended Beaulieu submit a formal letter to the next selection board, detailing additional information from the court of inquiry not included in the letter of reprimand or Beaulieu's official response. Beaulieu's operational commander at the time of the collision, Captain Raymond W. Allen, also submitted a letter supporting Beaulieu's selection for promotion. In the recommendation, he criticized the letter of reprimand as "stark and barren" and missing important facts from the court's report. His recollections of *Hartley*'s crew during an Operational Readiness Inspection only weeks before the collision were of "a well-trained team

---

[14] Francis J. Fitzpatrick to Reo Beaulieu, January 27, 1967, Washington, DC.

[15] *Formal board of investigation to inquire into the circumstances surrounding the collision of USS Hartley (DE-1029) and motor vessel Blue Master and possible subsequent grounding of Hartley.*

efficiently operating a well-maintained ship and well prepared to carry out assigned tasks" when Allen made recommendations Beaulieu immediately acted on them.[16] Allen further commented that "Lieutenant Commander Beaulieu['s leadership] was severely tested during and immediately after the collision, and as established by the Board of Investigation, he was not found wanting."[17]

Notwithstanding Admiral Loughlin's experience, selection board proceedings are secret, so while we cannot know for certain whether these letters made the difference, the fact remains that the next selection board selected Beaulieu for Commander. He later commanded a Navy Recruiting District before retiring after 20 years of service to spend time with his family. He currently resides in Lincoln, Rhode Island.

USS *Frank E. Evans* and HMAS *Melbourne* - 1969

On June 3, 1969, United States, Australian, New Zealand, and British naval vessels took part in a South East Asia Treaty Organization exercise called "Sea Spirit."[18] Two of the ships, the *Allen M Sumner*-class destroyer USS *Frank E. Evans* (DD-754) and HMAS *Melbourne*, collided. *Melbourne,* a British built light aircraft carrier 702 feet long and 20,000 tons cut the 2,200 ton and 376 foot long *Frank E. Evans* in two, killing 74 of her sailors.

Around 9 p.m. the evening prior, Commander Albert Sydney McLemore finished writing his instructions for *Frank E.*

---

[16] "Comments and Observations regarding Lieutenant Commander Reo A. Beaulieu, USN, 565850/1100," Raymond W. Allen to Chief of Naval Personnel, April 12, 1967.
[17] *Formal board of investigation to inquire into the circumstances surrounding the collision of USS Hartley (DE-1029) and motor vessel Blue Master and possible subsequent grounding of Hartley.*
[18] United States, Department of the Navy, Commander, Seventh Fleet, *Report of the Combined USN-RAN Board of Investigation into the Collision Between HMAS Melbourne and USS Frank E. Evans convened by COMSEVENTHFLT and ACNB*, Jerome King (Washington, DC, 1969). 4.

Evans' night watches. These "Night Orders" supplement, alter or elaborate on an individual captain's "Standing Orders" - written instructions for the conduct of shipboard watches. Within these orders are routine reporting requirements, specific nighttime events and special instructions for them, and often admonitions to remain alert, report unusual actions, and so on. Around midnight Commander McLemore retired to his sea cabin for the night, the night's officer of the deck having control of the ship's engines and rudder - within the realm of the Standing Orders, the supplemental Night Orders, and the rules governing the exercise. The ships were operating in a darkened ship condition, but the weather was calm, and the seas were glass, easily reflecting the ample moonlight.[19]

HMAS *Melbourne* was scheduled for flight operations that night, but McLemore was apparently not concerned. He made no mention of them in his night orders, and he commonly allowed his watch officers to conduct routine operations unsupervised. His actions were not unusual, at least not between commanders and well trained and trusted watch officers. Overlooked in his planning was assignment as the rescue destroyer.[20]

The Officer of the Deck, the positional senior officer on watch, was Lieutenant Junior Grade Ronald Ramsey. Ramsey was in his fourth month standing this watch. However, his formal designation was signed only ten days prior. His assistant, who directed the movement of rudder and engines, Lieutenant Junior Grade James Hopson, was in his nineteenth month aboard *Frank E. Evans*. He was an experienced, yet unqualified, watch officer.[21] Something not uncommon into the early 1970s, however completely forbidden in today's administratively guided Navy.

At 3:10 a.m. HMAS *Melbourne*'s commander, Captain John Phillip Stevenson, acting in his role as the group's tactical

---

[19] Ibid, 5-6.
[20] Ibid, 7.
[21] Ibid, 7.

commander, ordered *Frank E. Evans* to her rescue destroyer station, 1000 yards astern of the carrier. *Frank E. Evans* was somewhere to *Melbourne*'s port beam (left side) when she received her new station orders.[22] Later testimony showed that neither Ramsey nor Hopson had a full recollection, or possibly understanding, of their position relative to *Melbourne*, or where they needed to go. The only way for two ships to safely operate in proximity is with a clear understanding of at least one's course and speed. Knowing the other's course and speed is also helpful.[23]

During the discussion between the two watch officers, they did not contact the Combat Information Center. They also did not call the commanding officer, even though his Standing Orders required a call in the event of any changes in course, speed, or formation.[24]

Seeking to move quickly to the assigned station, *Frank E. Evans* turned as soon as *Melbourne* executed the signal sending her to rescue station. This right turn closed the range between the two ships and increased the closure rate.[25]

Captain Stevenson in *Melbourne* saw *Frank E. Evans*' turn and his seaman's eye told him something was wrong. He directed a signal to *Frank E. Evans* explaining the course he was steering. He also ordered *Melbourne*'s running lights to full brilliance. Compounding the course, speed, location errors, and eschewing available advice and counsel, Ramsey also incorrectly decoded the signal about *Melbourne*'s course, reading it as 160° rather than the correct 260°.[26]

Frank E. Evans finished her turn and steadied on a course the watch officers expected to take them to station. In

---

[22] Ibid, 8.
[23] Ibid, 9.
[24] Ibid
[25] Ibid, 9-10.
[26] Ibid, 10-11.

reality, they were perpendicularly crossing the carrier's bow on a collision course. As Ramsey and Hopson observed *Melbourne*, she did not move as they expected her to. Rather than fall away to the right, she moved leftwards and towards them.[27] Their confusion was so great they could not understand why *Melbourne* wasn't acting as they expected.

Captain Stevenson, far more experienced, ordered another signal to *Frank E. Evans*, "You are on a collision course." By now the two ships were within a mile of each other. Ramsey and Hopson in *Frank E. Evans* heard the signal and immediately turned right. Stevenson ordered *Melbourne* left. The range was now just over a thousand yards between the ships.[28]

Ships turn slowly, especially aircraft carriers. They slow down even more slowly. Seeing collision imminent, *Melbourne*'s watch officers first stopped the engines, then ordered all back full. Ships do not have brakes, and they slow down either with the friction of the water or by backing their engines and applying reverse thrust.

The two ships collided at 3:15 am. *Frank E. Evans* was rolled violently to her right and split in two. The forward section of the ship sank within nine minutes. At least 73 sailors died in the forward section, which included the forward fireroom, the Combat Information Center, and some berthing areas. 37 managed to escape the sinking section and survived. The after section remained afloat and all the crew stationed there rescued.[29]

Melbourne suffered extensive damage around her bow, both above and below the waterline.[30] Large ships, unlike smaller ships and as previously seen with *Wasp*, have a greater

---

[27] Ibid, 11.
[28] Ibid, 10.
[29] Ibid, 13-15.
[30] Ibid

capacity to withstand damage – more steel, more mass, and significantly more reserve buoyancy. After search and rescue operations concluded, *Melbourne* transited unassisted to Singapore, making 15 knots in her damaged state. *Frank E. Evans'* surviving stern section was towed to Naval Base Subic Bay in the Philippines and decommissioned on July 1, 1969.[31]

At the height of both the Cold War and American involvement in Vietnam, political considerations were more paramount than any objective search for truth. A joint United States and Royal Australian Navy board was formed to investigate the tragedy. It met only six days after the collision.[32]

The Australian members were Rear Admiral Hugh D. Stevenson, the Royal Australian Navy deputy chief of naval staff (no relation to *Melbourne* Captain John Stevenson), Captain E.W. Shands, and Captain John Davidson. Davidson was an unusual choice because he was a supply officer with little to no shipboard operational experience.[33]

U.S. Navy junior members were Captain Stephen L. Rusk and Captain Clyde B. Anderson, both former ship and squadron commanders. The senior member was Rear Admiral Jerome King, who at first glance was eminently qualified to lead the board. However, he was also the officer in charge of the exercise during which *Melbourne* and *Frank E. Evans* collided. Some thought that, in essence, he chaired a board investigating his command.[34]

In addition to the political issues (some Australians were already placing blame on *Frank E. Evans*), the board had press issues - at least the American board members had American press issues. The collision was the U.S. Navy's seventh major

---

[31] Ibid, 25.
[32] Louise Esola, *American Boys: The True Story of the Lost 74 of the Vietnam War* (Temecula, CA: Pennway Books, 2014). 238.
[33] Ibid, 240-1.
[34] Ibid, 241-2.

89

disaster in three years including explosions aboard USS *Enterprise* killing 27 men; the loss of nuclear submarine *Scorpion* with 99 men while on her post-builders shakedown cruise; and major fires in USS *King* (4 dead), USS *Franklin D. Roosevelt* (7 dead) and USS *Oriskany* (44 dead.)[35] An Associated Press article quoted unnamed U.S. Navy officers that destroyers were supposed to avoid carriers, and a congressman opined that the Secretary of Defense should take action against the Navy, citing a string of recent issues including the North Korean seizure of USS *Pueblo*, a reconnaissance aircraft shot down by the North Koreans, and a brand new submarine that sank at the pier.[36] To make matters worse, the July 1969 *Esquire* included a three-page story headlined "*Esquire's* Official Court of Inquiry into the Present State of the United States Navy" detailing sixty-seven incidents or accidents between July 1965 and March 1969.[37]

Australian Rear Admiral Gordon John Crabb was the first witness. Crabb was aboard *Melbourne* during the collision with *Frank E. Evans* and much of the testimony sought to determine whether or not he had operational command of the ships. In his day-long testimony he revealed that on May 31, 1969, USS *Everett F. Larson* (DD 830) passed within fifty feet of *Melbourne*. Because of this near miss ships were ordered to remain outside three thousand yards from the carrier, an increase over the standard two thousand.[38]

Despite the admonition to remain outside three thousand yards, the exercise commander, and senior board member, Rear Admiral King, was unhappy with American maneuvering and

---

[35] Jo Stevenson, *In the Wake: The True Story of the Melbourne-Evans Collision, Conspiracy and Cover-Up* (Alexandria: Hale & Iremonger, 1999). 10.
[36] Esola, 244.
[37] "Esquire's Official Court of Inquiry into the Present State of the United States Navy," *Esquire*, July 1969. 84-6.
[38] Esola, 274-5.

scolded the U.S. Navy captains the very evening before the collision. He was not unhappy with the ranges, or the close call. Rather, he was embarrassed by sloppy and un-seamanlike maneuvers.[39]

Commander McLemore testified for two full days as the board looked into every detail of how he ran *Frank E. Evans*. One of his most telling statements was that U.S. Navy ships conducted plane guard maneuvers differently from the norm during the exercise. U.S. ships would remain behind the carrier and when called into rescue destroyer station would just close in, then open the range back up after flight operations were over. The most revealing, however, was that no examinations, formal course, or any definitive experience were required before an officer qualified as Officer of the Deck.[40] The sole requirement was the commanding officer's trust. While today there are formal courses, examinations, and required demonstrations of experience, the Captain's trust remains the single most important element for qualification. This trust in Lieutenant Junior Grade Ramsey cost McLemore his career and 74 sailors their lives.

After three weeks and seventy-nine witnesses, the board placed blame on both ships, though the lion's share went to *Frank E. Evans*, in particular, Ronald Ramsey and John Hopson. Ramsey's misdeeds were called out on a single page; the actual word 'failure' used nine times; six times for Hopson. Commander McLemore was also found wanting. Not because he provided inadequate training, or set an unqualified watch, or provided inadequate instructions or failed to insure his orders were carried out. In fact, the board explicitly identified he provided each of these items. The board also found that McLemore did nothing to contribute to the collision. Rather, the board, citing Naval Regulations, "recognize[d] the inherent

---

[39] Ibid, 275.
[40] Ibid, 278.

accountability of a Commanding Officer for his ship, and his absolute responsibility for the actions of his ship."[41]

Likewise, the board shared the blame with *Melbourne* citing:

> as Task Unit Commander, he was responsible for the safe operation of all ships in the Task Unit. He failed to exercise due care in that he did not positvely[sic] direct the movements of EVANS at a time not later than when EVANS was determined by him to have come into a collision course. It is considered that the informatory signal sent at that time, that EVANS was on a collision course, was in the circumstances not positive enough...[also] Commanding Officer *MELBOURNE* should have backed his engines at the time he put his rudder over. Such an action, though not avoiding collision, might have lessened the effects thereof.[42]

An Australian court-martial tried Stevenson in August 1969. The judge dismissed all charges stating there was 'no case to answer.' Regardless, Stevenson's career was over. A plumb job he'd expected went instead to the supply officer board member, Captain Davidson. Stevenson retired the following year.[43]

Ramsey, Hopson, and McLemore faced American courts-martial where they answered charges of dereliction of duty; negligence; hazarding a vessel by failing to sound the collision alarm when the hazard of collision existed; failing to establish the correct position of *Frank E. Evans* in reference to *Melbourne*; and failing to ascertain a safe course of action for the plane-guard maneuver. McLemore's charges included dereliction of duty in that he permitted an "inexperienced and immature" officer of the deck to act unsupervised, and "failed to

---

[41] *Report of the Combined USN-RAN Board of Investigation into the collision between HMAS Melbourne and USS Frank E. Evans convened by COMSEVENTHFLT and ACNB*, 34.
[42] Ibid
[43] Stevenson, 173-192, 218-219.

require an alert and competent watch," two items specifically refuted by the joint board.

Ramsey pled guilty and lost seniority. Hopson was not court-martialed but punished administratively, and the details never made public. McLemore pled not guilty. Despite the board's findings he was convicted of the charges and reprimanded. McLemore retired in 1976. He died in 2001 and was buried in Fallon, Nevada.

In 1972, the surface navy created a course for newly commissioned officers to level the practical knowledge between graduates of the Naval Academy, Naval Reserve Officer Training Corps, and Officer Candidate School. Over 16 weeks these officers learned the basics of shipboard operations and administration.[44] In 1974, a formalized qualification process complemented the school and laid out the path for qualification as officer of the deck among other watchstations.[45] In 1975, Navy filmmakers created *I Relieve You, Sir* - a thirty-minute film based on the events leading to the collision between *Frank E. Evans* and *Melbourne*.[46] New surface warfare officers watched the film through the end of the twentieth century, and it remains available on YouTube. Unlike the Wall Street Journal "Hobson's Choice" editorial, *I Relieve You, Sir* provided clear and unambiguous lessons in practical shipboard operations without mythology or hyperbole. For the next three decades all officers received the same basic core training. Between 1975 and 2003 junior officer training, in fact all surface warfare officer training was stable with only minor and incremental changes to allow for new equipment.[47]

---

[44] Charles P. Vion, "The First Step Toward SWO Qualification," *Proceedings*, March 1978 and Robert S. Salzer, "The Surface Forces," *Proceedings* 102, no. 11 (November 1976):31.
[45] Hart, 41 and Vion
[46] Arthur Lenahan, "New Navy Film Dramatizes Collision of U.S., Aussie Ships," *Navy Times* (Tysons Corner), November 26, 1975.
[47] James T. Robinson, *Initial Training of Surface Warfare Officers: A Historical Perspective from World War II to 2008* (Fort Leavenworth, KS: U.S. Army Command and General Staff College, 2008). 53.

Two other notable events in these years were the much publicized 1966 removal from command of Lieutenant Commander Marcus Aurelius Arnheiter and the less publicized, but more sensational, 1975 removal of Commander Connelly D. Stevenson. Navy leadership summarily removed Arnheiter after only 99 days in command of USS *Vance* (DE 387). In those 99 days Arnheiter reportedly enforced discipline "with a martinet's fetish for shined belt buckles and shoes, but violated Navy regulations and the orders of his superiors whenever it suited him."[48] Arnheiter learned of his removal from command by a naval message from the Bureau of Personnel and six days later an investigation received sworn testimony detailing Arnheiter's behavior. Removing an officer first and ordering an investigation second is rare, so rare that this is the only known instance in naval history. Over two years, and against Arnheiter's public stand against his removal, the Navy maintained that it acted correctly. Arnheiter's actions, while in command, were of a personal leadership nature and only border on the idea of a crime of command. Poor leadership exists at all levels, as does poor judgment. Arnheiter exhibited poor leadership, something noteworthy but not new, while Connelly Stevenson's judgment, and the Navy's reaction, marked the beginning of a sea change.

Stevenson commanded USS *Finback* (SSN 670), a *Sturgeon*-class nuclear-powered attack submarine. After a port visit in Port Canaveral, Florida, Stevenson allowed a go-go dancer to perform aboard the submarine while the sub departed port. Three weeks later the Navy learned of the dance, canceled her patrol and ordered *Finback* to port, where Stevenson was removed from command "pending the investigation of a non-operational nature."[49] Stevenson eventually received a letter of

---

[48] Neil Sheehan, "The 99 Days of Captain Arnheiter," *The New York Times*, August 11, 1968.
[49] Robert A. Taylor, "Cat on a Cold Steel Dive Plane," *Naval History*,

reprimand from Commander, Submarines Atlantic, for not following standard procedures in embarking civilian guests and for demeaning his position as commanding officer.[50] The case was so well publicized that President Gerald R. Ford received a question about it during a press conference. While little known, Stevenson's removal presaged the Navy's coming approach to command responsibility and accountability for non-operational issues.

Early 1970s changes included more than the new division officer school. A series of boiler explosions that killed almost a dozen sailors over three years forced the Navy to instill a series of inspections intended to stem the tide of accidents from a lethal combination of high-pressure steam engineering plants, poor training, and poor maintenance.[51] Other changes included requiring all commanding officers to have some level of engineering expertise[52] and routing all commanding officers through an engineering course in Idaho.[53] These actions reversed the trend of engineering accidents,[54] but also began moving the surface Navy closer to the nuclear navy's technocracy. Engineering incidents remained crimes of command from which commanders might recover, or at least retain command. Collisions, especially those involving deaths, were now no longer recoverable.

USS *Belknap* and USS *John F. Kennedy* - 1975

Just over six years after HMAS *Melbourne* cut USS *Frank E. Evans* in half another carrier collided with her escort, and unsurprisingly the incident between USS *John F. Kennedy*

February 2010.
[50] Ibid
[51] United States, Naval Postgraduate School, *A Normative View of the Pre-Overhaul Planning Process*, by Michael Edward House (Monterey, CA, 1976). 33.
[52] McKearney
[53] Holloway, 358-9.
[54] Ibid, 359.

and USS *Belknap* shared many similarities with previous collisions. There were also some major differences, the most significant of which included the presence of nuclear weapons onboard both ships.

On November 22, 1975, *John F. Kennedy* and *Belknap* were operating in the Mediterranean Sea, 70 miles east of Sicily. Sunset was shortly before 5 p.m., the winds were light and the seas at six feet. Visibility was good, both ships showed navigation lights, and radar was in use. Communications between the ships were satisfactory.[55]

While *Belknap* was operationally proficient, underway for eleven days straight with the task force and a third of the previous ninety days at sea, this was her first day operating close to the carrier. The officer of the deck, Lieutenant Kenneth M. Knull, was experienced and had a reputation as the best officer of the deck in *Belknap*. Ensign C. M. Howe, Jr, the Junior Officer of the Deck, was new to *Belknap*, having reported aboard at the beginning of September. While not experienced in close maneuvering situations he was balanced by the more experienced Knull.[56]

From 6:45 p.m. on *Belknap* operated off *John F. Kennedy*'s port quarter at roughly two miles. At 9:45 p.m., *John F. Kennedy* informed *Belknap* that she was turning downwind to recover aircraft. Shortly before the scheduled 10 p.m. landings, Captain William Gureck, *John F. Kennedy*'s commanding officer entered his bridge.[57]

Aboard *Belknap*, the commanding officer, Captain Walter Richard Shafer, was watching a film in the officer's wardroom. The new direction was almost exactly opposite from

---

[55] United States, Department of the Navy, Commander in Chief United States Naval Forces Europe, *Investigation to Inquire into the Circumstances Surrounding the Collision Between USS John F. Kennedy (CV 67) and USS Belknap (CG 26) which occurred on 22 November 1975* (Washington, DC). 708.
[56] Ibid, 710.
[57] Ibid, 712-713.

their current course and *Belknap* could either slow down and let the carrier pass ahead then turn to the new course, or immediately turn and then slow down. The first option meant the carrier would cross *Belknap*'s bow. The second would have her pass alongside. The subsequent investigation showed that neither the JOOD or OOD ever agreed on how they would act and that the Combat Information Center misunderstood the plan.[58]

When *John F. Kennedy* sent her signal, she immediately commenced her turn, turning left and towards *Belknap*. *Belknap* turned right, towards the carrier. Between 9:52 p.m. and 9:57 p.m., *John F. Kennedy* continued her turn, slowly reducing the rate of turn and finally steadying farther right than the intended course. Captain Gureck ordered his watch team to keep an eye on *Belknap* and not turn left to the recovery course until *Belknap* was abaft the carrier's beam.[59]

During *Belknap*'s turn, Lieutenant Knull lost awareness of the carrier's orientation. Unable to determine whether he was looking at the carrier's bow or stern he was incapable of judging the relative motion between the ships. At 9:54 p.m. *Belknap* sped up and increased the rate of her left turn. At this point confusion among the watchstanders led to the helmsman's relief, and someone called Captain Shafer to the bridge.[60]

Captain Shafer arrived on the bridge at 9:57 p.m., just as *John F. Kennedy* called over the radio asking *Belknap* her intentions. *Belknap*'s Combat Information Center repeatedly recommended turning right, even as they observed the rudder swing from left to right then back to the left again. Captain Shafer could not pierce the confusion on his bridge as he received reports from his Officer of the Deck that did not match what he saw with his own eyes. To add to the confusion, the

---

[58] Ibid, 715-716.
[59] Ibid, 713.
[60] Ibid, 717.

ship's deck log, the official record of course and speed changes, was incomplete as that watchstander was busy with other tasks.[61]

At 9:59 p.m. Ensign Howe ordered a left full rudder and an increase to flank speed. Captain Shafer recognized a different position and immediately countermanded the order, ordering the ship right and an emergency backing bell. In making that order he took control of *Belknap*'s engines and rudder.[62]

At 10:01 p.m., *Belknap's* port superstructure struck *John F. Kennedy*'s port bow, dragging alongside the larger ship and shearing off most of her superstructure aft of the bridge in contact that lasted between seven seconds and three minutes. During the collision, *Belknap* severed pressurized aviation fuel lines onboard the carrier. The carrier's fuels officer depressurized the system and halted the fuel flow within minutes of the collision, but thousands of gallons of flammable aviation fuel had already poured out onto the damaged ship and surrounding water.[63]

Small fires broke out aboard the carrier. Smoke from fires onboard the carrier and *Belknap* forced the carrier to stop her engines and within three miles of the collision she was dead in the water dealing with her own engineering problems.[64]

Belknap's first fire occurred seconds after the impact, and the heavy fuel-fired smoke forced *Belknap* to secure her engines as well. The smoke was so bad watchstanders evacuated all four boiler rooms even as explosions damaged the vents near boiler rooms three and four. The emergency generator did not automatically start, and multiple fire pump issues meant little to no firefighting water was available for significant periods of time.[65]

Firefighting water came from USS *Claude V. Ricketts* who drove close alongside fighting the fires aboard *Belknap*.

---

[61] Ibid, 717-718.
[62] Ibid, 718-719.
[63] Ibid, 720.
[64] Ibid, 722.
[65] Ibid, 723.

Claude V. Ricketts and USS *Dale* also transferred medical personnel aboard *Belknap*. *Claude V. Ricketts* was so close that she repeatedly struck alongside *Belknap* as rescuers passed injured personnel from one ship to the other. Through the night ammunition aboard *Belknap* exploded in the fires, sending shrapnel into the air and over the assisting ships.[66]

Before midnight, USS *Bordelon* was pointed bow-on to *Belknap*'s port side pumping 750 gallons a minute onto fires still burning on the signal bridge. She also passed blankets and lifejackets to *Belknap* in the twenty-five minutes she was alongside.[67]

By 5:40 a.m., 23 November, the fires were out, and *Bordelon* took *Belknap* under tow. Search and rescue efforts continued until 6 p.m. that evening. Unlike *Hobson* or *Frank E. Evans*, deaths were relatively few. Of *Belknap*'s over 600 crew, only six died, and among *John F. Kennedy*'s over 3,000 sailors there was only one death.[68]

John F. Kennedy sustained significant damage on her port side. Repair and loss estimates totaled $2.3 million ($10.1 million in 2017). *Belknap*'s damage was catastrophic. All major equipment, sensors, antennae, and superstructure from aft of her bridge to her flight deck was either crushed in the collision or consumed in the fires. *Belknap*'s superstructure was aluminum, which is far more susceptible to damage from high heat fires than steel. The investigation was unable to provide a repair estimate for *Belknap*. She spent four years in reconstruction and was recommissioned in 1980 before ultimately hosting the Malta Summit in 1989 before her decommissioning in 1995.

Rear Admiral Donald Engen, Vice Commander of U.S. Naval Forces Europe, arrived onboard USS *John F. Kennedy* on November 23, 1975, and started his investigation. On November 24th he visited *Belknap*. Unlike previous cases which used a Board or Court of Inquiry, this was a one-person investigation,

---

[66] Ibid, 725, 727.
[67] Ibid, 726.
[68] Ibid, 728-736.

assisted by unidentified advisors and legal counsel. The team interviewed over ninety personnel over the next month. Within days the team determined that the probable cause of the collision was human, and not mechanical.[69]

With mechanical and equipment problems ruled out, the team designated two officers from each ship as 'parties to the investigation.' Doing so provided them with more rights but also notified them that they were under investigation. Captain Shafer and Lieutenant Junior Grade Knull in *Belknap* and *John F. Kennedy*'s Captain Gureck and his officer of the deck became the investigator's focus.[70]

As with previous carrier collisions, the investigator cleared the carrier's actions, and in the end, deliberated solely on *Belknap*'s actions. The final recommendations were to try Lieutenant Junior Grade Knull at court-martial and issue a punitive letter of reprimand to Captain Shafer. Shafer's punishment related to his absence from the bridge and failure to properly train bridge team members. The report also listed 19 other recommendations concerning training, equipment, and operations, closing with this statement:

> In retrospect this unfortunate and unnecessary collision leaves the question whether or not Commanding Officers and watch team leaders in our fleets are tending to place decreasing emphasis on the basics of seamanship and good sound operating procedures as well as on the utilization of the total watch team. There is a strong suggestion of a growing general acceptance of trainees' filling subordinate positions of responsibility with less than adequate command emphasis on qualification through demonstrated performance. If one collision of proportions much less than here can be attributed in the slightest degree to an

---

[69] Ibid, 704.
[70] Ibid, 704.

easing of our standards of excellence of established command elements at sea, then we should acknowledge a training problem and solve it.[71]

Unlike official opinions of the investigation, this closing statement was not required to list supporting facts. When combined with Shafer's recommended punishment one might assume that training discrepancies were causal to the collision. However, the findings of fact and opinions found that within *Belknap*'s watch team only the starboard lookout and bridge phone talker were not qualified for their positions. Only one of the other 100 opinions addresses deficiencies in bridge team training and provides contradictory information:

> That the bridge team training in *Belknap* was in need of greater command attention. There was evidence of individual and uncoordinated action. The Commanding Officer had counseled his Officers of the Deck with regard to shiphandling. The training that LTJG Knull had was excellent and his Commanding Officer placed the highest trust in him as OOD.[72]

The report was completed December 31, 1975, and ultimately endorsed and closed by the Chief of Naval Operations on September 7, 1976. In the interim, Commander in Chief U.S. Naval Forces Europe issued Captain Shafer a punitive letter. Ordinarily this would end any administrative or legal action. However, the Commander in Chief U.S. Atlantic Fleet referred Shafer to general court-martial on charges of two violations of Navy Regulations and three of dereliction of duty.

Captain Shafer requested a trial by military judge. Judge Advocate Captain Horace H. Morgan dismissed the two specifications of Article 0702, U.S. Navy Regulations, explaining that this regulation was "a guideline for performance and not an order to be enforced with criminal sanctions." The judge dismissed two charges on the grounds that the punitive

---

[71] Ibid, 763.
[72] Ibid, 759.

letter from Commander in Chief U.S. Naval Forces Europe addressed these alleged acts. The judge also dismissed one specification of dereliction related to supervision of the Officer of the Deck as an undue multiplication of the charge Shafer was ultimately arraigned on:

> "that through neglect he suffered the two ships to be damaged by failing to personally supervise and instruct his OOD and JOOD and by failing to post a fully qualified bridge watch section, in violation of Article 108, UCMJ, and one specification of negligently suffering the two ships to be hazarded, also by his failure to provide personal supervision and training to his OOD and JOOD and by his failure to post a fully qualified bridge watch section".[73]

Shafer pled not guilty, and after two days of testimony from eighteen prosecution witnesses, Captain Morgan granted a defense motion for findings of Not Guilty on charges because the Navy failed to establish that the bridge watch was improperly qualified or that Shafer was negligent in not personally supervising and instructing his watch officers.[74]

Morgan's ruling flew in the face of what many saw as both law and tradition. A San Diego Union editorial opined:

> The Navy...has inherited, ultimately from the Royal Navy of bygone days, an even sterner tradition: any captain who loses his ship, runs her aground, or is at fault in collision, must pay with his career. That has been the law of the Navy ever since John Paul Jones. It is a law founded not only in man's experience with the sea, but on the commonsense principle of the inseparability of a captain's total and awesome authority from corresponding total accountability.

---

[73] "Memorandum for All Flag Officers and Officers in Command," letter from J. L. Holloway, III, October 2, 1976, Washington, DC. 7.
[74] Ibid

> Because the authority of a captain is great, the price he must pay when he fails is great. And, by the same canon, when his ship, his people, or their common performance, fail, it is the captain who must pay.[75]

This editorial represented the view of so many that the Chief of Naval Operations, Admiral James L. Holloway, III, issued a letter to "All Flag Officers and Officers in Command" on October 2, 1976. It provided a summary of the collision's circumstances as well as administrative and judicial processes. The Navy did not publish the investigation; this letter provided the only detailed information for members of the Navy. It read, in part:

> A formal investigation held the Commanding Officer and the Officer of the Deck of *BELKNAP* accountable for the tragic incident. The Commanding Officer was subsequently referred to trial by general court-martial which resulted in disposition tantamount to acquittal on all charges and specifications. There has been some outspoken criticism of the outcome of the *BELKNAP* courts-martial. Much of that criticism reflects concern that the principle of command responsibility may have been imperiled as a result of the *BELKNAP* cases. I want to here address that concern, and to assure each of you that resolution of the *BELKNAP* cases will not in any way jeopardize the concepts of command responsibility, authority and accountability.
> There has always been a fundamental principle of maritime law and life which has been consistently observed over the centuries by seafarers of all nations: The responsibility of the master, captain or commanding officer on board his ship is absolute. That principle is as valid in this technical era of nuclear propulsion and advanced weapons systems as it was

---

[75] Robert D. Heinl, Jr., "Judge's Ruling Scuttles Accountability Law of the Navy," *The San Diego Union*, June 4, 1976, sec. B.

when our Navy was founded two hundred years ago. This responsibility, and its corollaries of authority and accountability, have been the foundation of safe navigation at sea and the cornerstone of naval efficiency and effectiveness throughout our history. The essence of this concept is reflected in Article 0702.1 of Navy Regulations, 1973, which provides in pertinent part that: "The responsibility of the commanding officer for his command is absolute, except when, and to the extent, relieved therefrom by competent authority, or as provided otherwise in these regulations."

To understand fully this essential principle, it must first be recognized that it is not a test for measuring the criminal responsibility of a commanding officer. Under our system of criminal justice, in both civilian and military forums, in order that a man's life, liberty and property may be placed at hazard, it is not enough to show simply that he was the commanding officer of a Navy ship involved in a collision and that he failed to execute to perfection his awesome and wide-ranging command responsibilities. Rather, it must be established by legally admissible evidence and beyond a reasonable doubt that he personally violated carefully delineated and specifically charged provisions of the criminal code enacted by the Congress to govern the armed forces-the Uniform Code of Military Justice-before a commanding officer can be found criminally responsible for his conduct. Military courts-martial are federal courts and the rules of evidence and procedure applicable therein are essentially the same as those which pertain in any other federal criminal court and the rights of an accused, whether seaman or commanding officer, are closely analogous to those enjoyed by any federal criminal court defendant. The determination of criminal responsibility is therefore properly the province of our system of military justice.

The acquittal of a commanding officer by a duly constituted court-martial absolves him of criminal responsibility for the offenses charged. It does not, however, absolve him of his responsibility as a commanding officer as delineated in U.S. Navy Regulations.

In summary, the Commander's responsibility for his command is absolute and he must and will be held accountable for its safety, well-being and efficiency. That is the very foundation of our maritime heritage, the cornerstone of naval efficiency and effectiveness and the key to victory in combat. This is the essence of the special trust and confidence placed in an officer's patriotism, valor, fidelity and abilities. Every day in command tests the strength of character, judgment and professional abilities of those in command. In some cases, Commanders will be called upon to answer for their conduct in a court of law. In all cases, they will be professionally judged by seagoing officers-a far more stringent accountability in the eyes of those who follow the sea. We in the Navy would have it no other way, for the richest reward of command is the personal satisfaction of having measured up to this responsibility and accountability. The loss of life, personal injuries, and material damages sustained in the collision of USS *BELKNAP* and USS *JOHN F. KENNEDY* serve as a tragic reminder of the necessity and immutability of the principle of command responsibility. The Commanding Officer and the Officer of the Deck of *BELKNAP* have been held accountable for that terrible loss of men and equipment. The concept of command responsibility has not been eroded.[76]

This letter was so important that it is included in every subsequent copy of *Command at Sea*. For most, this letter, and

---

[76] Holloway Memo, 1-4.

the occasional sea story are the only information they have of the collision between *Belknap* and *John F. Kennedy*. This is unfortunate as there are more than a few opinions presented as fact, and a few facts left to the wayside. From where did Holloway draw his assertion that "there has always been a fundamental principle...the responsibility of the...commanding officer on board his ship is absolute?" How is that principle of responsibility and accountability "the very foundation of our maritime heritage, the cornerstone of naval efficiency and effectiveness and the key to victory in combat"? Where is the process for judging commanders by other seagoing officers? Furthermore, how should the Navy, within the community of sea-going officers, hold others accountable? Are they held to account and their actions examined and questioned, or simply blamed and punished?

Holloway's comments are also curious because Admiral Engen's investigation made no direct statement of personal accountability. Holloway likely drew his statement from a separate unpublished Article 32 investigation which, while addressing the same incident, came to differing conclusions. The statement about Shafer's court-martial "which resulted in disposition tantamount to acquittal on all charges and specifications" is certainly crafted to cast aspersions on the court's decision. Even Holloway's summary shows Shafer was acquitted of the only charges brought to the court. Dismissal of a charge is more than "tantamount to acquittal." Dismissal is tantamount to uncharged.

Admiral Holloway cites no source for his statements that command responsibility is "the cornerstone of naval efficiency and effectiveness and the key to victory in combat" – they are opinion, even if they are professional and expert opinion. He also conflates the words accountability, responsibility, and culpability - even though he never uses the latter word. Nowhere is this more apparent than when he writes: "There has always been a fundamental principle of maritime law and life which has been consistently observed over the centuries by seafarers of all nations: The responsibility of the master, captain or commanding officer on board his ship is absolute." When taken in context, and in response to complaints about the trial's outcome, the intimations, however, are clear and in keeping with the San Diego Union editorial: "...when his ship, his people, or their common performance, fail, it is the captain who must pay."[77] By 1976 the movement from individual responsibility towards command culpability was complete and crimes of command no longer required personal action from the commander; the actions of his command sufficed. After almost twenty-five years, "Hobson's Choice" was realized. By the mid-1980s commanders were accountable for their subordinate's acts – criminal or otherwise.

USS *Ranger* - 1983

The 1980s saw increased spending on Navy procurement, personnel, ships, and aircraft. Even with new ships, better training, and more people the Navy retained some of the problems that plagued her over previous decades. Aircraft carriers remained dangerous and were still subject to fires and explosions.

Forrestal-class aircraft carrier USS *Ranger* (CV 61) was commissioned August 10, 1957 and served until July 10, 1993. She was one of the first "supercarriers" - fully 25% larger than her World War II predecessors. If carriers like *Bennington* were dangerous, then supercarriers were super dangerous. Her bigger engines produced more shaft horsepower and drove the ship slightly faster than her predecessors. She was 200 feet longer and carried more than a thousand more crew - almost 4,000 sailors.

Like all aircraft carriers, *Ranger* had her share of mishaps; some mechanical, some human. In 1982 Captain Dan Pedersen was censured for inefficient management after an

---

[77] Heinl

investigation into maltreatment of prisoners in the ship's brig. One sailor died from the mistreatment and the Navy disciplined 27 other crewmembers.[78]

Concurrent to the brig investigation, *Ranger* suffered a series of engineering safety challenges. In February 1982, she received an unsatisfactory grade on an Operational Propulsion Plant Recertification Examination (OPPRE) and failed a second examination in March. After a deployment and maintenance period, a May 1983 OPPRE was also unsatisfactory.[79] OPPREs began in 1972 in response to a series of engineering accidents related to a combination of high-pressure steam engineering plants, poor training, and poor maintenance.[80] Other engineering related changes included requiring all commanding officers to have some level of engineering expertise[81] and routing all commanding officers through an engineering course in Idaho.[82] While the inspection regime greatly increased safety and reliability, no system is perfect and *Ranger* validated the rule.

Despite the training and inspection program, but in light of the identified problems, it is no surprise that on November 1, 1983, *Ranger* experienced a major fire while operating in the North Arabian Sea (Persian Gulf). The fire began shortly before 10 a.m. and burned for ten hours, killing seven and injuring 35. Investigators estimated damages at $1.8 million ($4.3 million in 2017).[83]

---

[78] Kip Cooper, "Former Skipper Censured; CCUs Closed," *The San Diego Union*, October 27, 1982.

[79] "Results of Inquiry into the Chain of Command Responsibility for the USS Ranger (CV 61) Fire on 1 Nov 83," Letter to Commander in Chief, U.S. Pacific Fleet, July 16, 1984, Naval Air Station, North Island, San Diego, California.

[80] House, 33.

[81] McKearney

[82] Holloway, 358-9.

[83] "Informal investigation to inquire into the circumstances surrounding the fire on board USS RANGER (CV 61) which occurred in the Northern

The investigation revealed that a major fuel oil leak erupted from a sounding tube in #4 Main Machinery Room (MMR) while crewmen internally transferred fuel oil. Properly trained and qualified crewmen failed to conduct hydrostatic tests on the transfer system and failed to properly close valves to a fuel tank. Equipment failures, the heat, and smoke hampered firefighting efforts in #4 MMR. The investigation also noted that construction discrepancies in *Ranger* might have contributed to the fire. The investigation ultimately placed responsibility for the fire with the two enlisted watch standers who improperly aligned and operated the fuel oil transfer system. The Navy tried both at special courts-martial for dereliction of duty and violation of a lawful order.[84] The courts dismissed most charges. However, one sailor pled guilty and was sentenced to three months in the brig.

During the investigation's administrative endorsement process senior commanders requested more information and ordered an additional investigation.[85] The second report included a review of watchstander qualifications, written procedures, instructions, material conditions, training, responsible personnel and arrived at the same conclusions.[86] In directing the second investigation, Vice Adm. Thomas R. Kinnebrew, Deputy Commander in Chief, Pacific Fleet wrote: "...the absence of any finding of responsibility in the chain of command above that level lacks credibility. It is questionable that the actions of those two individuals can be totally isolated

---

Arabian Sea on 1 November 1983," Thomas R. Kinnebrew to Judge Advocate General, April 16, 1984, United States Pacific Fleet, Pearl Harbor, Hawaii.
[84] Ibid, Crawford A. Easterling to Judge Advocate General, March 16, 1984.
[85] Ibid, Sylvester R. Foley to Judge Advocate General.
[86] "Results of Inquiry into the Chain of Command Responsibility for the USS Ranger (CV 61) Fire on 1 Nov 83," Letter to Commander in Chief, U.S. Pacific Fleet, July 16, 1984, Naval Air Station, North Island, San Diego, California.

from the actions (or lack thereof) of their seniors."[87]

A third report documented declining performance in *Ranger*'s engineering department over the two years preceding the fire. This report attributed the decline to *Ranger*'s Engineering Officer,[88] Commander J. P. Melanephy who reported in October 1981 and transferred less than a month before the fire.[89] *Ranger* failed every single OPPRE while Melanephy was her Chief Engineer.

Even this third investigation was found wanting. In the final endorsement covering all three inquiries, Admiral James D. Watkins, the Chief of Naval Operations wrote:

> Actions of the prior endorsing officials imply that responsibility for decline in the *RANGER*'s engineering department rests solely with [the engineering officer] This implication is contrary to the Navy's fundamental principles of command responsibility, as was the determination in the original investigation that responsibility for the fuel oil fire rested entirely with the two enlisted crewmembers. While criminal responsibility for the fire and specific derelict actions associated with the engineering department's decline may be attributable to these individuals, our traditional principles of command responsibility impose a higher standard of accountability on the chain of command than the "reasonable doubt" test.[90]

---

[87] Thomas R. Kinnebrew to Judge Advocate General.

[88] "Results of Inquiry into the Chain of Command Responsibility for the USS Ranger (CV 61) Fire on 1 Nov 83," James D. Watkins to Judge Advocate General, November 9, 1984, Office of the Chief of Naval Operations, Washington, DC.

[89] Carol A. Guy, "Captains of USS Ranger CVA 61," USS Ranger CV/A 61 1957-1993, September 1, 2011, , accessed September 17, 2017, http://uss-rangerguy.com/captains_of_ranger.htm.

[90] "Results of Inquiry into the Chain of Command Responsibility for the USS Ranger (CV 61) Fire on 1 Nov 83," James D. Watkins to Judge Advocate General, November 9, 1984, Office of the Chief of Naval Operations, Washington, DC.

He went on to cite a familiar reference, U.S. Navy Regulations, Article 0702; the same article Captain Morgan deemed "guideline for performance."

> Commensurate with that responsibility is the commanding officer's unfettered authority over the command and a duty to exercise that authority to ensure the safety, well-being and efficiency of the entire command. The two officers in command of the *RANGER* during the year prior to the fuel oil fire failed to bring the full authority of their office to bear to resolve the serious engineering department deficiencies reflected in this report...Had these officers fulfilled their responsibilities, it is likely *RANGER* would have satisfactorily completed the Re-OPPRE examination scheduled for August, 1983, and, more importantly, the tragic fuel oil fire may have been avoided. Therefore these officers must be held accountable for their failings.[91]

Again, there is more to the story than the final judgment. While *Ranger*'s Commanding Officers may be accountable for the ship's failings, there were others who did not bear any form of accountability, even though the investigation pointed to their responsibility.

Ranger had a documented history of deficiencies in her fuel oil and ballast piping. Only six years earlier, repairs replaced all engineering space fuel oil transfer and service pipes. Three years before the fire, workers replaced the through-tank fuel oil service pipes for two of the four main machinery rooms. From 1980 until the fire, there were few fuel system repairs; however, the engineers conducted considerable tank preservation. In early 1983 Commander Naval Air Force Pacific worked with the ship to properly identify and document the material condition of the ship's piping, voids, and fuel tanks, and

---

[91] Ibid

established an incremental program to correct these deficiencies.[92]

In the 1982 OPPRE, *Ranger*'s fuel oil quality management program failed to conduct required fuel oil quality tests. The 1983 OPPRE reported the program was further degraded and assessed is "as ineffective overall and lacking in supervisory review."[93]

In 1981-1983 the Navy had an overall, severe shortage of senior petty officers which manifested in shortages of *Ranger*'s supervisory Boiler Tenders (BT) and Machinist Mates (MM). By October 1983, *Ranger* had 94% of her allotted BTs, and 94% of her MMs.[94]

Compounding the enlisted personnel problem was a higher than usual officer turnover; new officers assumed both the Damage Control Assistant and Main Propulsion Assistant positions in June 1983 and in September 1983 two different officers took each of these positions. On 17 October 1983, a new Chief Engineer reported aboard. Finally, *Ranger*'s captain at the time of the fire had been aboard less than six months.[95]

None of these were direct causal issues for the fire. However, they point to an overall challenge for *Ranger*, and her engineering department. In contrast, the only documented admonishment from *Ranger*'s seniors noted that her "performance in all areas except OPPRE in the interdeployment period has been unequivocally outstanding."[96]

In November 1984, a full year after the fire, Watkins ordered reprimands for *Ranger* skippers, Captain Arthur H. Fredrickson, who commanded during the fire and his

---

[92] Ibid
[93] Ibid
[94] Ibid
[95] Ibid
[96] "Operational Propulsion Plant Re-Examination," letter to Commanding Officer, USS Ranger (CV 61), July 7, 1983.

predecessor Anthony Less; as well as former *Ranger* executive officer, Captain Stephen Todd; and *Ranger's* former ship's chief engineer, Commander James P. Melanephy.[97]

Of *Ranger's* 29 commanders, 19 became Flag Officers, six rising to Admiral or Vice Admiral. Notable exceptions are the decade between 1974 and 1985. Of that decade's seven commanders, only two promoted to flag rank, a clear anomaly in promotion patterns. Captain Dan Pedersen, censured for "inefficient management"[98] as part of the investigation into maltreatment of prisoners in the ship's brig, retired as a Captain immediately after command of *Ranger*. Captain Frederickson, reprimanded for the fire and a collision only nine days after taking command,[99] retired as a Captain. Captain Anthony "Tony" Less, who commanded between Pedersen and Fredrickson from June 11, 1982, to July 8, 1983 - the critical period including all the failed engineering examination - was selected for and promoted to Commodore (the Navy's then one-star admiral rank) before receiving his reprimand.[100] Apparently, that was the last anyone thought of it. As a Flag Officer he was Director Political-Military Branch of the Joint Chiefs of Staff, Washington, 1985-1987; Commander Carrier Group One, Pacific, 1987-1988; Middle East Force, Manama, Bahrain, 1988-1989; Director Plans and Policy Navy Staff, Washington, 1989-1991; and Commander Naval Air Force Atlantic Fleet, Norfolk, Virginia, 1991-1994 before retiring as a Vice Admiral in 1994.[101] Even as a Flag Officer his career brushed with crimes

---

[97] "Skippers Must Share Blame for Fire" *The Washington Post* (1974-Current file); Nov 23, 1984; pg. A14.
[98] "The Skipper of the Carrier USS Ranger Vigorously Denied...," *United Press International*, September 28, 1981.
[99] "National News in Brief," *United Press International*, April 10, 1984.
[100] Cong. Senate, Congressional record, vol. 130, proceedings and debates of the 98th Congress, second session, 98th Cong., 2d sess. (Washington: Government printing Office, 1984).
[101] "Golden Eagles," Golden Eagles, accessed August 18, 2017,

of command. While commanding Middle East Force, USS *Vincennes* shot down Iran Air Flight 655, killing 290 passengers and crew and while Commander Naval Air Force Atlantic Fleet he attended the infamous 1991 Tailhook Convention in Las Vegas, Nevada. In both cases, Navy investigators rejected disciplinary action against Less.[102]

In the 19 years between 1965 and 1985, the Navy saw over 500 crimes of command removing 22 commanding officers, almost twice the number removed between 1945 and 1965. Not unsurprising, as there were twice as many incidents with far fewer ships and personnel. By the mid-1980s the rhetoric and buildup of President Reagan's 600 ship Navy captured American imaginations and new classes of ships entered the fleet. But new ships did not mean new attitudes. By 1985 the now modern concepts of accountability, responsibility and culpability were firmly entrenched in naval lore and of the 569 crimes of command, only 150 officers (1 in 4) recovered compared to 1 in 3 between 1945 and 1965. Some of the decreased recovery came from more incidents among fewer ships, some from the changing approach to command and command responsibility. By the early 1980s 'Hobson's Choice' was prevalent in officer training and fleet officers were thoroughly familiar with *I Relieve You, Sir*. The Navy accepted the idea that the commanding officer was wholly responsible for everything aboard ship. However, the next three decades saw even this concept reach towards excess.

---

http://www.epnaao.com/.
[102] "Limited Punishment Signaled in Jet Downing," *The New York Times*, August 14, 1988.

4: 1985-2015

Previous chapters introduced the ideas of command and crimes of command, presented the manner in which the early-Cold War navy dealt with crimes of command and showed the coming changes from individual responsibility to command culpability. This chapter shows the impact of those changes as commanders are now much less likely to receive the redemption afforded Beaulieu, Martineau, Loughlin and many others.

The last decades of the twentieth century proved tumultuous for the United States Navy. The promise of President Ronald Reagan's 600-ship Navy brought more and more advanced technology to the navy. Ships continued growing, but the dangerous steam plants gave way to more advanced, more reliable, more powerful, and far safer gas-turbine technology. Ships were safer, navigation more precise, and the training programs instituted in the 1970s were in full form. Major fires dropped from a mid-1980s high to an almost imperceptible statistical blip by the end of the millennium. Major collisions and groundings were, in comparison to earlier years, rare. However, while overall ships numbers dropped, from 571 in 1985 to only 287 in 2015 and personnel numbers fell from 579,000 in 1985 to 327,000 in 2015, the number of crimes of command remained steady. and removal from command skyrocketed. Where the first four post-war decades averaged roughly 25 incidents per year and the three following decades averaged 24 incidents per year, command removal jumped from 1 or fewer per year to average 10 per year between 1985 and 2015, with a clear increase as the millennium approached. Only two years, 2005 and 2006, had fewer than 10 command removals in the 21st century. Absolute blame and culpability for individual and collective action now resided in the individual commander. The weight of the command literally rested on one person's shoulders. While technology made operations safer, a safer world also reduced the margin for error.

The new *Arleigh Burke*-class destroyer was commissioned in 1991 and even thirty years later is the world's premier surface combatant. Over 500 feet long and displacing over 8000 tons, these ships are almost the size of McVay's *Indianapolis* with only a crew of 300 officers and men. By 1989 diesel submarines were gone from the force and the *Los Angeles*-class nuclear-powered submarines ruled the seas. These submarines are 362 feet long, displace over 6,000 tons with a crew of 129 officers and men. Capable of launching torpedoes and land attack guided missiles, no place on the globe lies beyond their reach. By the end of the millennium navigation systems integrate visual and radar information with the Global Positioning System (GPS) and electronic displays instantly show positions on charts relative to land masses, water depths, and even other ships. A worldwide system of satellite and underwater reconnaissance provides improved and detailed charts. Ships now determine where they are, to within feet, and like fires, groundings dropped to statistically negligible numbers. Improvements in radar, and fewer ships at sea, also meant fewer collisions. Crimes of command remained but the consequences are significantly different from previous decades.

The Navy never reached the 600-ship goal, suffering instead through a steady drawdown as the Cold War ended, counter-terrorism took center stage, and social and individual actions eclipsed operational issues. In previous decades, Connelly Stevenson and Marcus Aurelius Arnheiter were outliers but, by the late 1990s, the Navy removed far more commanders for personal failures than true crimes of command. However, over time operational crimes of command acquired the same taint as personal failings, and all misdeeds are corrected the same way - removal and administrative discipline. While leaders laid the foundation in the forty years after World War II, their successors erected and gilded the temple of accountability in the last years of the century. In these last decades the final movement from an individual commander's personal responsibility to one of command culpability was finalized and taken one step further. While professional actions of the commander or crew remained paramount, by the first decade of the twenty-first century, commanders were liable for the individual personal actions their crew took; like Captain Arthur Fredrickson in *Ranger,* modern commanders were now accountable for junior sailors knowingly turning the wrong valves and the actions taken by those sailors on liberty, at their homes, on travel or even vacation. By the end of the twentieth century commanders were wholly and completely accountable for every action within their commands – even as their authority eroded under increased communications technology and easier oversight and intrusiveness of supervisory commanders who were in turn less physically connected to the sea.

USS *Stark* - 1987

The 1970s-era *Oliver Hazard Perry*-class frigate was conceived as a low-cost supplement to carrier battle groups and as escorts for North Atlantic convoys expected to reinforce Europe in a war between the North Atlantic Treaty Organization and the Warsaw Pact. These 400-foot long, 4,000-ton ships were the true successors to World War II era destroyers and destroyer escorts like *Hobson, Frank E. Evans, Charles H. Roan, Hartley,* and *Brownson* in a way the *Arleigh Burke*-class cannot be.

However, without a major sea war and increasing global commitments, even these small ships ultimately operate on their own. At 9:09 p.m., on May 17, 1987, USS *Stark* (FFG 31), under Captain Glenn Brindel's command, operated alone in the central Persian Gulf where an Iraqi Mirage F-1 fighter jet fired two Exocet anti-ship cruise missiles at her. While the first missile did not explode, the second missile's explosion, both missiles' unexpended fuel and the weapons' impact killed 37 of *Stark*'s 200 sailors. Another twenty-one sailors were injured.[1]

---

[1] United States, Department of the Navy, Commander Cruiser Destroyer

It is reasonable for modern readers to forget that in 1987, the United States and Iraq were on friendly terms. After their 1979 revolution, Iran was the region's aggressor nation and the U.S.'s decades-long conflict with Iraq still in the future. *Stark* was in the area for a routine deployment, a peacetime mission sometimes called sea control or showing the flag. When she arrived in the Persian Gulf on February 28, 1987, Fifth Fleet intelligence officers briefed her captain and crew that "the probability of deliberate attack on U. S. warships was low, but that indiscriminate attack in the Persian Gulf was a significant danger."[2] Also briefed were Rules of Engagement which included an inherent right and obligation to self-defense:

> Nothing in these rules or in the absence of guidance herein, will be construed as preventing the responsible U.S. Commander from taking such action as is required by military necessity to defend his installation, aircraft, ship or unit from attack, or the imminent threat of attack.[3]

The rules included a concept of graduated response. If an unidentified aircraft, or identified aircraft with unknown intent, approached a ship the first action was a radio warning on the Military Air Defense frequency. The next step was to use fire control radars to illuminate and track the aircraft. Military aircraft can sense these radar emissions and recognize they are approaching a military ship. If the voice warnings do not work, the fire control radars should. All through March, April, and May 1987, *Stark* made many radio calls to warn aircraft, but she never used her radars when warning aircraft away.[4]

Group Two, *Formal Investigation into the Circumstances Surrounding the Attack on the USS Stark (FFG 31) on 17 May 1987* (Washington, DC, 1987). 1-2.
[2] Ibid, 6.
[3] Ibid
[4] Ibid, 7.

During the first part of May, Iraqi aircraft conducted repeated ship attack profiles (SAP) and Commander MidEast Force (CMEF) expected additional SAP flights for the remainder of the month. With this knowledge, *Stark* left Bahrain the morning of May 17th and steamed towards a radar picket station in international waters.[5] At 8 p.m. that evening, Captain Brindel entered *Stark*'s Combat Information Center (CIC) and learned that an Iraqi aircraft was flying over the Persian Gulf, headed south. He advised his Tactical Action Officer, Lieutenant Basil Moncrief, to monitor the aircraft and reminded him of the recent SAP flights. Brindel then climbed up one deck to the bridge to monitor a full power run, a standard engineering evolution designed to test engine capability.[6]

At 8:55 p.m., while still on the bridge, Brindel noticed that CIC was no longer tracking the Iraqi aircraft. The full power run finished early, unsuccessfully, and Brindel went to his cabin just behind the bridge. CIC regained contact of the Iraqi fighter but incorrectly labeled it as an unknown air contact. At 9:01 p.m., CIC prepared to record data for a Marine-Air Reporting System message about the aircraft. Four minutes later the Iraqi jet turned and pointed directly at *Stark*. Though the jet was only 33 miles away and held on radar, no one aboard *Stark* noticed the turn.[7]

At 9:07 p.m. the Iraqi jet fired her first missile at *Stark*. At the same time, *Stark*'s forward lookout reported a bright light off the port bow and Lieutenant Moncrief noticed the change in the Iraqi jet's course, realizing the jet was pointed directly at them. He directed an officer to call Captain Brindel and ordered watchstanders to issue radio warnings.[8]

As Moncrief moved watchstanders into weapons control

---

[5] Ibid, 8.
[6] Ibid, 10.
[7] Ibid, 10-11.
[8] Ibid, 12.

positions, calls to Captain Brindel's cabin went unanswered and he was not on the bridge. The Executive Officer, Lieutenant Commander Raymond Gajan, was in CIC on an unrelated administrative task.[9]

At 9:08 p.m. the Iraqi jet fired her second missile and *Stark* issued her first radio warning on Military Air Distress. Watchstanders took action to arm rocket launched chaff - a system intended to confuse anti-ship missile seekers. Within 45-seconds the chaff system was armed and launch control in CIC. None of the watchstanders placed the automated Gatling gun Close-In Weapons System (CIWS) online. This critical self-defense weapon remained in standby through the entire attack.[10]

At 9:09 p.m. one of the lookouts recognized the inbound missile as did the Junior Officer of the Deck. While watchstanders in CIC heard the report, no one informed the TAO. Shortly afterward the first missile struck *Stark*. In short order the ship sounded General Quarters, the second missile was sighted, the Captain entered CIC from his cabin, and the second missile struck. Both missiles impacted in the same location - port side and into one of the ship's berthing compartments. Thirty-one sailors died in the berthing compartment, three outside a radar equipment room, and three in Chief Petty Officer quarters.[11]

The impacts extensively damaged the forward part of the ship and *Stark* lost radio communications. Intense heat forced the bridge crew's evacuation. The resulting fires made most of the ship's interior uninhabitable. Crew not involved in fighting the fires relocated to the stern flight deck. They remained there until sunrise when the fires were contained enough to allow them to move forward and back into the ship.[12]

Somehow *Stark* maintained control of her engines and electrical plant, stopping only at 11 p.m. when lowering portable

---

[9] Ibid, 2, 11.
[10] Ibid, 12-14.
[11] Ibid, 15-17. 20-25.
[12] Ibid, 21.

pumps to provide firefighting water. At 11:30 p.m. a rescue tug arrived and helped cool the forward missile magazine, just forward of the missile impact site. Eventually sailors from four other ships provided personnel to help fight the fires; however, the number of personnel was the only negative the investigation found - damage control training and response was high[13] while combat direction was not. During the ten minutes from track to attack, *Stark* made no move to employ any of her weapons systems.[14]

    The rescue tug towed *Stark* to Bahrain where she moored alongside the Fifth Fleet flagship, USS *LaSalle*. On May 20th Rear Admiral Grant Alexander Sharp, Commander Cruiser Group Two, arrived in Bahrain to investigate the attack. A parallel investigation headed by Rear Admiral David N. Rogers of the Joint Staff, took place in Baghdad, Iraq. This second investigation dealt with the Iraqi actions and political ramifications. Admiral Sharp, son of a retired Admiral and a career surface warfare officer, and his team of six officers and five enlisted support personnel focused solely on actions aboard *Stark*. Captain Brindel, Lieutenant Commander Gajan, Lt Moncrief, and Ensign Jeffery Wright, Combat Information Center Watch Officer were designated parties to the investigation.[15] They were afforded one legal representative each, and no support personnel. Additionally, unlike the investigation team's sole focus, Brindel and his officers had obligations to *Stark*'s crew, forcing them to spend eight or more hours working on their defense and another eight or more hours in their normal duties.[16]

---

[13] Ibid, 27-30.
[14] Ibid, 15-18.
[15] Ibid, 4.
[16] Jeffrey L. Levinson and Randy L. Edwards, *Missile Inbound: The Attack on the Stark in the Persian Gulf* (Annapolis, MD: Naval Institute Press, 1997). 42-44, 56.

Damage estimates exceeded $142 million ($314 million in 2017).[17] The later investigation made a significant number of valor recommendations, but after awarding ten sailors (including Lieutenant Commander Gajan, and Lieutenant Moncrief) the Navy Marine Corps Medal, the Navy's highest non-combat award[18] Navy leaders made no other awards, ignoring or dismissing recommendations for the Purple Heart, Navy Cross, and Silver Star.

The investigation determined four factors caused the damage to *Stark*: failure to appreciate and respect the hazards in the region and the Mirage threat, in particular; improper watch manning and standing; failure to institute a proper level of weapon readiness; and misunderstanding of fire control radar as a less than lethal warning method. Over two dozen additional opinions detailed Captain Brindel's, and his watch team's, failures.[19] While each of those factors applied to *Stark*, it is unlikely they applied only to *Stark* – however no other ships were examined for readiness or compliance with procedures that might have protected *Stark*. *Stark* was hit, therefore she was investigated; no one else.

The report recommended removing Captain Brindle, Lieutenant Commander Gajan, and Lieutenant Moncrief from *Stark* and referring them each to General Court Martial.[20] All three were administratively removed from their positions by Central Command Commander General George B. Crist, citing a "lack of confidence."[21] Gajan's case was dealt with at Admiral's Mast, a nonjudicial punishment route authorized under the Uniform Code of Military Justice (UCMJ) and, ideally, less severe than court-martial.

On July 27, 1987, the Navy announced that it would not court-martial Brindel and Moncrief and reprimanded them at

---

[17] Commander Cruiser Destroyer Group Two, 31.
[18] Ibid, 42.
[19] Ibid, 31.
[20] Ibid, 45.
[21] Levinson and Edwards, 94.

Admiral's Mast. Navy statements indicated that Brindel chose to retire, meaning retirement as a Commander because he had insufficient time as a Captain, and that both Brindel and Moncrief "admitted and accepted accountability for the lack of readiness and inadequacy of measures taken to protect the *Stark*."[22]

A small detail often overlooked in the case lies in Captain Brindel's career timing. Before the attack, his change of command was scheduled for June 5. Instead of spending his final weeks writing awards and speeches, then preparing for a new job and potentially a new command, he spent his time writing condolence letters, eulogies, and working on his defense during the investigation and preparation for court-martial. Absent the attack, Brindel would likely have seen additional commands - despite the clear failures of forethought and leadership only exposed by the investigation.

Between 1987 and 2000 incidents and crimes of command dropped with only eight major explosions, 28 fires (a quarter of them in one year, 1990), 20 groundings, and just over 50 collisions. With this drop came a reduction in the Navy's size as ship numbers fell from 597 in 1987 to only 331 in 2000. Navy personnel went from over 602,000 in 1987 to 373,000 in 2000. With the end of the Cold War, the maritime nation no longer felt threated from sea.

While incidents of crimes of command dropped, removal from command intermittently rose and fell, with each rise noticed in the press. In 1992 and 1996 command removals spiked to 13 and 11 in respective years. The 1992 numbers stemmed largely from two incidents, the Las Vegas Tailhook Convention and a raucous party at the Miramar Naval Air Station. In Las Vegas, almost 100 men and women reported assaults during three days of drunken convention antics among over 4,000 Navy pilots, defense contractors, and guests between

---

[22] John H. Cushman, Jr., "Navy Forgoes Courts-Martial for Officers of Stark," *The New York Times*, July 28, 1987.

September 8th and 12th, 1991. After initial reports made it to the press, the Navy launched a massive investigation. That summer, emotions were still raw when fighter pilots staged a skit with disparaging references to Representative Patricia Schroeder during the annual "Tomcat Follies" gathering. Five commanders lost their jobs, but commanders later reinstated two of them.

By 1992 the initial investigation into Tailhook was scrapped and a Department of Defense Inspector General Investigation concluded the original investigation was deficient and was "the result of an attempt to limit the exposure of the Navy and senior Navy officials to criticism" and questioned the credibility of the Navy's entire flag officer community.[23] The ensuing investigation and alleged cover-up led to massive changes in Navy regulations, culture, and the removal of five admirals, a Chief of Naval Operations and a Secretary of the Navy. While over a hundred officers faced administrative sanction, not one was convicted at court-martial, with most legal cases dropped due to insufficient evidence.[24]

1996 did not have a specific reason for its spike. Removals that year included collisions, groundings, poor leadership and individual misbehavior. Before 1996, removal of ten commanders a year was unheard of. By 2002, removing ten commanders a year was normal. In 2000, the Navy was still deciding which direction to turn – remove more, or remove less. Meanwhile, the past returned to challenge the modern idealism of command.

USS *Indianapolis* - revisited

In 1975 Steven Spielberg's adaptation of *Jaws* introduced a new generation to *Indianapolis*. That summer Robert Shaw's Quint growled the now famous line "Eleven

---

[23] United States, Department of Defense, Inspector General, *The Tailhook Report: The Official Inquiry into the Events of Tailhook '91*, by Derek J. Vander Schaaf (Washington, DC). Introductory memorandum and X-9.
[24] Bray, 341.

hundred men went into the water, 316 came out, the sharks took the rest. June 29, 1945." and more than 50 million moviegoers wondered what happened. That short soliloquy emphasized the consequences of actions taken by McVay, Hashimoto, and the Pacific Fleet but did not mention any of the leading participants.

The modern technology of the video cassette allowed more generations to hear that line and wonder what happened. Surely the story was fiction? In time those interested learned the truth, or at least some of the truth and in 1996 Florida middle school student Hunter Scott, after watching *Jaws*,[25] found the story interesting enough to turn it into a school history project. Over the next six years Scott researched, reported, and eventually resurrected the history of 1945, ultimately redeeming Captain Charles McVay's reputation.[26]

Scott's was not the first attempt to clear McVay. Even before he killed himself in 1968 the survivors began lobbying Congress. McVay's suicide only strengthened the efforts. Over the next two decades they organized, gathered new information, wrote the Navy, their senators and congressmen. In 1975 the case was also investigated by Senators Vance Hartke and Thomas Eagleton but nothing came of it. Even when McVay's wife's cousin became Secretary of the Navy nothing was possible. A request to President Ronald Reagan in 1983 was denied because no authority allowed the changing of the court's findings and a presidential pardon was not possible because Secretary Forrestal remitted McVay's sentence, essentially pardoning him. In 1992, Republican Senator Richard Lugar of Indiana initiated a legal study of the court-martial again without

---

[25] Cong. Senate, Committee on Armed Services., *The Sinking of the U.S.S. Indianapolis and the Subsequent Court-martial of Rear Adm. Charles B. McVay III, USN: hearing before the Committee on Armed Services, United States Senate, One Hundred Sixth Congress*, First session, September 14, 1999, 106 Cong., Rept. (Washington: U.S. G.P.O., 2000). 20.
[26] Nelson.

result. After three separate Congressional inquiries in 1996 the Navy issued a report, supporting the findings of the court-martial.[27] By the time Hunter Scott came on the scene the battle appeared over.

After that first awakening, through research that contacted every living survivor, contact and exposure to Congressmen and the media, Hunter Scott took on a crusade to correct the injustice he saw in how the Navy handled McVay. By the time he was done he was an honorary member of the Indianapolis Survivors Association and had the world's foremost collection of information, artifacts, and documents related to USS *Indianapolis'* sinking and Charles McVay's court-martial.[28] McVay's family and the Indianapolis survivors sought for fifty years to clear him and in a matter of months the effort took on new life and coalesced around an unlikely hero.

Pressured by the survivors group and Scott's growing fame as a pre-teen challenging the U.S. Navy, on September 14, 1999 the Committee on the Armed Services held hearings into the sinking and subsequent court-martial. Chaired by senator and former Secretary of the Navy John Warner, the committee heard testimony from Hunter Scott, Dan Kurzman and twenty other survivors, the sister of a sailor killed in the sinking, McVay's son Charles B. McVay IV, and three Navy Department officials: Dr. William S. Dudley Director of Naval History, Rear Admiral John D. Hutson, Judge Advocate General, and Admiral Donald L. Pilling, Vice Chief of Naval Operations. The survivors and family member were unanimous in their opinion of the court-martial with the only differences being how angry or outraged they were over the conviction.[29]

McVay's son spoke of his father's, and his, thoughts on the Navy. They loved the Navy; both grew up in Navy families

---

[27] Nelson, 148-9.
[28] Nelson
[29] Committee on Armed Services (2000), 21.

and believed that "there was a right way, a wrong way, and the Navy way."[30] McVay's second son related that

> After my father's court-martial, I accepted the verdict without question, as did he. After all, the captain of a ship is supreme commander of that limited realm and is ultimately responsible for eve[rything] that occurs, good and bad. In that light, I shared my father's feelings after the court-martial. While the decision was personally a heart-breaker, we both knew that the Navy could not be wrong. My father believed that until his death, as did I. With command comes responsibility, and with responsibility one must pay the piper, no matter what the cost. This was the code by which my father lived.

After his father's suicide Kimo learned more about the disaster and what he learned eroded his belief in the Navy way. He testified that

> after over 54 years, it is apparent that my father was dealt a great injustice, an officer destined for distinction, then doomed to extinction, in order to hide the culpability that should have been borne by others in the Navy. I now believe that my father knew the injustice but bore it stoically for 'the good of the Navy.'[31]

The Navy's response, however, reasserted McVay's guilt. Rear Admiral John Hutson, Judge Advocate General of the Navy, personally read the record of trial and concluded that "the proceedings were fair and provided the due full process of law. Admiral McVay had every right applicable to trial by court-martial. The record clearly indicates Admiral McVay's counsel performed his duties well. In short, the proceedings were legal."[32] In fact, Hutson reiterates, at least six more times, that the trial and sentence were legal, reaffirming an opinion that was

---

[30] Ibid, 14.
[31] Ibid, 14.
[32] Ibid, 70.

never in doubt. Hutson also noted that "there is no authority under law to overturn or reverse a final conviction. Even if remedial action were warranted, no such action is legally available. For example, a presidential pardon does not overturn a conviction, but merely sets aside or mitigates the punishment imposed...findings of the Court of Inquiry are similarly final. Such administratively final acts may only be disturbed upon a showing of fraud, or mistake of fact or law.[33]

Vice Chief of Naval Operations Admiral Don Pilling, also defended the Navy's decision. In doing so he reaffirmed the modern interpretation of "Hobson's Choice" and is the first Navy official to use the word "accountability" in relation to Mcvay. Pilling's statement is the most concise endorsement of the Navy's modern view, even more so than Admiral Holloway in his 1976 letter to "All Flag Officers and Officers in Command."

> To understand why the Navy would bring an officer to trial in such circumstances, one must consider what the principles of a commanding officer's authority and accountability mean in the military context; more importantly, what those principles mean in the unique context of command at sea.
>
> The traditional scope and duties and accountability that attach to command at sea has no parallel in the military or civilian spheres. The commanding officer of a Naval vessel has tremendous authority; more independent authority than any other officer or officer of comparable seniority. It has often been described as absolute, and in combat, it effectively is, even today.
>
> With this authority comes an equally absolute counterbalance; accountability. A commanding officer is given full authority to command his ship, but never escapes absolute accountability for what he and that ship may do.

---

[33] Ibid, 74.

Again, uniquely, to command at sea, the commanding officer always remains responsible, not only for his own actions, but the actions or inactions of every crew member under his command.

For centuries, command at sea has demanded both full authority and full accountability. There cannot be one without the other.

From the first vessel commissioned under the Continental Congress until today, the United States Navy has enshrined these concepts as the cornerstone of command.

Accountability can be and must be a very severe standard. The commanding officer is charged with weighing every factor and circumstance which can be foreseen before he acts. If any of those judgments is in error, the commanding officer may be held accountable, perhaps at court-martial.

Each commander is separately responsible for his own deficiencies, without regard to the culpability of others. Admiral McVay understood these concepts perfectly. After his rescue, he told reporters, when asked about the sinking, "I was in command of the ship and I am responsible for its fate."

Later, during his court-martial, he stated, "I know I cannot shirk the responsibility of command." Indeed, the ultimate responsibility of command is for the command, itself, and the lives of the sailors who make up that command.[34]

Within those 274 words, accountability is mentioned seven times. Pilling's statement is the first overt acknowledgment that a commander is accountable, responsible, and culpable for the "actions or inactions of every crew member under his command." The absolute nature of command had never been so clearly described. In fact, Pilling closed his

---

[34] Ibid, 75.

testimony asserting that "the court-martial of Admiral McVay was not undertaken to attack him, but to defend the crucial principle of command accountability;"[35] even though no contemporary documents,[36] not the court of inquiry or court-martial, even use the word accountability or the concept of "command accountability."

Additional testimony furthered the final nature of McVay's court-martial when Pilling affirmed the legality of the conviction and added the word "fair" to the already stated "legal" and "proper."[37] He further opined that "the decision of the court-martial does not impugn the valor of Admiral McVay. He was an officer decorated for combat action. The Court took that valor into account by unanimously recommending full clemency for the very light, almost trivial sentence imposed."[38]

There are, however, some inconsistencies in the Navy's logic. Admiral Pilling asserted that "when a commanding officer's ship is lost in combat, and many of her crew die both on the ship and later, awaiting rescue, the commanding officer's actions and decisions will be scrutinized." Admiral Hutson affirmed that no one else was disciplined for *Indianapolis'* loss,[39] and that no other commanders were court-martialed after losing their ships.[40] There are also no records of commanders court-martialed for not zig-zagging. As with *Stark*, what mattered was not *that* a particular ship did not do something, but what happened *because* a ship did not do something. The crime was in the result, not in the action.

Hutson also noted that in 1945 courts-martial differed significantly from today. As seen in the aftermath of the *John F.*

---

[35] Ibid, 77.
[36] Ibid, 146-7.
[37] Ibid, 76.
[38] Ibid
[39] Ibid
[40] Nelson, 136.

Kennedy and *Belknap* collision, modern courts-martial are criminal trials intended to determine the guilt or innocence and award appropriate punishment. In 1945 courts-martial "were much broader in scope, often incorporating the function of fixing accountability and resolving vexing issues of command and discretionary action. In the modem Navy, it is safe to say that any court-martial conviction ends an officer's career. Before 1950, that was emphatically not the case."[41] Other than Admiral Nimitz, Hutson provided no other examples of officers who survived court-martial and also did not explain why, if courts-martial were so different then, the Navy used a modern standard to defend McVay's conviction.

In effect, the Navy's stance was: McVay did not zig-zag, was charged as such, and in a proper, legal, and fair trial found guilty. His sentence was trivial and recovery of his career was possible, especially after Secretary Forrestal remitted the sentence.[42] Yet, in the same testimony Pilling and Hutson accept the stigma brought by a court-martial conviction.[43]

Perhaps the real issue confronting the Navy was this, provided via questions for the record from Warner answered by Pilling and appended to the report:

> any attempt to "undo" the court-martial could only be construed as a finding that the Navy acted in an unjust manner [and] a judgment that the Navy acted in a "morally unsustainable" manner must impugn the character and integrity of the many high-ranking officers and officials who made decisions in that process-men such as Fleet Admiral King and Secretary James V. Forrestal, not to mention the seven combat commanders who served as the court-martial. In my judgment, that would unjustifiably tarnish the memory of these men, naval and even national heroes in their own right. Second, a finding that the court-martial was

---

[41] Committee on Armed Services (2000), 70.
[42] Ibid, 87.
[43] Ibid, 149.

somehow essentially wrong sets a precedent, at least in the minds of potential proponents of other causes, that final judgments can be revisited and reversed, long after the facts have been clouded by the passage of time. In fact, no new relevant facts have arisen in the 50-plus years since the court-martial took place. A repudiation of the court-martial now implies that later generations are free to substitute their judgment for the judgment of duly empowered tribunals and decision makers acting within the con-text of their times. While an extreme circumstance may sometime, somewhere justify such action, in my opinion, there is nothing in this case that approaches the level of justification necessary. These impacts on the Navy, though subtle in operation, might very well be significant in effect.[44]

The issue of McVay and his guilt, even the idea of revisiting the court-martial, had little to do with right or wrong and much to do with potential future actions.

The Senate disagreed with the Navy. As Senator Bob Smith, New Hamsphire, said:

> [The senate was] questioning whether it was morally right to have court-martialed [McVay] in the first place...That is not revisionism; that is the truth; that is trying to set the record straight.[45] You cannot court-martial somebody for an error in judgment, and then not court-martial everybody else who made errors in judgment that cost the lives of more men. You did not do it. That is why there is an injustice here. We should change injustices; not rewrite history, but change injustices.[46]

Smith saw injustice in the Navy's logical fallacy of

---

[44] Ibid, 146.
[45] Ibid, 4.
[46] Ibid, 89.

insisting that McVay was not court-martialed for losing his ship while simultaneously refusing to accept that the Navy would not have court-martialed McVay had the ship arrived safely in port. Smith raised this issue twice in testimony and the Navy never adequately answered him.[47]

On October 12, 2000 the Senate passed Joint Resolution 26. House Resolution 48 was passed the prior week. The resolution said, in part:

> Whereas Captain McVay thus became the first United States Navy commanding officer brought to trial for losing his ship in combat during World War II, despite the fact that over 700 ships were lost during World War II, including some under questionable circumstances;..[it] is the sense of Congress that-(1) the court-martial charges against then-Captain Charles Butler McVay III, United States Navy, arising from the sinking of the U.S.S. INDIANAPOLIS (CA-35) on July 30, 1945, while under his command were not morally sustainable; (2) Captain McVay's conviction was a miscarriage of justice that led to his unjust humiliation and damage to his naval career; and (3) the American people should not recognize Captain McVay's lack of culpability for the tragic loss of the U.S.S. INDIANAPOLIS and the lives of the men who died as a result of her sinking.[48]

October 12, 2000 was the same day terrorists attacked USS *Cole* (DDG 67) in Aden, Yemen killing 17 sailors. In years to come the similarities between the cases grew beyond a coincidental date.

In April 2001, the Navy announced it would revisit the case and seek the best method to change McVay's record. In July, the newly sworn Secretary of the Navy, Gordon R. England sent Senator Smith a letter stating he did not have the legal

---

[47] Nelson, 178-9.
[48] Committee on Armed Services, (2000). 8-9.

authority to overturn a court-martial or delete the findings from McVay's record. Instead he could only amend McVay's record including a copy of the Senate Resolution intending to change the perception that McVay was responsible for the loss of life.[49] In effect Navy leadership succumbed to the administrative pressure of a system the Navy created. Citing no authority to act was a poor answer because there was likewise no authority precluding action. The Navy made a choice, it just chose the wrong one. Even Captain Hashimoto, perhaps the only person really culpable for the sinking, recognized the problem when he said "Our peoples have forgiven each other for that terrible war. Perhaps it is time your peoples forgave Captain McVay for the humiliation of his unjust conviction."[50]

USS *Cole* - 2000

On October 12, 2000, coincidentally the same date as the Senate's vote on Joint Resolution 26, and shortly after 11 a.m., as the crew lined up for lunch, two men drove a small boat along USS *Cole*'s (DDG 67) port side and detonated blocks of C-4, Semtex, RDX (cyclotrimethylenetrinitramine) and TNT.[51] The explosion killed seventeen of the 296 crew and injured 42 others, ripping a 32-foot by 36-foot hole and causing extensive internal blast damage.

On August 8, 2000, *Cole* left her homeport of Norfolk, Virginia for a routine deployment which included operations in the Mediterranean Sea and the Persian Gulf. Through the first half of September, she patrolled the Mediterranean and made calls in Spain, France, Malta, and Slovenia. After departing

---

[49] Nelson, 186.
[50] David Stout, "Captain, Once a Scapegoat, Is Absolved," *The New York Times*, July 14, 2001.
[51] Kirk Lippold, *Front Burner: Al Qaeda's Attack on the USS Cole* (New York, NY: Public Affairs, 2013). 247.

Koper, Slovenia, the ship operated in the southern Adriatic Sea before transiting the Suez Canal on October 9, 2000. For political and logistics reasons, *Cole* stopped in Yemen to refuel. Aden was *Cole*'s first stop in the Central Command Area of Responsibility and was solely for fuel - the crew would not have liberty.

The crew had no warning; the boat pulled alongside mixed in with other support craft. The bombers did not look suspicious and did nothing to call attention to their behavior or boat. The ship immediately lost power, water poured into the massive hole and the crew worked for days to keep *Cole* from sinking to the bottom of the harbor. The damage was so great that *Cole* was towed from the harbor and transferred to a heavy lift ship. Brought back to Pascagoula, Mississippi, *Cole* spent almost a year in reconstruction at a cost the almost $250 million ($351 million in 2017).

The search for accountability started on October 14, 2000, and, despite numerous endorsements and actions by senior Navy and Department of Defense officials, remains a source of controversy. As the senior Navy officer, Admiral Charles W. Moore, Jr. assigned Captain James W. Holland, Jr. to investigate *Cole*'s role in the attack.[52] Holland commanded Moore's Task Force 53 supervising the logistics forces in the region. He was a prior enlisted officer and while he was senior to *Cole*'s commanding officer, Commander Kirk Lippold, he had never commanded a ship.

What was clear from the beginning of the investigation was that "this was not a random act, but rather an attack resulting from careful, deliberate planning."[53] However, as with USS

---

[52] Lippold, 231.
[53] United States, Department of the Navy, Central Command, *Command Investigation Into the Actions of USS Cole (DDG 67) in Preparing for and Undertaking a Brief Stop for Fuel at Bandar At Tawahi (Aden Harbor) Aden Yemen on or about 12 October 2000*, by James W. Holland, Jr.

Stark, the Navy investigator was tasked only with what happened inside *Cole*; specifically "to inquire into the facts and circumstances surrounding the actions of USS *Cole* (DDG-67) in preparing for and undertaking a Brief Stop for Fuel (BSF) at Aden Harbor, Yemen, on 12 October 2000."[54] The Federal Bureau of Investigation and Naval Criminal Investigative Service would look at the bombers and their planning. Removing this factor from Holland's purview drastically affected the investigation. In Holland's write up he was also paradoxically critical and supportive of the crew. Citing "initially the majority of the crew was fragile and extremely emotional" and "many instances, personnel had to be approached very carefully and gently, often they initially had difficulty discussing the incident or anything leading up to it" contrasted with

> Notwithstanding all of the stressful situations the crew encountered, they were all extremely helpful during the course of this investigation. They made themselves immediately available for interviews - in some cases multiple interviews over the course of several days. Several took the time to write detailed statements regarding the actions of the ship leading up to the time of the incident.[55]

> Holland covered what is now standard ground writing: The Commanding Officer is charged with the absolute responsibility for the safety, well- being, and efficiency of his or her command. The duties and responsibilities of the Commanding Officer are established by United States Navy Regulations, general orders, customs, and tradition. Of particular importance is the Commanding Officer's duty to take all necessary and appropriate action in self-defense of the command.[56]

(Washington, DC, 2000). 8.
[54] Ibid, 11, 132.
[55] Ibid, 17.
[56] Ibid, 94.

Holland cited Navy Regulations 0802, an updated version of 0702, which Captain Howard called a guideline for performance when he presided over the *Belknap* collision trial.

Cole's crew was well-trained with an active Force Protection Program and superb damage control organization. Commander, United States Second Fleet congratulated the crew for impressive performance in Force Protection and Anti-Terrorism pre-deployment training. *Cole* conducted frequent Operations/Intelligence briefings, continued and refreshed ship-wide Force Protection/Anti-Terrorism training and often discussed Force Protection during ship-led "Mediterranean-Arabian University" briefings. Despite all this training, the resulting investigation found that "the ship did not fully protect itself from attack because it lacked deliberate planning and execution of an approved Force Protection Plan."[57] This line is the briefest summation of what the investigator, and many others, believed about the attack.

Holland went on to write that this well-trained crew failed to adjust their thinking from a Mediterranean port to their new Central Command environment. He also accused ship leadership of "a notable absence of supervision...in implementation of the Force Protection Plan."[58] Holland believed the attack preventable, especially if *Cole* had implemented its entire Force Protection Plan. He specifically called out a dozen measures the ship intentionally set aside for the port visit.

Holland's final assessment? "Commander Kirk S. Lippold's performance as Commanding Officer did not meet the standards set forth in Navy Regulations...[and] That CDR Lippold's chain of command assess his accountability under applicable laws and regulations." Holland also criticized *Cole*'s immediate superior, Commander Task Force 50, saying he "also

---

[57] Ibid, 9, 97.
[58] Ibid, 98.

demonstrated a failure to think critically about USS *Cole*'s...posture."[59]

Holland completed his report on November 27, 2000 and forwarded over 200 pages with 134 separate enclosures including photographs and video to the Fifth Fleet Commander for review and comment. The Fifth Fleet Commander wrote 22 pages in his endorsement, five of which directly addressed "Why Aden?" and explained the rationale for *Cole*'s visit at the theater and strategic level. He also modified three of Holland's opinions, in each case moving the investigation away from finding fault with *Cole*'s leadership. "It is clear, however, that had USS *Cole* implemented the THREATCON BRAVO Force Protection Measures appropriately, the ship would not have prevented the attack. I am convinced THREATCON BRAVO Force Protection Measures were inadequate to prevent the attack."[60]

Admiral Robert Natter, Commander in Chief, Atlantic Fleet, moved the needle even more. Natter outright disapproved or modified half of the opinions, most specifically the one finding Commander Lippold's "performance as Commanding Officer did not meet the standards set forth in Navy Regulations."[61] Natter agreed with Moore that the attack could not have been prevented by any of the planned protection matters and that

> After careful consideration of the matter of personal accountability, I am firmly convinced, and conclude, that the Commanding Officer, Executive Officer, Command Duty Officer, Force Protection Officer, and other officers or crew of *COLE*, were not derelict in the execution of duty. Further, they did not act in violation of any regulation, order or custom of the Navy.

---

[59] Ibid, 105.
[60] Ibid, 127.
[61] Ibid, 150.

> Accordingly, no disciplinary or other adverse administrative personnel action is warranted.[62]

On January 4, 2001, Admiral Natter sent his endorsement to Vern Clark, Chief of Naval Operations. Five days later Clark wrote:

> After carefully considering the investigation and endorsements, I concur with the conclusion of Commander in Chief, U.S. Atlantic Fleet (CINCLANTFLT) to take no punitive action against the Commanding Officer or any of his crew for this tragedy. I conclude, along with the previous endorsers, that the tools and information at the Commanding Officer's disposal on 12 October 2000, coupled with the lack of any indication of hostile intent before the attack, severely disadvantaged the Commanding Officer and crew of *COLE* in trying to prevent this tragedy. Likewise, I concur that the investigation clearly demonstrates that *COLE* was a well-trained, well-led, and highly capable ship.[63]

For all practical purposes, Holland's investigation was reduced to the facts with any opinions on accountability removed or refuted. One area that everyone, from Holland to Clark, agreed on was that some level of responsibility and accountability lay in the chain of command above *Cole*. Admiral Clark alluded to "separate actions [that] will be taken to assess the accountability of others in the chain of command." No such investigations were ever made public.

Commander Lippold remained in command of *Cole*. Over the next year, he traveled and met with the family members of sailors killed in the attack. Some were open to his visit, others not so. Lippold spoke to classes of prospective Commanding and Executive Officers, detailing his experiences in, and after, command of *Cole*. In 2002, Kirk Lippold was selected for

---

[62] Ibid, 141.
[63] Ibid, 153.

promotion to Captain. Here is where the second half of his saga begins.

All military officer promotions above the grade of Lieutenant must receive Senate confirmation. From the summer of 2002 until August 2006, Virginia Senator John Warner and former Secretary of the Navy, bowing to reelection pressures and the wishes of two Virginia families who lost sailors aboard *Cole*,[64] threatened to reopen hearings into the attack if the Navy insisted on promoting Lippold. The Navy held fast, but only so far. The Navy did not acquiesce to Warner and did not formally withdraw Lippold's promotion, however, the Navy also did not press the issue. Lippold was selected, but not confirmed, as a Captain, his promotion held in limbo for four years. Eventually, Warner outlasted two Chiefs of Naval Operations and two Secretaries of the Navy. Finally, in August 2006, Clark's successor as CNO, Admiral Mike Mullen, informed his staff he

> ...recently recommended to SecNav that he permanently remove CDR Kirk Lippold from the FY03 O6 Selection list, and yesterday he approved that recommendation. My recommendation was based principly [sic] on what occurred - and what didn't occur - before the explosion, and on the fact that CDR Lippold, as CO of USS *Cole*, was the accountable officer when his ship was attacked and 17 sailors lost their lives. My expectation for CO's is that they anticipate that which no one else can...In CDR Lippold's case, his preparations for entering Aden, Yemen were neither timely nor sufficient to deal with the uncertainties associated with entering port. His judgement demonstrated constrained thinking that prevented him from seeking more information and creating other options. There was a routineness and immaturity in his leadership unsuitable to the circumstances.
>
> My recommendation is also based on the accumulation

---

[64] Lippold, 313.

of facts and errors in the professional decision-making displayed by CDR Lippold, my expectations for CO's and the exacting standards to which they must be held, and my firm conviction that leaders who fail to satisfy these standards are held to an exacting level of professional accountability. There is a professional accountability that must be satisfied and, in my judgement, a decision to not promote CDR Lippold fulfills that standard of accountability based on his performance as CO of USS *Cole*.[65]

Mullen vacated Admirals Moore, Natter and Clark's opinions, reverting to Captain John Holland's original language. Navy leaders were unwilling to risk a fight with Congress over a lowly commander. On May 24, 2007, Commander Lippold retired from active service. He continues speaking about *Cole* and her tragedy. Differing significantly from other commanders, he wrote about his experiences and included pages of the back and forth between the Navy and Senator Warner. One of the more interesting parts of Lippold's epilogue is a comparison between his case and Captain McVay of USS *Indianapolis*, including Senator Warner's role in both cases.

Lippold's case was unusual. To that time no officer cleared of wrongdoing was kept in command, and selected for promotion and then blamed and removed from the promotion list. However, the context around Kirk Lippold and *Cole* alters the landscape.

In the years after the attack in Aden, Navy budgets rose in response to the War on Terror, the invasion of Afghanistan and later invasion of Iraq. Navy procedures for force protection changed significantly after *Cole*'s attack, and since then there have been no successful terrorist attacks against Navy ships. However, this timeframe is also the period with the greatest recorded removals from command.

Between 2000, when terrorists attacked *Cole*, and 2007

---

[65] Michael G. Mullen, "CDR Kirk Lippold," e-mail, August 15, 2006.

when Lippold retired, 95 commanding officers were removed from command. From 5 in 2000, the annual numbers gradually increased to high of 18 in 2003, followed by 17 in 2004. From the outside, Lippold was handled just like approximately 100 other officers who failed to command to Navy standards. Prompted by the 2003 and 2004 spikes, and accompanying press coverage, Navy leaders commissioned a study into what happened. Neither study found linkages between the removals or reasons for the trends, noting that removals are rare, largely for individual behavioral problems, and there are no links related to race, gender, age, naval community or career path. Each study assessed that the removals might be cast as anomalous. Both studies also accepted the removals as correct and proper. Neither looked into the history or rationale of removal. By 2004 removals for crimes of command, or personal failings of commanding officers, while rare, were also accepted and familiar.

In 2005 and 2006, command removals dropped to half of previous years; some of the reason was more careful commanders; some of the reason lay in senior commander decision making as leaders worked to stem what some saw as a bloodletting.

USS *McFaul* and USS *Winston S. Churchill* - 2008

At 1:28 p.m., August 22, 2005, *Arleigh Burke*-class destroyers USS *McFaul* (DDG 74) and USS *Winston S. Churchill* collided. The day was clear, the sun shone, and in the thirty minutes prior to the collision both commanders personally controlled their ships, spoke to each other via radio and on occasion even waved to each other. While no one was injured, the collision caused over $2 million in damages only weeks before both ships deployed.[66]

---

[66] United States. Department of the Navy. Commander Carrier Strike Group Twelve. *Investigation into the Collision at Sea of USS McFaul and USS Winston S. Churchill*. Washington, DC, 2005. 4, 20-22.

The two ships were participating in the *Nassau* Expeditionary Strike Group Exercise, *Winston S. Churchill* defending *Nassau* and her group of six ships. *McFaul* and two other ships served as opposition forces. Commander, Strike Force Training, Atlantic supervised the exercise off the coast of North Carolina and Virginia.[67]

The morning of the collision the day's exercise was one of "escalatory rules of engagement" with an expectation that opposition force ships close the strike group and use the International Rules of the Road to influence the strike group's movements. [68] Essentially driving in front of, or close to, the other ships and forcing them to veer off without violating the rules. As seen in previous collisions, collisions themselves violate the rules and at some point, both ships are obliged to act and avoid collision.

To mitigate possible collision, exercise leaders established a 1000-yard stand-off range between ships. Early in the exercise, the strike group commander requested, and exercise controllers approved, an increased stand-off range to 2000 yards. [69]

Starting at 10:30 a.m., opposition forces closed in on the strike group. By 1 p.m., strike group ship USS *Laboon* intercepted USS *Cole* and *McFaul*. *Laboon* drove within 500 yards of the opposition forces. [70]

At 1:14 p.m., Commander Todd William Leavitt entered *Winston S. Churchill*'s bridge and anticipating close maneuvering, took personal control of the engines and rudders. He planned to drive between *Nassau* and *McFaul*, forcing *McFaul* to remain clear of *Nassau*. [71] Over the next ten minutes,

---

[67] Ibid, 4.
[68] Ibid, 7.
[69] Ibid
[70] Ibid, 11.
[71] Ibid, 11-12.

watchstanders on *Winston S. Churchill* and *McFaul* traded barbs related to the exercise with *McFaul* claiming right of way under the rules of the road. In this time the ships closed to within 150 yards of each other, both steaming at 25 knots. [72]

Commander Leavitt later said that the range (100-150 yards) was much closer than he "imagined we would be" but seeing *McFaul*'s commander, Sean M. Connors on his bridge wing he felt safe. Leavitt and Connors knew each other, and Leavitt thought Connors a "good shiphandler." From time to time the two commanders waved to each other. [73] At 1:24 p.m., Commander Connors believed the ships were too close and in imminent risk of collision. He ordered engines "back emergency full" and opened the range between the ships, falling back and turning left behind *Winston S. Churchill*. He then sped back up to 25 knots, believing the risk of collision passed. Neither ship used radio during this time. [74]

In *Winston S. Churchill*, Commander Leavitt saw *McFaul* fall back and believed the harassment exercise was over. As *McFaul* sped up and turned left, Leavitt realized his mistake and turned left towards *Winston S. Churchill*. At this point, *Winston S. Churchill* was to the right and 300 yards in front of *McFaul*. *McFaul* was steady on her course while *Winston S. Churchill* was in a left-hand turn and increasing speed to 30 knots. Within a minute the range was halved. [75]

Again, *McFaul*'s captain sensed danger and backed his engines. With the ships at 150 yards, *Winston S. Churchill*'s captain saw an imminent collision and again increased speed, turning towards *McFaul* hoping to swing his stern clear of the oncoming bow. Neither his swing nor *McFaul*'s backing bell avoided collision and *McFaul* struck a glancing blow on

---

[72] Ibid, 12.
[73] Ibid, 13.
[74] Ibid, 13.
[75] Ibid, 13-16.

Winston S. Churchill's port quarter. Both ships sustained damage topside; there was no damage below the waterline. *Winston S. Churchill*'s damage was estimated at $1.1 million and *McFaul*'s at $250 thousand. Repair estimates were 40 and 20 days respectively.[76]

A seven-person investigation team of two Captains, two Commanders, two Lieutenant Commanders, a JAG Corps LT and three administrative support personnel, took statements over three weeks. The report mentions but does not explain, a September 6 change in team leadership. All team names are redacted from the report.[77]

The investigation team collected numerous statements from the crews of four ships, examined ship's logs, legal records, relevant navigation data, exercise message traffic, exercise e-mail, chat room discussions, and Aegis combat systems data. With all this data and 73 enclosures, the investigator opined that "As with all investigations, challenges existed in an effort to reconstruct events as they transpired; ascertain guidance, direction and policies that were promulgated and assess and verify command and control procedures."[78]

The team found that all watch team members on both ships were qualified. There were some procedural errors with the watch teams, mainly in failing to advise each ship's respective captain. However, since both captains were clearly and closely involved in the ship's maneuvers the investigator found that:

> The cause of the collision between [*McFaul*] and [*Winston S. Churchill*] was the result of a number of errors in judgment and lack of professional performance by both Commanding Officers to include:
> a. Failure to distinguish between real world and exercise environments...
> b. A lack of appreciation and understanding of their

---

[76] Ibid, 17, 20-22.
[77] Ibid, 5-6.
[78] Ibid, 5.

vessel's shiphandling capabilities and limitations...
c. No understanding of when either a risk of collision existed or when a collision was imminent...
d. Failure to properly utilize their watch teams and employ available equipment to their full potential for the close quarter situation in which they came involved. [79]

The report also cited the opposition force commander as negligent for not defining tactics including "intercept," "harassment," and "shouldering." None of these terms were then, or are now, defined in naval doctrine or tactics. The report recommended administrative and disciplinary action against both Leavitt and Connors, as well as the opposition force commander. [80]

Carrier Strike Group 12, under whose command both ships fell, ordered the investigation. In his endorsement, Rear Admiral Ray Spicer did not concur with disciplinary action against either captain but did concur with administrative action, writing:

> What separates this incident from previous at-sea mishaps are two mitigating circumstances that must be taken under consideration:
> (1) the collision occurred while these vessels were preparing for a wartime deployment, during an exercise period involving "escalatory" Rules of Engagement. This was an inherently dangerous training event requiring aggressive shiphandling and high-speed, close-aboard maneuvering required to "shoulder" the [opposition force] vessel away from the high value unit it was attempting to close and attack.
> (2) while certainly not the cause of the incident, the lack of formal, unambiguous safety guidance...was a contributing factor. From the viewpoint of the

---

[79] Ibid, 22-23.
[80] Ibid, 31.

[opposition force] ships, direction to them to "utilize inherent right to freely operate on the high seas IAW international rules of the road to advantage" and "interfere with [the strike group] formation" conflicted with previous guidance to [opposition force] to maintain a 2000-yard separation between ships. Had this separation distance clearly and formally disseminated to both [opposition force] and [the strike group], adhered to and enforced, it likely would prevented these ships from closing within a distance and geometry that set the stage this incident.[81]

Admiral Spicer also pointed out that there were no watch team qualification discrepancies and highlighted the two captains' "stellar performance," the two captains' capability to overcome the incident, and the impact on the crews and ships readiness if the commanding officers were relieved just prior to deployment. He closed with a recommendation that "To the extent that close-aboard approaches and/or shouldering-techniques are exercised, I recommend a tactical review be conducted to determine whether such tactics are valid in the current operating environment."[82]

In the second and final endorsement, Commander Naval Surface Forces, Rear Admiral Michael Nowakowski, agreed with Spicer and neither captain faced court-martial. The results of administrative censure are rarely released and were not in this case.[83] Both retained command.

Todd Leavitt completed his command tour on March 1, 2006. He retired August 1, 2007, as a commander and as of 2014 worked for Northrop Grumman Corporation in the Maritime Systems Division. Sean Connors completed his command tour of *McFaul* on June 21, 2006. He served a tour as the Reactor

---

[81] United States. Department of the Navy. Commander Carrier Strike Group Twelve. *Investigation into the Collision at Sea of USS McFaul and USS Winston S. Churchill.* Washington, DC, 2005. 2.
[82] Ibid, 4.
[83] Ibid, 38.

Officer aboard USS *Dwight D. Eisenhower* (CVN 69) before retiring on March 31, 2009, as a commander.

USS *William P. Lawrence* - 2013, and unfinished

On September 22, 2013, during operations in the Red Sea, a wave struck a helicopter shortly after it landed aboard USS *William P. Lawrence* (DDG 110) breaking the helicopter free of its moorings and sending the helicopter and its pilots into the ocean. Both pilots died.

The morning of the fatal accident, USS *William P. Lawrence* refueled and replenished stores alongside USNS *Rainier* (T-AOE-7). As the battle group ships finished replenishment ships rotated positions and *William P. Lawrence* was urged to make best speed towards USS *Stockdale* (DDG 106) so she could begin her replenishment. Seas were two to three feet high with a swell of two to four feet. Winds were strong at 28 knots but the skies were clear with visibility out to six nautical miles with haze. There were no thunderstorms, turbulence, or precipitation. The weather was within the safe limits for flight operations.[84]

At 12:37 p.m., Indian 617, a Sikorsky SH-60S Knighthawk helicopter assigned to Helicopter Sea Control Squadron 6, landed aboard *William P. Lawrence* to deliver flu vaccines and transfer crew members. Two minutes later the helicopter was properly secured with chocks and chains, verified by a helicopter crewman and the ship turned towards her next assigned mission. Over the next eight minutes,

the ship took a large roll to port followed by a larger

---

[84] United States, Department of the Navy, United States Pacific Fleet, *Command Investigation into the Circumstances Surrounding a Class Alpha Mishap Involving HSC-6 MH-60B Aircraft, BUNO 167985, Which Occurred at N 22° 34' 18" E 037° 25' 29" Resulting in the Deaths of LCDR Landon L. Jones, USN and CWO3 Jonathan S. Gibson, USN on 22 Sep 2013* (Pearl Harbor, HI, 2014). 9.

correcting roll to starboard. This resulted in a wave of unknown size impacting the starboard aft portion of [*William P. Lawrence*]'s hull, which in turn resulted in a large amount of water impacting the rotor blades, pushing them down and possibly impacting the fuselage. This caused the tail to break off and the helicopter to shake violently....The violent shaking, in turn, resulted in the breaking free of the chocks and chains, and also left and right pilot doors to detach from the helicopter then moved forward and starboard while the rotor blades and other parts of the helicopter impacted surrounding structures. [*William P. Lawrence*] took another strong roll to port, which resulted in the helicopter continuing the clockwise rotation while the rotor blades came apart and the empennage section rotated into the forward port corner of the flight deck. At this time, the [tail assembly] broke off the fuselage and remained on [*William P. Lawrence*] while the fuselage slid overboard off the port side of the flight deck [taking LCDR Jones and CW03 Gibson with it].[85]

In their recommendations, the investigators did not provide for administrative or disciplinary action; neither are mentioned. They did recommend that destroyer flight deck cameras include recording capability, something ordered for aircraft carriers in 1971,[86] and they also recommended that "investigation should be conducted into material modifications to DDG class ships or changes to standard operating procedures in order to mitigate risks of water impacting helicopters on deck. Potential solutions could include modification of flight deck nets to provide a solid barrier to deflect water, disengaging rotors, or maneuvering restrictions."[87]

Over the next two months, five commanders endorsed

---

[85] Ibid, 6,11.
[86] Dunn, 160.
[87] United States Pacific Fleet (2014), 17.

the investigation. Because this accident involved an aircraft aboard a surface ship, three chains of command participated in the investigation: an operational chain of command, a surface ship administrative chain of command, and an aviation administrative chain of command. *William P. Lawrence*'s immediate superior, Captain H. Thomas Workman, Commander of Destroyer Squadron 23 and a former frigate commander concurred with the findings and "respectfully submit[ted] that no punitive or non-punitive action is required for any of the parties involved." He also called for "further review of wind, sea state, pitch, roll, ship's speed, and wave height/period parameters governing MH- 60 aircraft operations aboard DDG- 51 Class ships."[88]

The helicopter squadron's immediate superior was Captain Kevin Mannix, commanding Carrier Air Wing 11. An F/A-18 fighter pilot and former squadron commander, Captain Mannix recognized the report highlighted "the dangers of operating helicopters on DDG- 51 class ships. Operations were conducted in accordance with regulations, procedures and good headwork, yet catastrophic events still occurred."[89]

Mannix and Workman's boss, Admiral Michael S. White in command of Carrier Strike Group 11, wrote that he was "satisfied that negligence was not a contributing factor by anyone within HSC- 6 or USS *William P. Lawrence* (DDG 110). Therefore, I do not believe any disciplinary action or administrative corrective measures are warranted in this case." Two vice admirals, John W. Miller and Thomas H. Copeman, III, Commander, U.S. Naval Forces Central Command and Commander, Naval Surface Force, U.S. Pacific Fleet respectively, concurred without comment on the previous endorsements.[90]

At this point, two investigators, two Captains in command, a strike group commander and two vice admirals

---

[88] Ibid, 23.
[89] Ibid, 22.
[90] Ibid, 24.

believed and accepted that an accident occurred, and however tragic, there was no individual culpability, responsibility, and therefore no need for accountability. This all changed when Vice Admiral David H. Buss, Commander of Naval Air Forces, Pacific, endorsed the report. Like *Bennington*, it turned out that Navy leaders were aware of the material issues contributing to the accident, but were not known to the ship's leaders. Unlike *Bennington*, *William P. Lawrence*'s accident occurred in the time of a commander's exposure to command culpability.

Admiral Buss previously commanded an attack jet squadron, two ships including USS *John C. Stennis* (CVN 74) and Carrier Strike Group 12. He modified five opinions, in all cases adding specific language chastising Commander Jana Vavasseur, *William P. Lawrence*'s commanding officer. The other two modified opinions lessened the original investigators' opinion that *William P. Lawrence* had a documented safety climate and also included ship's course and speed as causal factors for the accident. He also directed a number of actions which are redacted from the report. His added statements indicate the direction this investigation was taking:

> However, based on the trust and confidence imbued in our selected leaders, I believe there is more that could have, and should have been done by the Commanding Officer of the USS *William P. Lawrence* (DDG 110) in properly and thoroughly assessing the totality of risk factors present at the time of the mishap...This hallmark of professional seamanship and airmanship shall be a defining characteristic of all Commanding Officers, ensuring that we only accept operational risk when the benefits far outweigh the potential cost, particularly when operating at or near the edges of the envelope.[91]

Normally the investigation would end here. However, Admiral Buss had no authority over ship captains. To take action against Commander Vavasseur, the investigation needed to

---

[91] Ibid, 30.

move up another level.

When the total investigation, including Admiral Buss' endorsement, arrived with Admiral Harry Harris, Commander of U.S. Pacific Fleet the new direction continued and expanded. The overall investigation is twenty pages, four of which simply list the number and type of enclosures. There are six pages of opinions and recommendations. Admiral Harris' endorsement is ten pages, almost all of them modifying or adding new opinions. Again, as with Admiral Buss, the changes all pointed in one direction - towards Commander Vavasseur.

Admiral Harris is a career aviator. As an anti-submarine P-3C Orion naval flight officer he never commanded a surface ship, aircraft carrier, or carrier strike group. Though he concurred with all the findings of fact,[92] to understand how much of the investigation he changed, one must first start with:

> This mishap was the product of (1) accepting unnecessary risks during routine, yet inherently dangerous, shipboard helicopter operations, (2) failing to systematically train frigate and destroyer Commanding Officers on previous mishaps, and (3) failing to incorporate the findings of these mishaps into NATOPS procedures...the primary cause was the Commanding Officer's failure to fully account for the combined effects of wave height and starboard quartering seas, exacerbated by maintaining a speed of over 30 knots.[93]

These conclusions are radically different from the original investigators. Harris did allow for blame to fall elsewhere, specifically on the "the surface and aviation communities [who] should have done more to train the CO on similar mishaps" however, "she was ultimately responsible for the safe operation of her ship."[94]

While placing some blame on the communities for not

---

[92] Ibid, 31.
[93] Ibid, 32.
[94] Ibid, 33.

training Vavasseur, and in a repudiation of Captains Workman and Mannix, Harris also wrote: "The dangers associated with seawater intrusion over the flight deck of DDG 51/79 Class ships are well known."[95] Also, repudiating Workman, Mannix, White, Miller, and Copeman, Harris said he would "direct appropriate administrative action for CDR Jana A. Vavasseur."[96]

 Admiral Harris included an unusual conclusion, writing: The [*William P. Lawrence*] Commanding Officer's actions contributed to the loss of life, loss of an aircraft, and damage to the ship. While conducting flight operations, she maneuvered at flank speed and did not fully assess the environmental factors. She unnecessarily assumed increased risk during the helicopter evolution, which was unwarranted given the operational circumstance, and she did not communicate with given the HEC. In this instance, the Commanding Officer did not exercise the highest degree of judgment, seamanship, or prudence.
A Commanding Officer has absolute responsibility and accountability for the conduct of her unit's mission; Article 802[sic] of Navy Regulations addresses this. Her responsibility to execute operations and to manage risk across the full range of environmental conditions is ever-present. These environmental conditions are both naturally occurring (the wind, seas and weather in which our units operate) as well as operationally induced (the mission at hand, and the circumstances in which we are employing the unit, from peace through crisis and into war). The management of risk is a comprehensive calculus, an enduring requirement, and an integral element for successful command. Commanding Officers have an enduring responsibility to manage risk, which requires the finest sense of

---

[95] Ibid, 35.
[96] Ibid, 37.

judgment.

Commanding Officers must execute this most serious responsibility through a continuous assessment of all factors that affect our operations - whether at sea, in the air, or ashore. We achieve success by drawing from our experience, expertise, and operational traditions, all of which value seamanship and airmanship; and by developing a finely tuned understanding of the physical environment in which we operate. These factors combine in our assessment of risk, both risk to mission and risk to force, and how this assessment relates to safety -- foremost for our Sailors, our most valued of all resources, and for our ships and aircraft. A Commanding Officer is trusted to get this balance right…When viewed in isolation, at every moment, CDR Vavasseur's maneuvering was within the envelope…but I expect more from my Commanding Officers than simply the ability to stay within the written operating parameters. I expect Commanding Officers to exercise independent thought and sound judgment. In this case, the risks assumed by proceeding at 30+ knots and turning into quartering seas with a helicopter on deck with rotors engaged, did not correlate to the environment in which the ship was operating. The Commanding Officer failed to factor in the totality of the physical conditions (wind, sea state, course steered, etc.) and the perceived operational necessity to return to station at an ordered flank bell, given the mission at hand. There was time to rectify the situation by simply reducing speed after taking INDIAN 617 aboard; a significant reduction in speed, thereby creating a more stable platform, could have been achieved in seconds.

There are those who will contend that my conclusion is unreasonable, perhaps even harsh and uncompromising; they might say that it fails to recognize the challenges of Commanding Officers' positions and the factors beyond their immediate control; and that my conclusions will breed timidity instead of aggressiveness in our Commanding Officers. On the contrary, I believe that the missions we are regularly asked to perform -- and must be ready to perform in conditions of extreme adversity while in conflict -- together with the lives of those we are charged to lead, demand a trust in our leadership to employ every means available to make the right decisions. This means factoring in the totality of conditions affecting any given operation, and fully employing one's skills and experience to draw the right conclusions. No single set of operating procedures, instruction manuals, guidelines, or checklists -- while essential contributing tools -- relieves this enduring responsibility. This highest of all standards is demanded in the naval profession all the time.

Equally incumbent on the naval profession is an institutional obligation to provide the necessary foundation to support our Commanding Officers. *William P. Lawrence*'s Commanding Officer was ill served by us, who did not provide her all necessary information and training for a thorough operational risk management calculus. Specifically, there is no systematic process in the surface warfare community for disseminating a pattern of known hazards and incorporating them into refined operating parameters beyond the most general of notes, warnings, and cautions in NATOPS. Accordingly, and as noted by Commander, Destroyer Squadron [23]...the event warrants further review of wind, sea state, pitch, roll, ship's speed, and wave height/period parameters governing H-60 aircraft operations aboard DDG-51 Class ships. This analysis should address take-off, landing, and on-deck rotor operations across a broad range of expected operating conditions; and it must be jointly conducted by both the Naval Aviation and Surface Warfare enterprises.

In the case of the *William P. Lawrence*'s helicopter mishap, the Commanding Officer did not do all that should have been done. While she did not exceed published procedures and operating parameters, she failed to accurately evaluate the totality of the combined effects of ship's speed together with winds, sea state, and course. While procedural compliance is essential, the full scope of responsibilities in our profession extends beyond simple compliance and blind obedience -- we require more.[97]

Admiral Harris signed his endorsement on April 17, 2014 - almost a month after Admiral Buss', who was, in turn, a month after Admiral Copeman. Four months earlier, on December 17, 2013, Commander Vavasseur turned *William P. Lawrence* over to her relief in a normally scheduled change of command. Her boss, Captain Workman, was the guest speaker and told the guests and crew "You know your commanding officer as a superior tactician and ship handler, an impeccable manager, a strong communicator and a respected leader."[98] The change of command was two days after Workman endorsed the investigation.

Because Vavasseur was no longer in command when Admiral Harris indicated he would take administrative action he could not remove her from command. It also meant he did not have to announce any action he took. However, subsequent events indicate he likely took no action, or no permanent action. In December 2014, an administrative board selected Commander Vavasseur for Captain Command; a clear indication the surface warfare community continued to hold her

---

[97] Ibid, 37-40
[98] United States Navy, USS *William P. Lawrence* Public Affairs, "USS *William P. Lawrence* Holds Change of Command Ceremony," news release, December 17, 2013.

in high regard and no adverse information was in her record. In January 2015, a selection board selected her for promotion to Captain. However, similar to Kirk Lippold's case, pressure from the two pilot's widows prompted Secretary of Navy Ray Mabus to pull her name from the list sent to the Senate "pending a review." As of February 2018, Vavasseur's name had not reached the Senate for confirmation and she remains a commander. Jones' and Gibson's widows have sued the Navy for their husband's deaths alleging that the very material problems that Workman and Mannix were unaware of, but Harris claimed were well known, directly caused their husband's deaths. The lawsuit was dismissed in 2016. However, a new lawsuit was filed in February 2017.[99] Commander Vavasseur remains on active duty, her promotion still uncertain. While the investigation highlighted significant systemic failures and dysfunctions, no other personnel were disciplined for Jones' or Gibson's deaths.

Admiral Harris' actions epitomize the change between 1945 and 2015. Captain McVay was afforded a court of inquiry and a court-martial. He was afforded counsel and allowed to challenge his accusers. The Navy was forced to present a coherent and cogent case. Even with the resulting verdict one can at least recognize an openness in the process not available to any commander since the mid-1980s. *Stark*'s Brindel had counsel; Lippold, Vavasseur, Leavitt, and Connors did not. The latter group were never identified as interested parties because the Navy chose an administrative, rather than legal, investigative process. Over time the Navy increased its view of command accountability, while at the same time decreasing the formality of the process it used to enforce that accountability.

The shift of accountability towards the individual commander is readily apparent in the last four cases, even though none of those officers were removed from command. For

---

[99] "Theresa Jones, et al v. USA, et al," Justia Dockets & Filings, accessed October 02, 2017, https://dockets.justia.com/docket/circuit-courts/ca9/17-55234.

Commander Kirk Lippold, Navy leaders sought to protect a ship attacked without warning or provocation. For Commanders O'Connor and Leavitt, Navy leaders tried sending a message that mistakes were tolerated. For Commander Vavasseur the majority of her chain of command recognized an unexpected accident that no one could prepare for.

For each of those officers, the same crime of command in the 1950s, 1960s, or 1970s would not be noteworthy. *Cole* was attacked in a way more like a mine strike than the missiles *Stark* saw and was able to engage, even if she didn't. The collision between *Winston S. Churchill* and *McFaul* was more like collisions between *Charles H. Roan* and *Brownson*, or *Hartley* and *Blue Master* than those of *Belknap*, *Frank. E. Evans*, or *Hobson*. The helicopter crash aboard *William P. Lawrence*, largely caused by issues Navy leaders knew of but did not correct, is more like the explosion in *Bennington* than any other incident.

However, the lessons taught in *Command at Sea* through Admiral Holloway's letter about the *John F. Kennedy* and *Belknap* collision and the *Wall Street Journal* editorial on *Hobson* and *Wasp* turned those collisions into the exemplar of command responsibility, accountability, and culpability. The change in language regarding *Indianapolis* and Captain McVay shows how much changed between 1945 and today. The change is clear and apparent, easily proven when looked at with a long view. How this change happened, however, is a more difficult problem to understand.

5: The Reasons

The first part of this study looked at operational removals, the crimes of command that are truly and solely related to command. This chapter seeks to explain some of the reasons, beginning with the popularly accepted ones and proposing one not normally considered.

As culpability for crimes of command moved from that of individual responsibility to one that is command wide, the modern application of command removal also changed. To some degree this began with Connelly Stevenson's removal from command for letting go-go dancer Cat Futch dance on USS *Finback*'s sail, continued through *Ranger* and Arthur Fredrickson, and cemented itself in Tailhook's aftermath. In public consciousness command removal is now about personal misconduct, largely because personal misconduct is salacious and interesting. Where a landlocked citizen might forgive a ship collision, grounding, or major fire as part of doing business at sea, adultery, drunkeness or simple stupidity are all too universal, inexcusable, and palatable for removing someone from command. When more officers are removed from command for personal misconduct, then the operational crimes of command are subsumed into the larger group.

Over the past decade the Navy, individual naval officers, journalists, pundits and citizens offered their ideas of why the Navy removes commanders from command. All come to different answers in different ways. Women in the Navy is one answer. Changed societal norms another. The "tradition older than the country itself" is the most common, along with the idea that removing a commander is normal, common, and proper. At some level, removal from command is all that - normal, common, and proper. However, removal was far less normal or common in the 1950s through the 1970s so why is removal now common?

Ask anyone who follows or served in the Navy, or the

military, or even government and you will get at least one answer. Every few years another article, editorial, or even news story scratches at the problem. Is it alcohol? Women? Smaller Navy? Bigger responsibilities? Social media? Technology? Everyone has an answer and some even support the answer with anecdotes. With only four limited studies in recent history no one has a good grasp of the issues, or the changes, since the end of the Cold War, much less since the end of World War II.

Overall reasons or issues

Breaking the removal timeframe into three periods - 1945 to 1965, 1965 to 1985 and 1985 to 2015 provides part of the answer. In general, the Navy only addresses removals when they are publicized. In 2011, after the second 21st century spike, Chief of Naval Operations Admiral Gary Roughead, referred to this spike as "bothersome" but also noted that the Navy must uphold strict behavioral standards, even for off-duty personnel. He made a clear declaration that a commander's entire life was under scrutiny - "The divide between our private and professional lives is essentially gone. People can engage in the debate — does it really matter what a commanding officer does in their personal life? We believe it does, because it gets right to the issue of integrity and personal conduct and trust and the ability to enforce standards."[1]

Roughead highlighted one of the major contemporary changes - personal conduct. Between 1985 and 2015, there were 683 incidents resulting in 305 removals from command. Of those 305 removals, over one third (138) were for personal conduct not necessarily related to command, or even a classic crime of command. By comparison there is only one documented removal for personal behavior between 1965 and 1985. Modern ship operations are safer. Aircraft are safer. Social mores have changed. Unfortunately, the modern focus on

---

[1] Craig Whitlock, "Bad behavior sinking more Navy officers' careers," *The Seattle Times*, June 17, 2011.

personal behavior hides the historical approaches to crimes of command, as well as the historical resolution, or lack thereof, for personal misconduct.

The current response from Navy leadership is that firings are problematic, troublesome, or "bothersome." Ray Mabus, Secretary of the Navy from 2009 to 2017, said in 2011 that he didn't see a broader problem with the also routine response that only a tiny percentage of commanding officers are removed. Summing up the culture and how he saw the system holding commanders to account he said, "We hold absolute standards of conduct and if you breach those, you're going to be relieved, but I don't see a pattern."[2]

When studies look at very small populations, short time periods, or conflate anecdotes with data, the results, while possibly satisfying in the short term, are imprecise, inaccurate...or just wrong. Such was the case in 2011 with the second removal spike and interested parties grasped for answers. Personal misconduct was a clear statistical change, and alcohol abuse and sexual escapades grabbed headlines with vague terms and statements. In one article alone, two different time scales - six months and eighteen months - were used and the catchall phrase "offences related to sex, alcohol or other form of personal misconduct"[3] cast the removed officers as deviants and miscreants.

The reality is that over the eighteen months in question there were forty-four incidents ranging from major fires and pirate attacks to fraternization and drunkenness. Of those forty-four, thirty-five officers were removed from command. In addition to the pirate attack, there were four collisions, two crew deaths, one major engineering casualty, and two major fires. Two collisions resulted in removal. The remaining issues were either leadership (15) or personal behavior related (20), however only two involved alcohol use by the removed commander. Ten

---

[2] Ibid
[3] Ibid

removals resulted from some form of an inability to provide effective leadership, or a failure to act appropriately on wrongdoing. In those instances, alcohol use by others was a factor in at least three removals. On the surface, one reason for more removals or even removals in general is an increased focus on personal misconduct. However, the issue is deeper as the misconduct standard today is not what it once was, and the rationale for removal is applied not only to misconduct but also to operational incidents. Likewise, an officer removed for a crime of command - a collision or grounding - is as likely to end his career as an officer removed for theft, drunkenness, or sexual misconduct.

Alcohol

When expanding to include the 305 removals of the last three decades only 23 were for alcohol related issues, and those cluster between 2002 and 2015. Clearly alcohol was an issue at Tailhook, but those removed from command were removed not for their actions in Las Vegas, but for actions afterwards either in connection with the investigation or because officers in their commands committed misconduct. With such a small statistical finding, among a small statistical population, why is alcohol seen as a primary reason for removal from command? To understand this, we must understand the Navy's, and the American societal, relationship to alcohol.

The larger social issues of abstinence, prohibition, and other alcohol related concerns are beyond the scope of this study, however, post-war attitudes relating to alcohol use, alcohol abuse, and intoxication have some bearing - especially when within the constraints of how the Navy reacted to and changed in response to societal pressures. Perhaps the best frame of reference is America's approach toward driving under the influence (DUI), and since almost half of the 23 documented incidents involved DUIs this is a good place to start.

Driving while intoxicated was never fully accepted, but

also wasn't stigmatized or shamed through much of the twentieth century. Drinking aboard ship, while banned by Secretary of the Navy Josephus Daniels in 1914, continued in secret, or semi-secret through today. Alcohol and cigarettes remain two legal vices available to sailors, at least in legal moderation.

Barron Lerner's 2012 history of drinking and driving *One for the Road: Drunk Driving Since 1900* provides amazing insight into the changing social mores regarding DUI asserting that "we have become a society that concurrently condemns and tolerates drunk driving."[4] When combined with a Navy system that once tolerated alcohol excess the combination of condemnation and toleration provides for easy answers to complicated questions.

Post-war anti-drinking and driving activists, largely religious groups with moralistic views on alcohol, asserted that government and society either minimized or ignored the problem. For some, any alcohol use was immoral.[5] Through the 1970s there were periodic articles or lawsuits, but little open discussion of curbing drunk driving and in far too many cases, the victims were blamed for the circumstances of their injuries or death.[6] When drunk drivers were blamed, they were also seen through the lens of victims, victims of alcoholism as disease,[7] rather than someone who'd made a conscious decision to drink and drive.

In 1985 philosopher and bioethicist Bonnie Steinbock made the case that American society inadequately prevented people from driving drunk and inadequately punished them when they did, even when injury or death resulted writing: "It is

---

[4] Barron H. Lerner, *One for the road: drunk driving since 1900* (Baltimore: Johns Hopkins University Press, 2012). 3.
[5] Ibid, 5.
[6] Ibid, 8.
[7] Ibid, 4.

not unreasonable to require people to undergo great inconvenience to avoid killing other people."[8] Steinbock's premises underlie much of the Navy's approach towards alcohol - just making alcohol difficult to get reduces the problem, and if someone makes a mistake because of alcohol, punishment must be swift and severe to send a message and avoid needless deaths. Sometimes a single alcohol incident will kill a career, regardless of rank. For commanders, a personal alcohol incident or even a series of them within the crew, may be fatal to the career.

So, while alcohol is not a leading cause for command removal, it is a reason understood by American society, especially by its more conservative elements. The other well understood, and greatly overstated, reason for the increase in removals is sex.

Women

The entry of women into the Navy is another area some cite for increased removal from command. While Tailhook certainly provided an uptick in command removal and also signaled a clear direction for Navy leadership, command removals significantly increased well before Tailhook. Tailhook was just the most obvious symptom of a fully entrenched cultural movement related to the culpability of command. Twenty-five years later some believe that women are a core issue, but only two, retired Admiral and Chief Executive Officer of the United States Naval Institute, Peter Daly, and retired Captain Kevin Eyer, speak openly about it.

In 2012 Eyer penned an opinion piece asserting that "men and women are having sex with one another, regularly, and in blatant disregard of regulations" and " record numbers of misconduct-related Triad firings have occurred in the past few years, and this trend shows no sign of cooling."[9] In 2013, a

---

[8] Ibid, 13.
[9] Kevin Eyer, "Co-Ed Crew: Reality vs. Taboo," *Proceedings*, October 2012.

slightly repackaged version said "you cannot put young, healthy men and women into a small box, send them away for extended periods of isolation, and not expect them to interact dynamically with one another. They're like magnets being put into a box and shaken — they stick."[10] In each article he conflated authorized relationships with unauthorized. He repeatedly maintained that men and women are incapable of working together without seeking sexual relationships. Eyer believes that in the beginning "a healthy fear evident between the sexes" helped to keep instances of fraternization in check. That fear has since dissipated, and the result has been a growing number of firings for what he politely called "zipper failures."[11] Maintaining the theme, broken record style, Daly and Eyer, asserted that bringing women aboard ships was the largest factor in increased command removal.[12]

Anecdotally, Daly and Eyer have a point and might even be able to defend a correlation argument if challenged on causation. However, when looking at the numbers, between 1991 and 2015 (Tailhook through the end of the data set) of 282 removals, 123 were for personal behavior issues. Of those, only 10 were for sexual misconduct not related to fraternization while 18 were for fraternization, or 9% of removals over 2 years. 21 involved alcohol, making alcohol almost as prevalent as sex in removals. Leadership issues, like those seen with Captain Fredrickson in USS *Ranger* were the second largest non-operational category with 103 of 305 removals. While women might be related to the leadership issues, in reality a shift from individual culpability to one of the culpability of command is far more likely than anything else.

---

[10] Kevin Eyer, "Opinion: Why More Commanding Officers are Getting Fired," *USNI News*, October 1, 2013, accessed October 25, 2017, https://news.usni.org/2013/09/30/opinion-commanding-officers-getting-fired.
[11] Corinne Reilly, "Navy Takes Steps to Combat Poor Personal Choices," *Virginian-Pilot* (Norfolk, VA), June 18, 2012.
[12] Ibid

If alcohol and sex grab headlines but only account for ten percent of removals then something else must be the cause. Three things differ enough between the time before 1985 and the time since to cause change - fewer senior officers at sea, a shift towards less stringent and less formal fact-finding methods, and the rise of a nuclear technocracy.

Fewer senior officers at sea

While none of the Navy wide studies found either correlation or causation, there were three items noted as "contributing factors" in 2010.[13]

First, commanders were incapable of recognizing a poor relationship between themselves and the executive officer or command master chief (senior enlisted adviser). While a subordinate relationship, the only crewmember that a commanding officer can see as near peers in age, seniority, or experience are the executive officer and command master chief.

Second, many superior and supervising commanders did not properly supervise or evaluate subordinate commanders. In some cases, these superiors committed acts of omission by inadvertently not supervising or tracking available reports. In others they committed acts of commission by choosing not to look. Either way, these failings precluded early action to assist their subordinate commanders, especially for those who had bad relationships between the commanding officer, executive officer, or command master chief.

Third, and especially for cases of personal misconduct, some commanding officers were insufficiently self-aware and did not understand how their actions might be seen or interpreted. This problem was ascribed to the "Bathsheba Syndrome"[14] first presented by Dean Ludwig and Clinton

---

[13] Naval Inspector General (2010).
[14] Dean C. Ludwig and Clinton O. Longenecker, "The Bathsheba Syndrome: the Ethical Failure of Successful Leaders," *Journal of Business Ethics* 12, no. 4 (1993).

Longenecker in the *Journal of Business Ethics*.

The 2010 report, while identifying these three issues failed to note their common nature - awareness. The first problem is horizontal - the leaders within a command are not clearly, openly, and honestly communicating with each other. The second is vertical, where a commander and his commander (or a commander and his subordinate) are not communicating well. The third is an internal issue where a lack of personal self-awareness precludes reflection and introspection. Further, because the study only looked back five years it was incapable of recognizing that significant changes in Navy operations contributed to the problems.

During Pacific Fleet operations in World War II, the only operational commander not stationed aboard ship was Fleet Admiral Nimitz. Admiral Spruance spent most of his time aboard one flag ship after another, one of which was USS *Indianapolis* with Charles McVay. Spruance knew McVay well. As a four-star admiral at Saipan and Okinawa, Spruance was the most senior officer ever directly involved in modern combat at sea.[15] Of today's ten four-star admirals, none are afloat for more than a day - even fleet commanders. None have a personal, yet professional, relationship with captains or commanders in command unless a previous assignment brought them together. The same is true for all three-star admirals. The only afloat flag officers, strike group commanders, are one or two-star admirals and when deployed are aboard the aircraft carrier and get to know that ship's commanding officer. With only eleven carriers and all carriers commanded by aviation officers, combined with shortened flag officer tours the only real knowledge the admiral has of his flagship captain is from deployment.

The issue moves further down the chain of command. Groups of ships are called squadrons and are commanded by a commodore. While large amphibious ships have space to

---

[15] Michael D. Hull, "Modest Victor of Midway," *World War II*, August 19, 1998.

embark squadron commanders and their staffs, the relatively smaller destroyers and cruisers do not. As a result, the destroyer squadron commander will deploy aboard the aircraft carrier with the strike group commander. The destroyer commodore knows his boss and peers fairly well, but it takes real effort to get to his subordinate ships and work with them. In recent years the Navy has exacerbated the problem by placing ships in one port and squadron commodores in another. The relationship between commander and subordinate becomes one of strangers. Strangers are hard pressed to have open and honest communications or to have the command intuition to sense a problem before it is untenable.

While these relationships are less than they once were, the idea of culpability of command has not extended past the ship hull. Between 1945 and 2015 not one squadron commodore was removed from command for something one of his subordinate commanders did. In one case a submarine squadron commodore was removed from command because he personally contributed to a submarine grounding. In another case, a destroyer squadron commodore was administratively counseled for not properly advising a commanding officer during operations where the destroyer ran aground. The destroyer commander was removed from command.

Less formal fact finding

During the Congressional hearings into Charles McVay's court-martial, the Navy repeatedly reminded Congress that McVay's court was legal and proper. In the strictest sense, the Navy was completely correct. However, the Navy also ignored the new precedent which made McVay's case, despite its injustices, fairer and more equitable than any contemporary crime of command. Charles McVay faced a Court of Inquiry and a court-martial. Charles Loughlin faced a court-martial. Every case chronicled here between 1945 and 1983 had benefit of either a court or board of inquiry, or a court-martial. Marcus

Arnheiter and Connelly Stevenson are mentioned in passing because they mark the beginning of the change. Since Walter Shafer's not guilty verdict for *Belknap*'s collision with *John. F. Kennedy* only seven commanding officers have been court-martialed; four for personal misconduct - one for homosexuality, one for rape, one for sexual assault, and one for larceny and three for crimes of command - one for abandoning a group of boat people escaping from Vietnam, one for a grounding, and the last for a collision. Guilty verdicts came in three of the four personal misconduct cases, however only two crimes of command were found guilty. When Commander John Cochrane was found not guilty of negligence in the collision of USS *Kinkaid* (DD 965) in the Strait of Malacca in 1989[16] it marked the last time a commanding officer was court martialed for a crime of command. In 2011, Commander Jay Wylie plead guilty to raping two sailors[17] and in 2015 Captain James Duke was found not guilty of sexually assaulting his girlfriend.[18]

If crimes of command do not include personal misconduct, why address personal misconduct here? Again, partly because of misconduct's modern rise, but also because the changing approach to Navy discipline is so evident in command removal where personal misconduct cases are treated the same as crimes of command.

In the forty years between 1975 and 2015 only eight commanding officers were court-martialed. In that same time period there were 1004 incidents characterized as crimes of command and 145 commanders removed. So, of the 145 commanders removed from command, only seven were tried in

---

[16] From Staff and Wire Reports, "CALIFORNIA IN BRIEF: SAN DIEGO : Skipper Not Guilty in Collision," *Los Angeles Times*, May 24, 1990, accessed July 19, 2017.

[17] US Navy, "Navy Commander Pleads Guilty to Rape, Sex Assault," news release, October 28, 2011,
http://www.navy.mil/submit/display.asp?story_id=63547.

[18] US Navy, "Special and General Courts-Martial for February 2015," news release, March 17, 2015,
http://www.navy.mil/submit/display.asp?story_id=86095.

a court of law. The other 138 were administratively removed from command and administratively sanctioned.

Likewise, over that same time period only one commanding officer faced a court of inquiry, Commander Scott Waddle who commanded the submarine USS *Greeneville* (SSN 772) when she surfaced beneath Japanese fishing vessel *Ehime Maru* killing four high-school students, two teachers, and three crew members. Waddle was sanctioned, but not referred to court-martial.[19]

Why has the Navy stopped court-martialing crimes of command? Part of the answer lies in Admiral Holloway's letter to the Navy after Shafer's not guilty verdict. Another part of the answer, completely linked to the first, is as old a tradition as the Navy itself - control. In his social history of the early Navy, Christopher McKee found that dismissal, similar to modern administrative separation, was the predominant means Navy leaders used in removing troublesome officers. Between 1794 and 1815, one quarter of the officer corps' attrition came through administrative dismissal or strongly encouraged resignation.[20]

Even in the early days of the U.S. Navy, some officers recognized a need for legal culpability and accountability. In 1800, Commodore Richard Dale wrote

> I think in all cases the president has a right to dismiss an officer, because he holds his commission on them terms. But at the same time I think it more prudent, when it can be done, to hold court martials on officers when they commit faults that require it, [as it] has a much greater effect on the rest of the officers. It gives them an opportunity of knowing what the officer was

---

[19] Scott Waddle, *The Right Thing* (Integrity Publishers, 2002). 213-216, 234-5.
[20] Christopher McKee, *A Gentlemanly and Honorable Profession: The Creation of the U.S. Naval Officer Corps, 1794-1815* (Annapolis (Md.): Naval Institute Press, 1991). 430.

broke or punished for, [and] it impresses on their minds [that], if they are guilty of the like faults or behave improperly, they will be brought to a court martial and punished according to the crime they have committed.[21]

However, Navy leaders of the time apparently disagreed as fewer than ten percent of the officers dismissed from the service did so via formal courts - either courts of inquiry or courts-martial.[22]

When dealing with transgressions the early Navy was much like today's Navy - the sure, certain, and expedient was preferred over legally correct or thorough. Some of the reasons McKee found for administrative dismissal rather than court-martial included speed and simplicity, as well as remote naval stations with insufficient numbers of officers to convene a court, the significant distance between stations, and at the corporate level the small size of the Navy. However, the most telling and comparable answer lies in the uncontrollable nature of courts - where a court of inquiry or court-martial sought the truth and allowed impaneled officers to arrive at their professional decision using personal judgment, often that judgment was contrary to Navy leadership's desires. Administrative dismissal, was swift, sure, certain, and final.[23]

Admiral Nimitz had this problem with Eliot Loughlin's court-martial, enough so that he issued letters of reprimand to the court's members, deciding they had failed in their duties. The punishment imposed on the court was greater than the punishment they imposed on Loughlin. Likewise, when Captain Horace H. Morgan dismissed the charges against Walter Shafer, Navy leadership was forced into an internal and external public relations battle to maintain their ideal of absolute accountability.

In the 1950s, Admiral Arleigh Burke saw a problem with

---

[21] Ibid, 431.
[22] Ibid
[23] Ibid

courts-martial, but from a different perspective, writing of "too many inexperienced commanders of stations and ships (some of them rather senior) who use courts-martial to correct defects which should have been corrected by direct personal action of the division officers or the captain himself."[24] While Burke was said to not want unlucky commanders of ships,[25] he was also adamant that early action could prevent unwanted problems.

There is another reason the modern Navy remains focused on administratively handling personal misconduct and crimes of command - the Navy has a process to correct or absolve administrative matters where a court-martial is final. Recall that in the Congressional inquiry into Charles McVay's court-martial the Navy repeatedly insisted on two things - the legally proper nature of the court and the lack of any authority to alter the outcome. Had McVay been dealt with administratively the case could have been referred to the Board for Correction of Naval Records (BCNR), a common response to modern issues within naval administration.

Established in 1956[26], the Board for Correction of Naval Records serves to "correct errors and remove injustices from naval records."[27] Many of the corrected errors lie in name changes, performance, pay, disability and discharge characterization, however promotions, awards, and any other manner of administrative concern may be heard by the board. The board reviews over 12,000 petitions each year. Senator Smith, during the McVay hearings invoked the concept when he said that Congress was "questioning whether it was morally right to have courtmartialed [sic] [McVay] in the first

---

[24] Arleigh A. Burke. "General Discipline in the Navy" in *Selected Readings in Leadership* Malcolm E. Wolfe and F. J. Mulholland ed (Annapolis, MD: United States Naval Institute, 1960). 89.
[25] Rudy Abramson, "Age-Old Tradition: Sea Skippers Must Answer for Tragedy," *Los Angeles Times*, June 6, 1981, accessed December 19, 2016.
[26] 10, § 79-1552 (1956).
[27] http://www.secnav.navy.mil/mra/bcnr/Pages/MIssion-and-Overview.aspx

place...That is not revisionism; that is the truth; that is trying to set the record straight."[28] However, since McVay's case was both a court-martial and prior to 1956, the BCNR was not available. McVay's case was clearly an injustice, even it if was legally correct.[29]

Modern removals rarely seek relief through the BCNR. In some cases, the removal is incontestable, the removed officer accepts the command accountability precedent, or the removal does not constitute an injustice. That latter idea is difficult to sometimes grasp. A captain in command has a chance at selection to admiral, however the selection percentage is already small and any blemish on a record, or reputation, can be enough to halt a career. Tying a clear and definitive link between an incident and failing to select for admiral, then forcing the system to promote an officer, is less likely than selection to begin with. For commanders and junior, the opportunity for redemption is far greater, however in the last fifteen years only two Navy officers successfully petitioned the BCNR to expunge their removal from command. In both cases the Navy scrupulously followed its administrative process for documenting removal from command. Adherence to this process allowed the petitioners to later gather new information, new opinions, and successfully lobby for relief. Had those officers been removed from command in any other manner or given lukewarm fitness reports documenting lackluster performance the issues would have been more difficult to overcome.

Another area that impacts the modern removal from command and the less formal fact-finding processes is the professionalization of military law. Before 1967, Navy lawyers were officers from the line who were aviators, submariners, or surface warriors first and then attended law school. This made law a subset of military operations, but also allowed for significant errors in law and justice. It also provided the Navy

---

[28] Committee on Armed Services (2000). 4.
[29] Toti

with commanders who understood the law. With the professionalization of the Judge Advocate Corps, Navy lawyers are lawyers first, and sometimes only lawyers. They rarely serve afloat, are not qualified in aircraft, ships, or submarines, and are legally barred from command at sea. Removing the line officer from legal proceedings and handing them over to professional lawyers assisted the move towards administrative action.

The 2001 incident where USS *Greenville* surfaced into Japanese fishing vessel *Ehime Maru* is illustrative of the change. This international incident in U.S. waters provided multiple paths for assessment of culpability and accountability, however the U.S. government chose the internal Navy process. In its report the Court commented on the choice saying

> Given the circumstances of this incident, the decision to convene a Court of Inquiry was both necessary and appropriate...It is clear, however, that a Court of Inquiry should not be convened without full appreciation for its significant procedural and substantive requirements. The decision to convene a Court of Inquiry requires a careful balancing of all circumstances. Once committed, this form of investigative body requires investment of significant resources and time.[30]

While Courts of Inquiry were once the norm for even small collisions, by the end of the twentieth century the Navy was openly speaking of choices between resources and transparency.

With military law professionalized, commanders still needed some way to impose discipline, but something that was not within the realm of law. The solution was amended into military law in 1962 and provided specified commanders the ability to impose nonjudicial punishment (NJP) on those

---

[30] United States, Department of the Navy, Commander, U.S. Pacific Fleet, *Court of Inquiry into the Circumstances Surrounding the Collision Between USS Greeneville (SSN 772) and Japanese M/V Ehime Maru that Occurred off the Coast of Oahu, Hawaii On 9 February 2001* (Washington, DC, 1954). 6.

assigned to their commands. Article 15 of the Uniform Code of Military Justice actually codified long standing processes, and the Navy's form of Article 15 is called "Captain's Mast" or "Admiral's Mast" - a term found in the pre-war Navy. Captain's Mast allows for nonjudicial resolution of minor offenses. Punishments are limited to arrest in quarters, reduction in rank for enlisted personnel, loss of pay, punitive letters, or admonitions. Punishment is dependent on both the rank of the accused and the rank of the commander.[31]

Since Captain's Mast is nonjudicial, the proceedings are classified as administrative and each service can select its own level for burden of proof. Where a court-martial will seek to establish proof beyond a reasonable doubt, the Navy allows Captain's Mast determinations based on the standard of "preponderance of the evidence" which only requires the hearing officer believe that "the existence of a fact is more probable than its nonexistence."[32] Legal scholar Katherine Gorski summed up the intent of nonjudicial punishment.

> First, nonjudicial punishment avoids the stigma of a criminal conviction and instead is a necessary remedy purely insular to the military system. Second, the punishment meted out in nonjudicial punishment, such as restriction aboard ship for a period of no more than two months, is far more desirable than subjecting sailors to lengthy prison confinements. Because using nonjudicial punishment in lieu of a court-martial avoids the "unnecessary stigmatizations" and the lengthy confinements caused by a criminal conviction, it is more desirable than a court-martial.[33]

Additionally, modern legal requirements also impose significant burdens on court-martial authorities to allow the

---

[31] Katherine Gorski, "Nonjudicial Punishment in The Military: Why A Lower Burden of Proof Across All Branches Is Unnecessary," *National Security Law Journal* 2, no. 1 (2013):89.
[32] Ibid, 89-90.
[33] Ibid, 99.

accused counsel, the ability to question witnesses, and to present evidence in their defense. All of these add up to increased use of resources in a resource constrained system. An administrative process, controlled by the commander, is a far more certain way to handle minor offense. And since the commander can determine what a minor offense is, courts-martial are now largely reserved for only the most serious cases.

Court-martial statistics are only available from 1950 on, and nonjudicial punishment data from 1977 on. In both cases the numbers are aggregated, and not split among rank, paygrade, or even by officer or enlisted. As figure 3 shows, total courts-

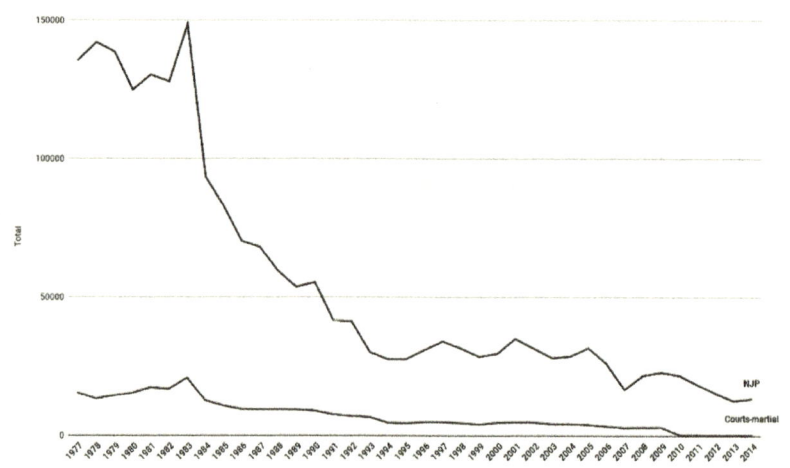

Figure 3. Total courts-martial and non-judicial punishment (NJP) from 1977 to 2014

martial and total NJP have consistently dropped since 1983. In both 1978 and 1983 almost a quarter of the Navy's sailors went to NJP - likely linked to crackdowns on drug use in the ranks. It is also clear that while NJP was once fairly common, in the last three decades less than one in ten sailors was disciplined via nonjudicial punishment.

Courts-martial are even rarer. 1960's courts-martial of over seven percent of the Navy indicated the high-water mark and since 1985 the number has remained below two percent, hovering at one tenth of one percent since 2010. Even with these numbers, and corresponding numbers for officers in recent years or making statistical interpolation about officer nonjudicial punishment, the reality is that many commanders removed from command are neither disciplined via nonjudicial punishment nor officially detached for cause. These actions, commonly called a "soft firing," preclude any form of appeal or later action through the BCNR. If a soft firing is unannounced, it is likely never known beyond the officer removed from command and the officer ordering it.

Historically, and part of the reason for a professional Judge Advocate Corps, commanders were overly harsh in punishing their subordinates. A 1946 Army panel found that wartime court-martial sentences were excessive and a subsequent clemency board reviewed tens of thousands of courts-martial, remitting or reducing 85 percent of the convictions or sentences. A Navy study reviewed 2,115 wartime trials, and found that nearly half involved "flagrant miscarriages of justice"[34] It is possible that there are similar issues today with nonjudicial punishment, but since it is extralegal the opportunity for review and modification are far more limited. While military justice is now more rational, systematic, and formally structured, a commander's individual influence and politics remains paramount.[35]

The issue is not new. Writing after Walter Shafer's acquittal, Captain John E. Greenbacker recognized that the "Navy will not again, in like circumstances, attempt to use the court-martial as a vehicle for enforcing the professional accountability of those in charge of its ships at sea." He also recognized that a substitute was necessary, but a substitute that still allowed for publicity, disgrace, recording performance, and removal from command - "if the absolute responsibility of the captain for his ship is to be upheld."[36]

While accepting the concept of absolute accountability,

---

[34] Bray, 292.
[35] Ibid, 341.
[36] John E. Greenbacker, "The Cruel Business of Accountability," *Proceedings*, August 1977. 28.

Greenbacker did recognize that the system had no variability, that there "seems to be little difference in the treatment of the commanding officer whose ship is severely damaged or lost and one whose ship is temporarily grounded or suffers a relatively minor collision." He was however, also focused not on the commander's judgment, but on the resulting outcome - something Congress recognized as flawed logic in its hearings on McVay[37] but generally goes unremarked in other cases.

Greenbacker recognized the issues of both the loss of courts-martial and the rise of the sole commander's opinion. If a single commander chose to punish a crime of command, then that punishment was no more likely fixed and certain than a commander who chose to exonerate a crime of command. Jana Vavasseur and Kirk Lippold are modern examples of the fickle nature of command decisions. Neither went to nonjudicial punishment, neither were removed from command. At many levels in their chain of command both were absolved of personal culpability for their crimes of command. However, both fell to the single act of a determined commander unconstrained by justice. Had either officer been tried via court-martial, or Greenbacker's "collective judgment of a panel of disinterested professional peers" either their culpability, or exoneration, would have been more impactful than the action of a single member of the chain of command.[38]

Changes focusing more on victim's rights and the scandal of accusation over the Constitutional rights of the accused[39] also provide depth of understanding to the Navy's changes, and while each of these arguments provide part of the picture, none of them stand on their own. In the complex system of crimes of command, the foundational concept of absolute accountability had its roots not in administration or justice, but technology. Today's Navy looks at accountability and responsibility as completely synonymous and does so because

---

[37] Ibid, 28-9.
[38] Ibid
[39] Lerner, 9.

of an officer who held command at sea for only six months, but was also the longest serving admiral in American history - Hyman G. Rickover.

Rickover's Technocracy

Perhaps the greatest impact on Navy culture, manning, training, leadership, and accountability came from Hyman G. Rickover - a limited duty engineering officer who served roughly six months in command before World War II, rose to flag rank through Congressionally coerced special Navy action, and served as an admiral for over thirty years. Admiral Rickover, now over thirty years after his death, remains a man of mythic proportions. Almost no one serving today served with him, however, his name is known to the officer corps and stories of his leadership approach, especially how he interviewed prospective nuclear officers, are legend. Rickover is simultaneously on the pillar and the pillory for everything good, or bad, in the Navy. More has been written about Rickover than all of the case studies presented here - and none of those writings, not even Rickover's own, capture the full extent of his influence, legacy, or complexity. In fact, one of the problems with Rickover's legend is that too often he is reduced to a caricature or truncated version of reality. However, his approach to responsibility is one he repeated, often, and is deeply embedded in today's Navy.

In his 2014 book on Rickover and leadership, retired Admiral David Oliver wrote that "Rickover was known to hold his subordinates strictly accountable [with an] absolutist view...that one strike was often more than sufficient to cause doubt as to an individual's good judgment."[40] Oliver, in writing solely about Rickover, is still unable to move past a shorthand version of Rickover's approach. A more contemporary view of

---

[40] Dave Oliver, *Against the Tide: Rickover's Leadership Principles and the Rise of the Nuclear Navy* (Annapolis, MD: Naval Institute Press, 2014). 38-9.

Rickover opens Francis Duncan's mildly hagiographic *Rickover and the Nuclear Navy*. Beginning as an Atomic Energy Commission historian, Duncan worked with and for Rickover from 1959 until the admiral's death in 1986. As Rickover's accepted, if not official, biographer, Duncan wrote that his conversations "with Admiral Rickover revealed a very complex man, far more complicated than the demanding, ruthless, and dictatorial individual portrayed by popular anecdote."[41]

Those anecdotes, however, are part and parcel to the Rickover myth, a myth that moved the Navy into nuclear propulsion and established a system that remains incident free. This was no small feat. Rickover's system created an aura that the commanding officer of a nuclear ship or submarine worked for both an operational commander and the director of Nuclear Reactors.[42] The system emphasized engineering and propulsion as the most important parts of a ship.[43] Rickover's meant that even a reporter's visit to a shipyard resulted in an incident report sent to a four-star admiral[44] or an unread letter might mean dismissal.[45] However, this same system ensured that each and every person working with nuclear power was trained and supervised so that nothing could go wrong.

While rooted in fear, the fear is not misplaced. Nuclear power is more unforgiving than the sea, and with two unforgiving masters, Rickover became a third. By focusing on absolute responsibility - by "applying implacable responsibility arbitrarily to naval or industrial personnel with equal ruthlessness"[46] Rickover created a system in which the people

---

[41] Francis Duncan, *Rickover and the Nuclear Navy: The Discipline of Technology* (Annapolis, MD: Naval Institute Press, 1989). xxi.
[42] Norman Polmar and Thomas B. Allen, *Rickover: Controversy and Genius: A Biography* (New York: Simon and Schuster, 1984). 348
[43] Ibid
[44] Ibid, 331.
[45] Ibid, 332.
[46] Duncan, xii.

controlled the machinery. A system that did not rely on zero-defect machines, but instead on ensuring that people performed with knowledge and intelligence.[47] Complex systems evolve, and Rickover's system both evolved and expanded.

Background

Hyman G. Rickover was born in Makow, Poland in 1900, emigrating to the United States in 1906. Growing up poor, he nevertheless finished formal schooling and entered the United States Naval Academy in 1918. Graduating 107th out of 540 his first shipboard assignment was in USS *La Valette* (DD 315), a new destroyer where he rapidly rose to engineering officer, the youngest in the destroyer squadron.[48] In 1925 he reported to USS *Nevada* (BB 36), again serving in engineering, this time as electrical officer. He applied for aviation training, was medically rejected,[49] and began graduate studies in electrical engineering. He married in 1931, while assigned to submarine duty. By 1933 he was qualified for command of submarines but did not fit in with the other submarine officers and once again transferred ashore. After two years in the office of the Inspector of Naval Material he returned to sea as the assistant engineer officer in USS *New Mexico* (BB 40).[50] Aboard *New Mexico* he trained a group of ensigns who later rose to flag rank, among them were Edgar H. Batcheller, William A. Brockett, Charles A. Curtze, and Charles E. Loughlin.[51]

In 1937, Rickover promoted to lieutenant commander and reported to command the minesweeper USS *Finch* (AM 9) in China. He commanded less than six months before acceptance into the newly created engineering duty officer program.[52] It was

---

[47] Polmar and Allen, 332.
[48] Duncan, 8.
[49] Ibid, 25.
[50] Ibid, 9.
[51] Ibid, 54.
[52] Ibid, 10.

as an engineering duty officer that Rickover made his mark on the Navy.

Three incidents impacted Rickover's career and are relevant to his mythos. At Annapolis, Rickover was quarantined as a possible diphtheria carrier. When he returned to class he was behind and in order to catch up Rickover violated academy rules to study after taps. His classmates did not approve, but Rickover saw his actions as necessary, despite their illegality.[53] The second incident was aboard *La Valette*. When the ship's navigator incorrectly plotted a course in fog, the ship went aground, and the captain was court-martialed. One biographer noted that "the concept of personal responsibility was vividly impressed upon the young ensign."[54] The third incident occurred when Rickover applied to submarine school and was rejected as too old. A fortuitous meeting with one of his *Nevada* commanding officers led to senior level intercession and a waiver of the age requirement.[55]

From those three instances one can extract that Rickover was aware of and understood responsibility, but that he was also not limited to blind rule following and would use his contacts as necessary to further his goals. He took this attitude with him through the creation of the nuclear program and his own definition of responsibility, even if he did not always hold himself to that same standard.

On responsibility

Rickover repeatedly wrote and spoke on responsibility. In 1961 he testified in Congress that

Responsibility is a unique concept: it can only reside and inhere in a single individual. You may share it with others, but your portion is not diminished. You may

---

[53] Theodore Rockwell, *The Rickover Effect: How One Man Made a Difference* (Lincoln, NE: IUniverse, 2002). 22.
[54] Ibid, 23.
[55] Ibid, 29.

delegate it, but it is still with you. You may disclaim it, but you cannot divest yourself of it. Even if you do not recognize it or admit its presence, you cannot escape it. If responsibility is rightfully yours, no evasion, or ignorance or passing the blame can shift the burden to someone else. Unless you can point your finger at the man who is responsible when something goes wrong, then you have never had anyone really responsible.[56]

In *The Rickover Effect* acolyte and long-time Rickover associate Theodore Rockwell wrote that "the point about the inescapability of responsibility was basic Rickover dogma, and he never missed an opportunity to drive it home." According to Rockwell, Rickover shared an eclectic group of writings among his staff, but one, John Grier Hibben's "Essay on Responsibility,"[57] provides insight into where Rickover obtained his concept of responsibility.

John Grier Hibben was a Presbyterian minister turned academic who succeeded Woodrow Wilson as Princeton University president. He wrote a series of essays and books on diverse subjects including logic, philosophy, patriotism, and ethics. His "Essay on Responsibility" was published as a chapter in the 1911 *A Defence of Prejudice and other Essays.* Hibben's premise was simple - that responsibility was misunderstood. In very formal style, but unwavering clarity, Hibben repeatedly attacked the idea that responsibility might in any way be shared, or lessened. Hibben instead asserted that responsibility "can be divided among many, but it is not thereby diminished in degree"[58] and that responsibility "belongs to the class of things

---

[56] Radiation safety and regulation: *Hearings before the Joint Committee on Atomic Energy, Congress of the United States, eighty-seventh Congress, first session, on radiation safety and regulation, June 12, 13, 14, and 15, 1961* (Washington, D.C.: United States Government Printing Office, 1961). 366.
[57] Rockwell, 127.
[58] John Grier Hibben, *A Defence of Prejudice: and other essays* (Charles

which, when divided, each part is equal to the whole."[59] In reading through the essay, Rickover's stance on responsibility stands out. As one reads more on Rickover and his statements on responsibility, Hibben's influence is profound.

In 1911, Hibben asserted "If one would thus seek to minimize his sense of obligation as regards that which may be placed in his keeping as a trust, he should not forget that his share of responsibility is not a part, but the whole, undiminished and untransferable[sic]."[60]

In 1952, Rickover told his subordinates, in response to an issue he learned of later than he desired,

> Dammit, then it's your responsibility to tell me so. One hundred percent your responsibility. It's also 100 percent Marks's[sic], because the pumps and valves are his. And if he weren't out of town, he'd be here and I'd be chewing him out too. And it's 100 percent Panoff's, because he's submarine project officer. And it's 100 percent Geiger's, because he's in charge of the Pittsburgh office. The existence of these other guys doesn't change your responsibility one whit. Do you guys all understand that? I don't want to have to keep going over that point again.[61]
>
> In 1982, speaking at Columbia University Rickover said Unless the individual truly responsible can be identified when something goes wrong, no one has really been responsible. With the advent of modern management theories it is becoming common for organizations to deal with problems in a collective manner, by dividing programs into subprograms, with no one left responsible for the entire effort. There is also the

---

Scribner's Sons: New York, 1911). 498.
[59] Ibid
[60] Ibid
[61] Rockwell, 126-7.

tendency to establish more and more levels of management, on the theory that this gives better control. These are but different forms of shared responsibility, which easily lead to no one being responsible—a problem that often inheres in large corporations as well as in the Defense Department.[62]

Hibben even wrote of large organizations or businesses, and recognizing that he wrote in a time before telephones, computers, or email, his admonition is still valid.

> A person who is at the head of a large business enterprise cannot be omnipresent or omniscient; but he is responsible for the kind of men who are his partners in responsibility, and also for the atmosphere which pervades his business, for the general morale of the service, for the discipline that is enforced, for the prevailing policy and method pursued, and for the spirit and tone which characterize all departments, however various they may be.[63]

Simply having greater technology does not bestow omnipresence or omniscience, but Rickover didn't need either to retain personal responsibility. In 1961, Rickover testified to Congress

> the fact that a nuclear ship may go to sea for 2 months at a time, and be away from the United States, does not in itself relieve me of my responsibility even though an operational commander has charge. I have been responsible for the design of the reactor plant, the training of the crew, the installation and test, the issuance of instructions. So no matter where an accident might happen, I am still personally responsible.[64]

And in 1982 Rickover said

> Attention to detail does not require a manager to do

---

[62] Hyman G. Rickover, "Doing a Job" (speech, Columbia University, New York, 1982).
[63] Hibben, 499.
[64] Joint Committee on Atomic Energy, (1961). 366.

everything himself. No one can work more than twenty-four hours each day. Therefore, to multiply his efforts, he must create an environment where his subordinates can work to their maximum ability. Some management experts advocate strict limits to the number of people reporting to a common superior-generally five to seven. But if one has capable people who require but a few moments of his time during the day, there is no reason to set such arbitrary constraints. Some forty key people report frequently and directly to me. This enables me to keep up with what is going on and makes it possible for them to get fast action. The latter aspect is particularly important. Capable people will not work for long where they cannot get prompt decisions and actions from their superior.[65]

Hibben's assertion that "he who is responsible for a particular task is relieved of that responsibility only when there is evidence that the given work has been done"[66] pairs well with an oft quoted Rickoverism: "Unless you can point your finger at the one person who is responsible when something goes wrong, then you have never had anyone really responsible."[67]

Hibben saw that "a person may not be held responsible for failure to see some obvious circumstance when his eyes are shut; but he is responsible for his eyes being shut when they ought to be open."[68] Rickover insisted that

> One must permit his people the freedom to seek added work and greater responsibility. In my organization, there are no formal job descriptions or organizational charts. Responsibilities are defined in a general way, so that people are not circumscribed. All are permitted to

---

[65] Rickover (1982).
[66] Hibben, 499.
[67] Duncan, 275.
[68] Hibben, 499.

do as they think best and to go to anyone and anywhere for help. Each person then is limited only by his own ability.[69]

Rickover spoke of and demanded absolute individual responsibility, however as seen with his admittance to submarine school and study habits at Annapolis, he was able to adjust his perception as he saw fit. In his career, two major instances of adjusting responsibility are his promotion to admiral and the later loss of USS *Thresher* (SSN 593).

Promotion

In August 1951, *Time-Life* correspondent and World War II submariner Clay Blair Jr. wrote a story on the Navy's growing nuclear power program. He became fascinated with the program and with Rickover. Blair captured Rickover's focus as a "war on naval indifference."[70] Rickover's star rose in the public eye, and in Washington he was called to brief President Truman on the propulsion program. Events over the next two years show the contentious relationship between Rickover and the Navy that culminated in Rickover's promotion to admiral.

Rickover briefed Truman in February 1952 and later persuaded a friendly senator to ask the President to speak at the June keel laying ceremony for the first nuclear powered submarine, USS *Nautilus* (SSN 571). Only days before the ceremony, Rickover aides discovered that he was not slated to sit in the stands with the other dignitaries. The aides worked with the shipbuilder, Electric Boat, who issued an invitation to Rickover in his role as chief of the Naval Reactors branch of the Atomic Energy Commission (AEC).[71] Rickover attended, in his role with the AEC, and appropriately wore civilian clothes to the military ceremony.

During the ceremony Rickover was repeatedly singled

---

[69] Rickover (1982).
[70] Duncan, 118.
[71] Ibid, 119.

out for praise, but the die was soon cast in the biggest issue of his career. Only weeks later the Navy's admiral selection board reported its results, and Rickover was not on the list. Despite recognition at the highest levels of government, the Navy was finished with Rickover and he would have to retire within a year.

The AEC, Congress, and Clay Blair were all concerned - no one else had the background to run the Navy's nuclear power program and the AEC could not see converting Rickover's role into a civilian one. In August, *Time* magazine published a Blair-penned story hinting at anti-Semitism and overtly charging that the Navy was unwilling to accept technical specialists and willing to end the career of "a brilliant officer who developed the most important new weapon since World War II."[72] Rickover's associates met with friendly congressmen and lobbied for their assistance. The Senate Armed Services Committee considered investigating the promotion.[73] Ultimately, the Senate Armed Services Committee began considering withholding votes confirming the selection board results.[74]

By now the story was making headlines in the *Washington Post, Washington Times-Herald, New York Times, Boston Herald*, as far away as Tulsa, Oklahoma in the *Daily World*.[75] Congress began receiving mail about Rickover and decided to hold up confirming thirty-nine captains to rear admiral while it investigated the overall promotion system.[76]

Eventually a compromise was reached. First, Rickover's billet description was changed from that of a captain to rear admiral.[77] Second, the Secretary of the Navy announced he

---

[72] Ibid, 121.
[73] Ibid, 125.
[74] Ibid, 125.
[75] Ibid, 126.
[76] Ibid
[77] Ibid, 128.

would convene a new selection board to retain engineering duty captains on active duty past their mandatory retirement date. This board made Rickover eligible for the ensuing 1953 flag promotion board, which was charged with selecting for promotion "an engineering duty captain experienced and qualified in nuclear propulsion."[78] There was only one.

While Rickover's fans delighted, not everyone was pleased. Famed submarine captain and author, Edward L. Beach, Jr, wrote of the incident in the preface to Duncan's *Rickover: The Struggle for Excellence.*

> ... secretary of the navy, Robert B. Anderson, ordered a special selection board to sit. With some shuffling of feet it did what it had been ordered to do, and neither Congress nor the press cared that the navy's carefully created promotion system had been violated. Ninety-five percent of navy captains must retire regardless of how highly qualified because there are only vacancies for 5 percent of them to become admirals, and although vindictiveness has sometimes played a part in determining who shall fail of selection for promotion (thus also violating the system), never before or since have pressures from outside the navy overturned this form of career-termination.[79]

Rickover was promoted three more times and eventually retained on active duty by an annual Congressional vote that waived statutory rules. The system which normally bowed to no one, bowed to this one man.

Thresher

While the personnel system bent to support Rickover, the engineering systems were sometimes different. By 1963 the Navy operated twenty-six nuclear submarines and had thirty more planned or under construction. Rickover was still

---

[78] Ibid
[79] Ibid, ix.

intimately involved in the program; however, he was largely limited to the propulsion side. Nuclear powered ships were entering the mainstream.

On April 10, 1963, USS *Thresher* (SSN 593) departed Portsmouth Shipyard on a post-overhaul operational test. Diving slowly towards half-test depth, something went wrong and *Thresher* sank, killing her entire crew. Later investigations determined that an improperly joined salt-water system pipe failed, dooming the submarine and crew; however it is Admiral Rickover's reaction and later actions which are pertinent.

Rickover was quickly advised of the sinking and he immediately called the Navy's Office of Information and Admiral Ralph K. James, Chief of the Bureau of Ships offering his assistance. James related that Rickover "called to remind me on that occasion that he was not the submarine builder, he was simply the nuclear-plant producer... Rickover went to great extremes to disassociate any likelihood of failure of the nuclear plant from the Thresher incident. I considered this thoroughly dishonest."[80] Recall that just two years earlier Rickover testified that

> The fact that a nuclear ship may go to sea for 2 months at a time, and be away from the United States, does not in itself relieve me of my responsibility even though an operational commander has charge. I have been responsible for the design of the reactor plant, the training of the crew, the installation and test, the issuance of instructions. So no matter where an accident might happen, I am still personally responsible.[81]

In time, some accepted Rickover's position, partially buoyed by his testimony at the ensuing Court of Inquiry. Testifying for twelve minutes in open session and more behind closed doors one attendee said "I was damn impressed by his

---

[80] Polmar and Allen, 430-1.
[81] Joint Committee on Atomic Energy (1961), 366.

intellectual honesty. When the chips were really down, when lives were at stake, he acted intellectually humble."[82]

The Rickover Process

Rickover's longevity with the naval service allows us a look at his process. It is one thing to have an idea, another to implement it, and still another for that idea to permeate and change an organization. Unlike any other naval officer, Rickover was able to use a process, largely the same process, over four decades. First, he would assess an organization. If it was not performing as he wanted, he changed the organization. Sometimes people, sometimes processes, sometimes both. In all cases he ensured that any task had someone, and only one someone, totally responsible for that task.

Assigning this responsibility carried a price - Rickover also accepted responsibility for his subordinate's actions and that meant creating the conditions for success. Rickover saw his role as forcing an individual to think and Rickover used inspections and reports to get that individual to assess the present, past, and future.[83] Rickover saw jobs as profession and profession as calling. Service to the United States was a moral imperative and neither tactics nor strategy mattered if a ship could not operate. Rickover believed that a commander had only two duties: train the crew and keep the ship ready to fight. Any commander who shirked these duties was traitor to himself, his crew, and his country.[84] As a result, Rickover judged failure harshly. If a ship was below average in too many he areas, he called the commander and chastised him "in a torrent of bitter language, casting doubts on the man's ability, intelligence, and strength of character." Rickover's tirade was not malicious. He

---

[82] Polmar and Allen, 431.
[83] Ibid, 284.
[84] Ibid, 260.

Over time, Rickover attained legend status, well before retirement or death. This status, and the organizational growth of the nuclear navy created detractors, and over time they too grew in status and stature. None in the Navy dared openly challenge the Father of the Nuclear Navy until 1978.

Navy Lieutenant Ralph Chatham was commissioned through Naval ROTC, served aboard a diesel submarine, and had a doctorate in physics. He was headed for service as a nuclear submarine navigator when the United States Naval Institute published his article, "Leadership and Nuclear Power" in July 1978.[91] Chatham challenged many long-accepted Rickover practices, from the personal authority that Rickover took and wielded over individual commanding officers to the direct control Rickover asserted in everything from power plant design to individual shipboard personnel assignments - in submarines and surface ships. Chatham recognized and lamented that nuclear trained junior officers did not realize Rickover's ways differed from the rest of the Navy's operations.[92]

Chatham identified a series of characteristics in nuclear power: insistence on rote obedience, an obsession with the propulsion plant over everything else, a desire to keep all problems within the family of nuclear power, a need for affirmative approval for each action, the reluctance to praise, and defining success as never making a mistake which in turn created a habitual distrust of people. Chatham saw nuclear power eschewing initiative and independence, relying instead on a pattern of rule following. Chatham summed the culture up as one where officers were

> Given responsibility, but not authority, [and] the natural reaction is to ask to be told exactly what to do, to request rudder orders. An officer working in a nuclear billet can become a commanding officer if he simply

---

[91] Ibid, 348-9.
[92] Ralph Chatham, "Leadership and Nuclear Power," *Proceedings*, July 1978.

makes no major mistakes. Leadership is not nearly so important a criterion of success. A leader who does what he is told and ensures that he is told everything that he must do does not make mistakes. This is an awful lesson for the highly intelligent nuclear-trained junior officer to learn. It has been my experience that too many of the 36% who stay with the Navy do learn it.[93]

Chatham's essay was the first from within the Navy, however he was clearly influenced and inspired by recently retired Chief of Naval Operations Admiral Elmo R. Zumwalt. Zumwalt was not nuclear trained but served enough in Washington D.C. to see Rickover's program first hand and over decades. Zumwalt is seen as one of, if not the, most influential CNO of the twentieth century, but even he could not influence Rickover. As frustrating as that was, Zumwalt was aware of the issue early on.

Zumwalt was closely associated with Secretary of the Navy Paul Nitze and in 1967, while serving as Nitze's aide, Zumwalt recalled of Rickover that

> while he was meeting with Paul, Rick began bragging about how strongly he encouraged dissent and debate in his shop, how he ran it on the basis of an adversary process, in fact. When Paul expressed polite skepticism, Rick offered to send over some officers in training for top nuclear command, to give their account of how his personnel system operated. Sure enough, a few days later two such officers did call on the Secretary. They told Paul essentially the same story Rick had. On their way out, one of them took me aside and said, "Bud, I have now carried out my orders from Admiral Rickover to say exactly what we have just said to the Secretary. However Admiral Rickover did not tell me what to say to you. Be sure to tell the Secretary that we said to him

---

[93] Ibid

what we were told to say to him, and that the Rickover system doesn't work that way at all." Crude, you say? Well, Rick is not subtle, just devious.[94]

Zumwalt wrote of this exchange a decade later in his autobiography, *On Watch*, which Chatham also quoted in his own writing, noting that Rickover used safety and inspection systems to enforce control over every aspect of nuclear power.[95] Zumwalt dedicated an entire chapter of his memoir to Rickover, most of which related to retelling two personal interactions with the older admiral.

Elmo Zumwalt was every bit the visionary his reputation gave him. At his most bitter, he allegedly once said the "enemies of the U.S. Navy were the Soviet Union, the U.S. Air Force, and Admiral Rickover." He later amended it to list Rickover second, behind the Soviet Union. Zumwalt believed that Rickover's influence was so pervasive that no one could "accurately portray what has happened over the years as the force of Admiral Rickover's out-of-channel, executive branch-unsupervised, Byzantine, bureaucratic operation has perverted the process. Only when one has access to the files of his office can the true story be portrayed."[96]

Rickover's Impact

Zumwalt was correct - the depths of Rickover's impact were such that only the superficial is readily seen and deeper changes must be sought out. In 1990, four years after Rickover's death, Captain Edward Beach wrote "Our navy is...indebted to Admiral Rickover in ways it still does not fully understand."[97] Rickover served for so long that in 1974 when Admiral Holloway, the first nuclear trained officer to reach four-stars, became CNO Rickover was still serving - and Holloway was

---

[94] Elmo R. Zumwalt, *On Watch* (New York: Quadrangle Books, 1977). 100.
[95] Chatham citing Zumwalt, 113.
[96] Polmar and Allen, 479.
[97] Duncan, x.

born the year Rickover graduated from the Naval Academy. CNO Holloway was the second Admiral Holloway Rickover worked with. The elder Holloway was Chief of Naval Personnel in the nuclear program's early years and the officer who helped Rickover get, and maintain, control over the personnel within the program.[98]

After Holloway, five of the next eleven CNOs were products of Rickover's nuclear power training. The two most recent, Admirals Jonathan Greenert and John Richardson, both career submarine officers, were interviewed by Rickover for selection into nuclear power. Those CNOs who were not nuclear trained, three surface warfare officers and two aviators, still attended SOSMRC and were influenced by Rickover's expanded influence.[99]

Rickover served on active duty from 1922 to 1982 - and from 1953 to 1982 as a flag officer. He died in 1986, four years after retiring, or being forced out, depending on whose version you accept. Thirty years after his death a generation and a half of naval officers have served and now by looking back it is possible to begin seeing what Rickover wrought.

Admiral James Watkins, CNO from June 1982 to 1986, said of Rickover's impact:

> We've all been talking about the personal impact Rickover had on us and on people we know. That's important, but one could argue that it's subjective and ephemeral. But he left behind two very solid legacies that can be seen by anyone. First, the entire Navy-not just the nuclear part-has now formally adopted his approach to engineering. A hands-on training facility was set up, first in Idaho and now at Newport, Rhode Island, for skippers, squadron commanders, and even flag officers dealing with major combat vessels-destroyers and larger. The training program and the

---

[98] Polmar and Allen, 479.
[99] Edgar F. Puryear, *American Admiralship: The Art of Naval Command* (Minneapolis, MN: Zenith Press, 2008). 407.

proficiency inspection system were modeled directly after Rickover's. It isn't perfect, but the framework is there, the goals and procedures are spelled out in official documents, so there's a clearly visible standard to work against.[100]

This visible standard, one of an accident free approach to engineering and a comprehensive training program, are Rickover's legacies and directly impact the Navy's approach to crimes of command.

Accidents

At the most obvious level is the number of nuclear submarines and ships in the Navy, and the continuing operation without major accidents. Rickover firmly believed in the fallibility of both people and machines - and neither machine nor technology could be commanded, but people could. Further, his concept of responsibility, tied to the command of people, insisted that "without acceptance—unlimited acceptance—of complete responsibility by the individual you cannot avoid ultimately having accidents."[101] The clear inference is that unlimited acceptance of responsibility was the way to avoid accidents.

In 1961, responding to a question about a nuclear meltdown at experimental Army reactor SL-1, Rickover stated that the accident was avoidable, citing the possibility of design errors, inadequate training, or faulty operation. Rickover believed an accident required a combination of things, that one error alone would not cause an accident. In each instance of an accident Rickover believed that

> had there been adequate training and proper operation the design alone would have not caused the accident. Proper training even with faulty design could have prevented the accident. Good supervision could have

---

[100] Rockwell, 381-2.
[101] Joint Committee on Atomic Energy, (1961), 361.

prevented the accident, even with faulty design and bad training. All nuclear accidents that have happened so far could have been avoided if the training and operation had been adequate.[102]

Rickover made these statements without having visited the SL-1 site, relying instead on a report from one of his engineers. The official report on the accident would not come out for six more months. However, Rickover made his point at a time it would resonate with Congress, even more so since the accident was on a reactor outside his program. With the official report unfinished, no one could refute Rickover's statement.

People

Rickover's approach to accidents revolved around people - training, supervision, and system design (which is done by people). While many focus on the number of ships, or reactors, the real impact lies in the people. Of the officers who first entered the nuclear power program, seven of the ten commanders of the first ten nuclear submarines became admirals.[103] By 1972, a quarter of the Navy's vice admirals were nuclear trained[104] and over 4,000 officers and 22,500 enlisted men had passed through Rickover's program - more people than were in the Navy when Rickover was born.[105] These people learned, and perpetuated Rickover's ideals and process with Admirals Holloway and Watkins among the most influential.

Holloway, who commanded USS *Enterprise* (CVN 65), was CNO when *Belknap* collided with *John F. Kennedy* and the Navy worried it was losing hold of command accountability and responsibility. Holloway also brought engineering duty into the fore of naval careers. He believed that engineering was neglected in favor of command and control and weapons

---

[102] Ibid, 367.
[103] Polmar and Allen, 336.
[104] Ibid, 337.
[105] Ibid, 335.

systems. He saw propulsion systems that were poorly designed, poorly maintained, and poorly led - which in turn were killing sailors. While engineering officers were diligent and well meaning, they were poorly trained, and largely ignored by commanders unfamiliar with engineering duty.[106] Holloway's solution was to duplicate Rickover's approach. Holloway mandated that officers complete tours and qualify in engineering before taking command of ships. In 1977 he assisted Rickover in mirroring the nuclear power training program with the Senior Officer Ship Material Readiness Course (SOSMRC) using isolated locations, hard work, and top-notch instructors.[107] Holloway's approach and initiatives mirrored Rickover's 1961 testimony:

> But the education and training does not stop there, because after they are assigned to a ship they must continue to learn. Even after he is on a ship he must remain qualified or he will be detached. We have adopted a new practice for ships completing at a shipyard where, instead of the shipyard or Navy yard employees testing the propulsion plants, getting them ready to go to sea and operating the plants on sea trials, we have that done by the officers and crew. This is different than the practice on other naval ships where the yard personnel do all the testing and conduct the sea trials.[108]

This program, and a series of inspection boards and examinations including those mentioned with USS *Ranger*, were not created to increase Rickover's hold on the Navy. The surface Navy in the late 1960s and early 1970s had real problems within its engineering control systems and personnel. Insufficient personnel with insufficient training and

---

[106] Holloway, 355.
[107] Ibid, 358.
[108] Joint Committee on Atomic Energy (1961), 362.

deteriorating material conditions within engineering plants in 1974 meant Navy inspectors failed 85% of inspected ships. Deadly explosions in two ships, USS *Dewey* (DLG 14) and USS *Goldsborough* (DDG 20) accentuated the need for reforms.[109]

Into the 1970s[110] and through today the totality of officer accession programs are geared towards producing sufficient numbers of officers to enter, and complete, nuclear power training,[111] even though nuclear ships make up less than thirty percent of the overall fleet, and nuclear trained officers are roughly seven percent of the officer corps[112]. In order to meet the recruiting demands for the nuclear power program, including an expected 60% rejection rate, at least 80% of every year's officer accessions must have technical degrees.[113] As such we now have multiple generations of naval officers well-grounded in science, math, and engineering who are also woefully uneducated in the arts, humanities, and social sciences.

Responsibility

However, Rickover's most lasting impact, embedded in the Navy via people and process, related to responsibility. That same 1961 testimony is where Rickover provided his definition of responsibility

> Responsibility is a unique concept: it can only reside and inhere in & single individual. You may share it with others, but your portion is not diminished. You may delegate it, but it is still with you. You may

---

[109] House, 33.
[110] Polmar and Allen, 464.
[111] See Naval Service Training Command Instruction 1533.3A dated May 28, 2009.
[112] As of January 2, 2018, the Navy had 3,876 nuclear trained officers at all ranks and 54,303 officers.
[113] John F. Lehman, *Command of the Seas* (Annapolis, MD: Naval Institute Press, 2001). 25-26

disclaim it, but you cannot divest yourself of it. Even if you do not recognize it or admit its presence, you cannot escape it. If responsibility is rightfully yours, no evasion, or ignorance or passing the blame can shift the burden to someone else. Unless you can point your finger at the man who is responsible when something goes wrong, then you have never had anyone really responsible.[114]

Rickover's 1961 statements, of the unique, indivisible, and non-transferable nature of accountability combined in Chief of Naval Operations Admiral Watkins. Watkins, a submarine officer and early entrant to the nuclear power program served as executive officer of USS *Long Beach* (CGN 9), the first nuclear powered cruiser, after commanding USS *Snook* (SSN 592). More influentially, Watkins served multiple tours in the Bureau of Naval Personnel, one as the distribution officer for all nuclear personnel and then as the first director of enlisted personnel. As a flag officer he served as Chief of Naval Personnel under Admiral Holloway. Watkins was also instrumental in setting up Holloway and Rickover's Senior Officer Ship Material Readiness Course (SOSMRC). By the time Watkins became CNO in 1982 he'd worked for three decades with and for Admiral Rickover. Watkins was CNO when Rickover retired and for Rickover's death and funeral. As CNO, Watkins delivered Rickover's eulogy.[115] Watkins' actions as CNO during the problems aboard USS *Ranger* detailed in chapter 3 show the depths of Rickover's influence.

In 1982 a sailor died aboard *Ranger* because of improper leadership and poor conditions in the ship's corrective custody unit. In assessing culpability and accountability for the ship's commander, Captain Dan Pedersen, Watkins issued a statement that read:

---

[114] Joint Committee on Atomic Energy (1961), 366.
[115] James D. Watkins, "Oral History," interview by Gary Weir, *Oceanography: The Making of a Science People, Institutions and Discovery*, May 11, 2000.

> both the Chief of Naval Operations, Admiral James Watkins, and Lehman decided that the commanding officer is the trinity of authority and responsibility on his ship. The doctrine of accountability has always been a part of command and a very active part of that doctrine is that you cannot delegate responsibility and authority to another.[116]

This is the first open and official linkage of authority, responsibility, and accountability and their indivisible nature. From 1982 onward, the ideal of culpability of command was set and became part of command. The questionable assertion that it had always been such went unchallenged.

Watkins also took Rickover's ideas outside the Navy. After retiring as CNO, Watkins remained active in government, first as Chairman of the Reagan commission on the HIV epidemic then as Secretary of Energy for President George H. W. Bush. At Energy, Watkins brought Rickover trained people to assist him. He told Ted Rockwell that

> You can tell [Rickover associates], 'Look into this mess, and tell me what we should do.' You don't have to define look into, or mess, or what options of action are permissible, possible, or adequate. And you know they're not going to tell you what they think you want to hear, or try to protect the people they're reporting on, or second-guess your motives. And they will be technically competent and will understand what they're investigating. It's incredible how hard it is to find people like that.[117]

Watkins was not the only one to take Rickover's ideas outside the Navy. Admiral Robert L. J. Long, nuclear trained and Vice Chief of Naval Operations under CNO Holloway, headed the commission investigating the 1983 Beirut barracks bombing. The report opened with this statement:

---

[116] Cooper.
[117] Rockwell, 378.

> The commission holds the view that military commanders are responsible for the performance of their subordinates. The commander can delegate some or all of his authority to his subordinates, but he cannot delegate his responsibility for the performance of the forces he commands. In that sense, the responsibility of military command is absolute. This view of command authority and responsibility guided the commission in its analysis of the effectiveness of the exercise of command authority and responsibility of the chain of command charged with the security and performance of the United states multinational force.[118]

Admiral Long later related that he believed the press and Marine Corps were supportive of the report, that they appreciated that accountability and transparency were preserved. However, neither the Secretary of State, George Shultz, nor European Command's General Bernard W. Rogers agreed. Rogers reportedly sent a message "demand[ing] that the commission come to Europe and explain to him why he should be held accountable."[119]

When historian Edgar F. Puryear interviewed Watkins for *American Admiralship: The Moral Imperatives of Naval Command* he asked Watkins about accountability. Watkins quoted Rickover's testimony on responsibility.[120] Admiral David Oliver similarly conflated accountability and responsibility when he asked

> Do you agree with Rickover's concept of accountability? He phrased it thusly: "You may share it with others, but your portion is not diminished. You may delegate it, but it is still with you .... If responsibility is rightfully yours, no evasion, or

---

[118] Long and Stillwell, 395.
[119] Ibid, 396.
[120] Puryear, 596.

ignorance or passing the blame can shift the burden to someone else." Does this definition say anything about current philosophical flirtations with group or team responsibility in the workplace?[121]

Thirty years after Rickover's death his ideas and concepts remain part of Navy leadership culture. His beliefs, and his process, changed the Navy more than anyone will ever properly recognize. His harsh and unyielding statements on responsibility became statements on accountability and when combined with his legendary status make him easy for reference without context. Edward Beach summed the issue up saying "In Rickover's case, even his warts, like them or not, somehow contributed to the extraordinary success of what he accomplished."[122] However, one remains responsible for how the "warts" impact others and Rickover cannot escape responsibility for how his process and legacy changed the Navy. He was "a great man to whom the nation and all who strive for excellence owe much"[123] and Rickover's legacy also provides the way forward to restore the separation between responsibility, accountability, authority, and culpability.

---

[121] Oliver, 38-9.
[122] Duncan, xiv.
[123] Duncan, 313.

6: Towards Forgiveness

Why does the Navy remove commanders from command? As with all decisions and actions within human systems, it is not the system which acts but rather individual leaders. Those leaders are shaped by their culture, by the organization's education and training, and their own personal moral development and experiences. The Navy does not so much remove commanders from command as other commanders remove their subordinate commanders from command. A senior officer removes a subordinate one because crimes of command violate the command ideal – the crimes insult the honor of command, and by extension the honor of the senior commander. Flag officers and investigating officers act as they do in order to defend the honor of command. Command is not an impersonal concept, but a personal and closely held belief based on experience and ideology.

While Navy commanders are removed for a variety of failings, the removal decision and punitive actions for a collision, drinking and driving, crew misbehavior, or sexual assault are largely the same. In today's Navy an officer's career is ended, there is virtually no hope of recovery or redemption, and removal from command is a public sacrifice on the altar of accountability. These removal actions also show that the Navy sees the words accountability, responsibility, and culpability as synonymous. David Oliver showed how Hyman Rickover's concept of responsibility became one of accountability. Ralph Chatham claimed that Rickover's culture provided for greater responsibility with decreased authority. With expanded responsibility conflated with accountability, culpability is never mentioned. With the movement from semi-legal proceedings in courts-martial to purely administrative procedures, culpability is reserved for legal scholars and lawyers; accountability becomes an administrative action. This is not simply an issue of etymology - the precise use, or misuse, of language is central to crimes of command.

Words have meaning and words make up part of language. Rickover understood this in his insistence on formal and precise language:

> Take the matter of formality—giving and acknowledging commands and reporting data in exact prescribed terms. Inevitably, men became slack and took to slang or private jargon. Misunderstanding was bound to occur, and accidents had no better breeding ground than the haze of confusion.[1]

Dictionary definitions for accountable and responsible provide complementary or synonymous meanings, and we see such in common usage. Since language lives and changes, the synonymization is not incorrect, however users must also recognize when one word is used in place of another and the meaning is thereby corrupted.

Accountability is the condition of someone who is accountable. Being accountable or to give account entails the need to explain one's actions or to provide a balancing of sums. Responsibility is different, even when synonymous. *Responsibility* is the condition of being responsible - that of an obligation or power to act or respond. Responsibility carries additional subtext of claim, credit, or blame and sometimes trust.

Culpability is the state of being culpable and often defined as being responsible for a fault or deserving blame. Different from either other definition, culpability is solely associated with blame. Culpability looks back after an action. As does accountability - one gives account for an action. Responsibility is the only word with both a forward looking (power to act) and backward-looking component (the power to respond). While commonly used together or in place of each other, their conflation provides one of the issues which leads to crimes of command residing in the same bin as personal misconduct.

---

[1] Duncan, 260-1.

While the change from individual responsibility to the culpability of command is clear, the rationale is less so. Likewise, the grouping of operational crimes of command with individual crimes might seem odd. A poor leader who abuses the crew should not be grouped with a respected commander whose ship runs aground, but because the options are limited, the actions taken against both are often the same. Personal behavior and operational issues are tossed together, partly because of the misunderstood approach to accountability, but also because of a reductionist and simplistic approach to process, professionalism and ethics. The process problem was addressed in the previous chapter, and all too often *professionalism* is conflated with *preferred*, and *ethics* is reduced to "a remembrance of a childhood morality learned at home and in the school-yard."[2] Neither is true, yet both affect how the Navy, and her commanders, act. When combined with lax language the Navy is rife for a culture of "ready, fire, aim" responses to crimes of command.

Navy culture has lost the ability to properly separate and distinguish between culpability, accountability, and responsibility. Navy culture no longer fully understands ethics and ethical dilemmas. Navy culture now sees administration and bureaucratization as professionalism. These issues are interrelated, but all lead to one inescapable conclusion - Navy culture must change. Navy culture must rediscover the core of its language. It must understand the truth behind the myth and rhetoric of command if it is to continue into the future and remain relevant. Making these changes will come from those who have both experience and education, practice and theory - from those who can properly perceive a situation, have the

---

[2] David K. Hart, "Administration and the Ethics of Virtue: In All Things, Choose First for Good Character and Then for Technical Expertise," in *Handbook of Administrative Ethics*, ed. Terry L. Cooper, 2nd ed. (New York, NY: Dekker, 2001). 132.

appropriate feelings about it, can properly deliberate about what was appropriate in those circumstances, and to act.[3]

Acknowledging that words are important ensures that we speak of the same things with understanding and without miscommunication; if we use the same words in different ways we talk past one another, creating and exacerbating misunderstanding.[4] Having addressed the separation between accountability, responsibility, and culpability we must now look at three words with individual meanings who are combined into a compound noun, retaining some of their original import but also becoming something else: professional military ethic. Before we digest the term, we must understand its parts.

Entire books are written on professionalism or the professionalization of organizations. A number of them focus on the formation and professionalization of the U.S. Navy, however these all stop at World War I. Donald Chisholm's *Waiting for Dead Men's Shoes* covers the professional promotion and personnel system up through World War II. Any writings on the Navy since then focus either on individuals, specific ships or actions, or in some cases leadership issues in a decade. The modern Navy is so obsessed with technology that even its historians forget to write on people and processes. This forces prospographers to look to the larger world of military sociology.

In the early years of the Cold War two scholars broke ground with studies on military professionalism. In 1957 Samuel Huntington's *The Soldier and the State* focused on the military's political and institutional roles and kick-started the concept of civil-military relations. Morris Janowitz' 1960 *The Professional Soldier* approached the same subject but from a sociological perspective. Huntington and Janowitz, when combined, provide a dated but clear description of Cold War U.S. military

---

[3] Barry Schwartz and Kenneth Sharpe, *Practical Wisdom: The Right Way to Do the Right Thing* (New York: Riverhead Books, 2010). 5.
[4] Gortner, 522-3.

profession, organization, culture, and position within American society. Over half a century later, both authors' conclusions remain largely valid, fully relevant, and are foundational to any modern study of the military as institution.[5]

Huntington established three distinguishing characteristics of a profession; expertise, responsibility, and corporateness.[6] Expertise denoted possession of "specialized knowledge and skill in a significant field of human endeavor....acquired only by prolonged education and experience."[7] Responsibility denoted that professional work lay in a social context - that "the client of every profession is society, individually or collectively."[8] Within corporateness, Huntington wrote that "members of a profession share a sense of organic unity and consciousness of themselves as a group apart from laymen."[9] This unity arose from the aforementioned prolonged education and experience, a common bond of work, and the shared social responsibility. These three elements coalesce in a select group of professionals who formalize their organization and establish specific standards for the group. Membership, and abiding by these standards, gaining expertise, education, and social responsibility distinguish that which is professional.[10]

Other scholars see profession as "a body of expert knowledge, on which basis the public accords certain privileges in exchange for, an understanding that the members of the profession will self-regulate and, operate for the common or

---

[5] Richard D. White, *Ethics and hierarchy: the influence of a rigidly hierarchical organizational design on moral reasoning* (1997). 76.
[6] Samuel P. Huntington, *The Soldier and the State: The Theory and Politics of Civil Military Relations* (Cambridge: Belknap Press of Harvard University Press, 1957). 8.
[7] Ibid
[8] Ibid, 9.
[9] Ibid, 10.
[10] Ibid

public good."[11] Historically doctors, lawyers, and clergy comprised professions. Another concept lists "expertise in the knowledge and skills of the profession; autonomy in action and decision-making related to clients; identification with others in the profession; commitment to a life's work in the field; a sense of obligation to render unselfish, neutral service; and a belief in self-regulation by members of the profession."[12]

In a 2015 working paper on ethics, Admiral Walter E. Carter, President of the U.S. Naval War College, wrote that professionals are "granted a high degree of collective autonomy; allowed to control their own education, certification, promotion, and dismissal; and given considerable discretion and latitude in how they apply the unique professional knowledge they possess."[13] While using different words the similarities are also clear - specific knowledge, specific privileges, a requirement for group self-regulation. For our purposes, Admiral Carter's definition suffices, even if he uses some words others do not.

Huntington, in defining the professional military ethic also specified his idea of military action. Military action related solely to state sanctioned violence and its application was split between officers and enlisted personnel. Enlisted personnel were subordinate to the officer corps but were not professionals in the same sense that officers were. Enlisted personnel comprised a trade where officers populated a profession. Enlisted personnel are "specialists in the application of violence"[14] while officers were "specialists in the management of violence."[15]

---

[11] Pauline Kaurin, "Questioning Military #Professionalism – Pauline Kaurin – Medium," Medium, January 22, 2015, accessed January 15, 2018, https://medium.com/@queenofthinair/questioning-military-professionalism-f00d34f6e1ac.
[12] Gortner, 521.
[13] Walter E. Carter, *Ethics in the U.S. Navy*, working paper, United States Naval War College (2014). 5.
[14] Huntington, 17-18.
[15] Ibid, 11.

Officers, across all services and countries, provided a common competence in managing violence.[16] Huntington ascribed three duties to military officers including: "the organizing, equipping, and training of th[e] force; the planning of its activities; and the direction of its operation in and out of combat."[17]

Huntington did not clearly separate professional from military or ethics. Huntington saw conflict as universal and believed that violence is rooted in the permanent biological and psychological nature of man.[18] His view of the military professional is Hobbesian, accepting that while man possesses goodness, strength, and reason, he will act wickedly, weakly, and irrationally. To ameliorate the wicked, weak or irrational Huntington maintained that the military must be disciplined and rigid, eschewing flexibility, tolerance, or emotion. The military, at its core is both bellicose and authoritarian. Huntington emphasized the importance of the group over the individual, believing that battlefield success demanded the subservice of the individual to the will of the group.[19]

Ethics is not just about establishing and following moral rules. Rather, ethics is about "figuring out the right way to do the right thing in a particular circumstance, with a particular person, at a particular time."[20] An ethical dilemma arises when "two or more competing values are important and in conflict. If you serve one value you cannot serve another, or you must deny or disserve[sic] one or more values in order to maintain one or more of the others."[21] In the study of ethics, the questioning of right and wrong or determining how man should live, scholars sort concepts and theories into separate schools of ethics. In each case an adjective precedes ethics, altering the meaning - e.g.

---

[16] Ibid, 13.
[17] Ibid, 11.
[18] White (1997), 639.
[19] Ibid, 640.
[20] Schwartz and Sharpe, 5-6.
[21] Gortner, 509.

normative ethics, meta-ethics, and applied ethics. However, when we begin looking beneath the major schools and see the intersection between applied and normative ethics, real ethics in practice, the adjective-noun phrase takes on a life of its own. Bioethics is both a specialized and paradoxically larger discussion of ethics of life, science and technology. For businessmen business ethics is synonymous with ethics. For professional soldiers, military ethics runs along topics from personal behavior to the behavior of nations. In many cases these subsets of applied ethics draw from differing concepts within normative and meta-ethics, sometimes to the detriment of application. Most people are said to see ethics as either consequentialist or utilitarian;[22] they focus on the results of an act rather than the intent or corresponding moral duty. Another school of thought, intuitionism, holds we should consult our conscience to determine the ethically correct action.[23] While scholars choose schools for debate, people rarely do so, instead moving from school to school as each situation shifts or changes. Schools of ethics are helpful for debate and taxonomy, less so for predicting or analyzing behavior.

Military ethics normally conjures thoughts of war, the legitimate use of violence, just war theory, the virtue of courage, bravery under fire and a host of other weighty and somber issues. Even professional ethicists have difficulty defining or limiting military ethics. After listing a series of activities ranging from recitation to exhortation and training, the editors of the Journal of Military Ethics wrote "Nobody has exclusive authority to dictate, of course, which of these activities might properly be worthy of the title 'military ethics'."[24] Fortunately, they go on to

---

[22] Toner, James H. *Morals under the Gun: The Cardinal Virtues, Military Ethics, and American Society*, 1969
[23] Ibid,
[24] Henrik Syse and Martin L. Cook, "New Editors Introduction," *Journal of Military Ethics* 9, no. 1 (2010): doi:10.1080/15027570903554490.

provide their own definition, while allowing others to do the same. Their definition serves our purpose here as well: "military ethics is part of professional ethics; that understanding the Law of Armed Conflict (the modern codification and instantiation of just war theory) is part of that professional ethic; that history and religion inform and shape military ethics; and that there is a place for exhortation, storytelling, and exemplars."[25]

Even this definition allows much to be grouped under the idea of professional ethics, relegating the other portions of the definition to just war, history, religion, and explanation. The first part of the definition leaves much to be desired and the authors recognize such. While calling military ethics "practical and professional" they also recognize that it is akin to "a large jigsaw puzzle where many different and unequally-shaped pieces make up the whole. Sometimes an odd-looking piece may come our way, which [possibly] helps us see the larger picture…"[26]

Focusing military ethics discussion solely on just war theory, or military actions uncommon to everyday life allows us to separate military ethics from personal ethics, something Cook and Syse did in their definition. Their definition highlights the common discussion over the difference between professional ethics and personal. Much of that discussion revolves around the adjectives – personal or professional – but little of the discussion focuses on the noun – ethics. The military has an ethics problem, but the problem is not in the ethical failures of the professional soldier, sailor, airman, or marine but instead in the general understanding of the very concept of ethics. The modern armed forces must move past the adjective and focus on the noun.

Two articles clearly and simply illustrate the dilemma. In 2013 philosopher Alasdair MacIntyre presented a paper entitled "Military Ethics: A Discipline in Crisis." The next year journalist James Joyner wrote a piece titled "The US Military's Ethics Crisis." From the titles one would think the subject matter

---

[25] Ibid
[26] Ibid

would be the same – military ethics in crisis. Yet, even a cursory read shows the marked difference in how ethics is seen, and understood, by military members and observers.

As a philosopher MacIntyre focused on the traditional moral issues of military ethics – courage as a virtue, the very concept of war, and the relationship between prudence and justice. Weaving in classical just war theory, his own concept of virtue ethics, and a strong understanding of changing social mores and technological capability MacIntyre stays at what we might call a higher level of ethics, focused solely on specific and peculiar military actions.

Joyner has a completely different approach and understanding. His article says nothing about just war theory, combat, or violence. He writes instead of: "massive cheating scandals with Air Force and Navy nuclear officers and Army National Guard recruiters to general and admirals abusing the perks of their office or sending wildly inappropriate emails…have many seeing an ethical crisis in the American armed forces."[27] Joyner is not the only one focusing on the baser human failings and seeing them as an ethical crisis; military leaders have as well and in March 2014 Secretary of Defense Chuck Hagel selected Navy Admiral Margaret Klein as his "senior advisor for military professionalism" with the task to "work directly with the service secretaries and chiefs on the Defense Department's focus on ethics, character and competence in all activities at every level of command with an uncompromising culture of accountability."[28]

Military ethics separated themselves from just war theory long before Admiral Klein was appointed to advise senior military leaders. In the same way that just war theory led to the

---

[27] James Joyner, "The U.S. Military's Ethics Crisis," *The National Interest*, February 13, 2014.

[28] United States, Department of Defense, "Statement by Secretary of Defense Chuck Hagel Announcing His Senior Advisor for Military Professionalism," news release, March 25, 2014, Defense.gov, accessed August 8, 2015.

creation and enforcement of laws of war governing actions of military forces in war, military ethics birthed rules and laws concerning actions and behavior outside of combat. Much of the separation began in the Korean War after North Korea treated prisoners of war very differently than either Germany or Japan had just a decade earlier. This changed social context forced the creation of new resources to help soldiers understand their rights, obligations, and duty when captured.[29] The resulting "Code of Conduct" began the evolution of modern military ethics standards and also began the bifurcation of just war theory and military ethics. Over the next five decades a combination of social change – desegregation, the All-Volunteer Force, women in the military, and the long vilification to current acceptance of homosexuality - and technological change - the Cold War, nuclear weapons, the internet and social media – created a new level of concern for accountability in the personal moral behavior of military members. However, as MacIntyre noted, since it is uncommon for Americans to receive "the kind of early moral training and education that Aristotle and Aquinas take to be a prerequisite for the development of virtues"[30] and militaries are founded on discipline and order the instantiation of military ethics acquired a deontological divine command theory foundation with the United States government assuming the role of the divine. The same challenges which created the divisions within normative ethics created friction and partition within military ethics.

On the surface, divine command theory is a comfortable fit for military ethics. Orders are orders, soldiers do as they are told, and all is well in the world. Yet, changing social norms and Nuremberg's rejection of the "I was just following orders"

---

[29] Troy Daland, "Home," The Military Code of Conduct: a brief history, February 09, 2011, accessed January 16, 2018, http://www.kunsan.af.mil/News/Commentaries/Article/414344/the-military-code-of-conduct-a-brief-history/.

[30] in George R. Lucas, *Routledge Handbook of Military Ethics* (London: Routledge/Taylor & Francis Group, 2015). 5.

defense created a category of "unlawful orders." This schizophrenic idea cleaved military ethics from divine command theory (with government as divine) and placed ethical action back in the realm of individual choice, without replacing or supplanting the foundation of divine command theory. Orders retain the presumption of lawfulness, even as the meaning of "lawful" is debated. A dilemma arises when one is expected to weigh each order in terms of lawfulness, do so instantaneously, and balance each order against another. Because of the complexities of the system of rules and regulations, it is possible to follow each lawful order given but at the same time violate any number of other orders - an issue commonly found within investigations of crimes of command.

Like Jana Vavasseur, it is possible to violate no orders and still face accusations of poor judgment. When this happens, it is less an indication of unethical behavior and more a reflection of the clash between the schools of normative ethics. For the deontologist, following the rules is sufficient regardless of the end result. For the consequentialist the end result is more important than any rule set and violating a rule is permissible. Despite a rule's latitude, acting more conservatively within the rule boundaries is desired if the outcome is foreseeable. Yet no one has precognition and foreseeable outcomes are generally only identified in hindsight. Kirk Lippold in USS *Cole* and Jana Vavasseur in *William P. Lawrence* exemplify the problem.

Some ethicists ascribe to a school of absolutism where "there is hardly a difference between a crime and a mistake, between a felony and a misdemeanor, between the seven deadly sins and the social 'lies' we tell every day."[31] Absolutism is a concept the military sees in its approach to ethics. Admiral Carter opined that the Navy's "predominant approach to ethics is legalistic in content and often negative in tone...At best, we employ a checklist of what not to do, and at worst, ethical

---

[31] Toner

development of our people is a chore or a burden that takes away from getting the job done."[32] How does one reconcile combining the words professional, military, and ethic into a single compound noun?

Recall that Huntington prescribed three aspects to a profession: expertise, responsibility, and corporateness. The military is focused on the application of violence. Ethics involve the search for right way to live, for the resolution between conflicting moral positions. The professional military ethic links the application of violence with conflicting moral positions. The officer must possess and maintain expertise in the management of violence, and expertise in resolving moral dilemmas. The officer will always be faced with competing duties - the responsibility to defend or preserve life, while risking or taking life to do so. The officer acts on behalf of society, and not autonomously or selfishly.[33]

Some seek to separate the military from ethical dilemmas by according military personnel special status. In *Moral Issues in Military Decision Making*, Anthony Hartle insists on a clear and coherent professional military ethic compatible with the America's fundamental societal values, and that the military must have and deserves a "partially differentiated status."[34] In other words, the military has "the right and responsibility to violate an ordinary person's moral restrictions, a role which morally justifies actions that would otherwise be immoral."[35] Hartle gives comfort to the absolutist or consequentialist and excuses the moral dilemma posed by killing.

Huntington, Hartle, and other writers on the professional military ethic also cite a cooperative spirit, an emphasis of group

---

[32] Carter, 5.
[33] Huntington, 14-5.
[34] Anthony E. Hartle, *Moral Issues in Military Decision Making* (Lawrence (Kan.): University Press of Kansas, 2004). 35.
[35] White (1997), 84.

over individual, service to the state, and a hierarchical structure demanding instant and loyal obedience of subordinates.[36] This obedience, combined with the partially differentiated status creates more ethical issues than it absolves. One author summarizes the professional military ethic as one that is "pessimistic, collectivist, historically inclined, power-oriented, nationalistic, militaristic, pacifist, and instrumentalist in its view of the military profession."[37] Huntington would likely disagree, of if he agreed would accept the commentary as positive affirmation rather than criticism. Huntington's model goes so far as to place obedience as the highest of military virtues.

This idea of loyalty as a virtue leads us to the next step. Are loyalty and obedience sufficient virtues for military personnel? Are the two even virtues? Are there differences between officer and enlisted personnel? Are commanding officers separate from other officers?

Loyalty is important, but is it loyalty to the organization or loyalty to the superior? Recall that Secretary of the Navy Matthews called Admiral Dennison disloyal for simply visiting the fired Chief of Naval Operations, Louis Denfeld.[38] John Lehman, Secretary of the Navy from 1981 to 1987 reportedly said "Loyalty is agreeing with me."[39] Are officers who protect the Navy from airing dirty laundry loyal to the institution, or disloyal to the country?[40] There is some evidence that senior officers protect each other to the detriment of the overall organization, seeing the admiralship as a fraternity.[41]

If ethics is not just about establishing and following moral rules but about what to do in the right place at the right time, then is the Navy's legalistic approach to ethics the correct one? If one may act unethically by following the rules or being

---

[36] Ibid, 77-8.
[37] Ibid, 77.
[38] Dittmer, 162-3.
[39] Vistica, 15.
[40] Ibid
[41] Ibid, 26.

loyal, then is a rule-based ethics appropriate? Is focusing on the consequences of actions, teleological or consequentialist ethics, more appropriate for organizations who manage violence? If those were the only two possible schools of ethics, we would certainly face a dilemma. However, there is another option. Virtue ethics is not concerned with *doing things* so much as with *becoming someone*; the emphasis on being rather than doing.[42] By being good, one inherently does good. One does not solely depend on rules to direct or constrain goodness.

In addressing virtue ethics, we must address virtue. Virtue theorists generally take a broad view and include virtues encompassing physical, intellectual, aesthetic, and moral aspects.[43] Some virtue theorists seek to appeal to or appease deontologists by creating lists of virtues. Lists of virtues are commonplace, almost legion. Aristotle provided a list, as did Benjamin Franklin. After the 1898 Battle of Manila Bay, Navy Admiral George Dewey attributed the victory to the virtue of foresightedness, writing that "It was the ceaseless routine of hard work and preparation in time of peace that won Manila....Valor there must be, but it is a secondary factor in comparison with strength of material and efficiency of administration."[45] In

Table 1. Cardinal Virtues and Deadly Sins[44]

Virtue	Sin
Faith	Greed
Hope	Anger
Charity	Lust
Fortitude	Sloth
Justice	Envy
Prudence	Pride
Temperance	Gluttony

---

[42] Toner
[43] Hart, 132.
[44] Ibid, 137.
[45] "George Dewey: Virtues of an "Ordinary" Naval Officer," *Naval History*

the twentieth century notable virtue lists come from statesman-scholar Sir Harold Nicolson and former Secretary of Education William Bennett.[46] In general, however, the lists normally derive from or default to seven cardinal virtues, contrasted with seven deadly sins (table 1.). What all these lists have in common is a shared theological and philosophical heritage.[47]

Virtue ethics, by design, does not provide a clear and explicit answer to any questions. A pure virtue ethicist will see any list as advisory in nature. What virtue ethics does provide is a frame of reference to discuss the questions of ethics and morality. And any real exploration or instantiation of virtue ethics requires more than three virtues. The Navy's articulated core values - honor, courage, and commitment - are simply not enough. However, prescribing specific virtues is also insufficient. Each rational individual derives his own golden mean, her own ethical principles. Each develops strength in virtue. As each individual becomes more virtuous, we all become more virtuous.

This concept, that as each individual becomes more virtuous, we all become more virtuous, is the core of virtue ethics. Virtue ethicist Alasdair MacIntyre, who wrote on the crisis in military ethics, provides a path and rationale for virtue ethics in his book *Dependent Rational Animals*. We are dependent on each other and need help when disabled, either permanently or temporarily. We need different resources at different times and different circumstances.[48] We may stray from practical reasoning, the core of maturity, because of either intellectual or moral error. To protect ourselves from error, or

---

Blog, January 23, 2011, accessed January 17, 2018, http://www.navalhistory.org/2011/01/23/george-dewey-virtues-of-an-ordinary-naval-officer.
[46] Toner
[47] Toner
[48] Alasdair C. MacIntyre, *Dependent Rational Animals: Why Human Beings Need the Virtues* (Chicago, IL: Open Court, 1999). 99.

recover or repent from that error, we need friendship and collegiality.[49]

MacIntyre writes that in "developing some range of intellectual and moral virtues we cannot first achieve and then continue in the exercise of practical reasoning."[50] This statement is either in marked contrast or fully in concert with his earlier recognition that most Americans do not receive the moral education and training to properly develop virtues. MacIntyre further attributes this failure to develop virtues with the inability of parents to properly educate or demonstrate virtue.[51] Military leaders, supervisors and role models fill the same ethical education mode and model as parents. If military leaders cannot inculcate virtue in others then those subordinates fail "to acquire an adequate sense of oneself as an independent person with one's own unity as an agent."[52] While we are dependent on others for assistance in creating and maintaining virtuous lives, too great a dependence leads to an inability to act as our own person – which has deleterious effects for adults in general and disastrous impact when manifested in military leaders. It is one thing for a child to look at a parent for reassurance or affirmation – something entirely different when one adult consistently relies on another for affirmation.

If there is one area where modern technology inhibits military leadership and the exercise of virtue, it is being one's own agent, of acting autonomously. Before radio was invented ship captains received orders which were necessarily general and vague. Even after radio the speed of transmission was such that orders were more in the form of guidelines than specific instructions of who, what, where, when, why and how. Today, orders are not just more detailed, but can be instantaneously changed and changed again – to the point that an admiral can pull a string and control his puppet ship half a world away and

---

[49] Ibid, 128.
[50] Ibid, 128.
[51] Ibid, 117.
[52] Ibid, 113.

do it now, now, now. Or, the officer in charge of a ship in port, rather than act to handle a situation well within the officer's ability and authority can call the commanding officer and ask "what do I do?" rather than report "this is what I did." Often the question supplants the statement out of a fear that making an error will result in a reprimand, or a bad fitness report and end that officer's career. While acting unless otherwise directed is a core part of naval culture, it is one that has faded in recent decades.

Aristotle, when first proposing virtue, suggested that character improved by acquiring virtuous skills. Man is not born with virtue, Aristotle argued, but is created by nature to receive virtue through education, example, and practice. The natural tendencies of youth - erratic, aggressive, and impatient behavior - can through the practice of virtue, turn instead into a life of maturity, modesty, and wisdom.[53] The practice of virtue also might temper man's penchant for wicked, weak, or irrational behavior.

The United States already has a legal requirement for commanders to practice virtuous behavior. Article 5947 in Title 10 of the U.S. Code, titled "Requirements of Exemplary Conduct," requires all commanding officers and others in authority to exhibit a good example of "virtue, honor, patriotism, and subordination; to take all necessary and proper measures to promote and safeguard the general welfare of persons under their command or charge; and to be vigilant in inspecting the conduct of those persons and to correct them when necessary."[54] If virtue exists in law, and has for over five decades, why are there still ethical problems?

Every high school student who studies Hamlet knows that pride can easily turn into hubris. Likewise, each virtue can be expanded or twisted into a vice; what is virtuous becomes

---

[53] White (1997), 52.
[54] 10 U.S.C § 5947

vicious.[55] As pride becomes hubris, justice becomes merciless, fortitude forces acceptance of sleep deprivation, and temperance leads to austerity. Over time changes in language or action can change a virtue into a vice, or a vice to a virtue.

One problem lies in culture. As mentioned with alcohol use, while temperance movements existed for more than a century it wasn't until the 1980s that they gained popular cultural sway. Even the Prohibition movement did little to change the cultural acceptance of alcohol the way Mothers Against Drunk Driving and the crackdown on driving while under the influence did. The competing ideals of individual self-reliance and collectivist team spirit create a core dilemma that shows itself in other areas.

To begin with, there is a tendency towards moral relativism where the ends justify, excuse, or rationalize the means. If a bad decision leads to an acceptable result, then the decision wasn't bad - it was just risky. Loyalty leads to a demand for, and acceptance of, blind obedience. Successful young people are recruited to the service and that same drive promotes careerism. Careerism begets a zero-defects attitude that rewards the absence of failure over all else.[56] Ethics is reduced to "a remembrance of a childhood morality learned at home and in the school-yard."[57] In time, norms deviate and that deviance becomes the norm.

Identifying the trend was the intent when in 1993 Democratic politician and sociologist Daniel Patrick Moynihan wrote "Defining Deviancy Down" writing that "by defining what is deviant, we are enabled to know what is not, and hence to live by shared standards."[58] In an essay gathering diverse elements, Moynihan maintained that American society was accepting behavior once considered deviant, and that deviance

---

[55] Toner
[56] White (1997), 642-3.
[57] Hart, 132.
[58] Daniel P. Moynihan, "Defining Deviancy Down," *American Educator*, Winter 1993/1994. 10.

was no longer understood. To some degree this was an acceptance of people as people. In others it was an outgrowth of the anything-goes ideas of the 1970s and 1980s. As Moynihan wrote "we have been redefining deviancy so as to exempt much conduct previously stigmatized, and also quietly raising the 'normal' level in categories where behavior is now abnormal by any earlier standard."[59] While Moynihan never mentioned the Navy, a slow normalization of social deviance occurred throughout the 1960s, 70s, and 1980s, culminating in the excesses of Tailhook.

The Vietnam War and long deployments to the Pacific began the trend. Impoverished Filipinos who would do literally anything for money made the naval base at Subic Bay the Navy's best kept secret.[60] Any manner of sexual fetish, menial labor, or drunken debauchery was not only accepted, but expected and encouraged. Presaging the modern Las Vegas advertising campaign, commanding officers told their crews that "what happens on deployment, stays on deployment."[61] The Navy's acceptance of moral deviance created significant social problems and exacerbated an already wide disparity between men and women.[62] Men became stereotypes of masculinity; women, stereotypes of sexual playthings.

One admiral who received good fortune when suffering his own crime of command later repeatedly doled out harsh punishment to others who failed. His actions ranged from raging over a soggy sandwich to using his own car to chase down a speeder on a military base. In the meantime, he also exerted undue command influence in pressuring subordinate commanders to punish lower ranking officers.[63] Other admirals

---

[59] Ibid, 11.
[60] Vistica, 243.
[61] Ibid, 244.
[62] Ibid, 245.
[63] Ibid, 364-5.

had no issue with repeatedly using foul language, making lewd jokes, berating their subordinates, or even physically assaulting them. These attitudes extended into all ranks even as those senior officers insisted that officers, and commanding officers, exhibited and were held to a "higher standard."[64]

This twisted virtue led to arrogance which in turn created a culture of "bending of rules and regulations to an art form."[65] It is not surprising that a byproduct of this attitude was the breakdown of honesty and integrity within the officer ranks, especially at the more senior levels. Intentionally ignoring misdeeds and rule-bending became almost as ingrained as the morning reveille. In the starkest terms - moral corruption had taken hold in the system.

The issues affected administration as well. Secretary of the Navy John Lehman repeatedly altered promotion board results using an exceptionally broad interpretation of law.[66] He pressed hard to expand what is now his legacy - the 600-ship Navy - but did so knowing that the increased ship numbers would later cripple Navy budgets.[67] Leaders used every tool in their arsenal to stifle dissent, even co-opting psychiatric evaluations to silence critics. Eventually Congress was forced to pass legislation outlawing the practice.[68]

Clearly, bad or even evil leaders can abuse otherwise virtuous individuals through deception.[69] Organizations can also hinder autonomous action. The 1960s Milgram Experiments, where subjects routinely shocked others because they were prompted to - delivering pain for no other reason than to reinforce an error. In 1974 the researcher behind the experiments, Stanley Milgram, provided his theory of obedience
    . . . the virtues of loyalty, discipline, and self-sacrifice

---

[64] Ibid, 81-2, 89, 116, 135, 194, 366.
[65] Ibid, 415.
[66] Ibid, 247.
[67] Ibid, 416.
[68] Ibid, 420.
[69] Hart, 141.

that we value so highly in the individual are the very properties that create destructive organizational engines of war and bind men to malevolent systems of authority. Each individual possesses a conscience which to a greater or lesser degree serves to restrain the unimpeded flow of impulses destructive to others. But when he merges his person into an organizational structure, a new creature replaces autonomous man, unhindered by the limitations of individual morality, freed of humane inhibition, mindful only of the sanctions of authority.[70]

Virtue ethics is based on the moral obligation to transcend one's own self-interest.[71] Researchers like Milgram and behavior of leaders like Lehman show that Aristotle's ideas may be more malleable than he thought. Integrity and good character are important, but individual situational factors also have great influence on actual behavior.[72]

One undiscussed aspect of virtue lies in corrective behavior, in virtuous punishment or discipline. Yes, punishment can, and should, be virtuous otherwise it is simply revenge or retribution, diminishing all. Ideally, as each individual establishes a personal moral standard, the personal concept of good, that individual will also recognize personal bad behavior and act to atone. Understanding where to go with virtue ethics, how to move from the current legalistic ethics regime, requires understanding how Americans, military personnel, and naval personnel respond to sins or mistakes.

There is a distinction between sin and mistake, a distinction sometimes forgotten. Mistakes are inadvertent wrongs. Mistakes are unintentional. Sins are a deliberate choice to commit wrong. Mistakes should be forgiven, sins might be forgiven. Conflating the two leads to misunderstanding and a

---

[70] Stanley Milgram, "Obedience to Authority," *Rain*, no. 3 (1974): doi:10.2307/3032069.
[71] Hart, 133.
[72] Carter, 7.

loss of virtue. Understanding their difference requires an understanding of culture.

Culture, the historically derived and socially transmitted ideas, practices, artifacts, and institutions are products of past action and influence future action.[73] Culture determines how we think and feel about sins and mistakes - our own or someone else's. A number of empirical psychological studies support the idea that different cultures differently measure, value and treat sins, mistakes, shame, and guilt.[74]

Individuals experience shame or guilt after violating standards or norms. Shame arises from group condemnation; guilt from self-condemnation. Feeling shame is generally negative, feeling guilt may be positive.[75] A 2007 study by Tsai and Wong asserted that shame and guilt differ between cultures promoting differing views of the self.[76] They began by establishing that "shame" and "guilt" are "feelings associated with being negatively evaluated (either by the self or others) because one has failed to meet standards and norms regarding what is good, right, appropriate, and desirable."[77]

The idea of shame and guilt cultures began with Ruth Benedict's pre-World War II writings on Japanese culture in *The Chrysanthemum and the Sword*. She proposed that Japan, as a collectivistic culture, focused both self and society on shame, while the United States, as a society based on individuality and moral standards, was a culture which focused on guilt. In a guilt culture, sinners can seek relief though confession, an open admission of wrongdoing and request for absolution. In shame

---

[73] Wong, Y., & Tsai, J. (2007). Cultural models of shame and guilt. In Jessica L. Tracy, Richard W. Robins, and June Price. Tangney, *The Self-Conscious Emotions: Theory and Research* (New York: Guilford, 2008). 210.
[74] Ibid, 209.
[75] Ibid, 211.
[76] Ibid, 209.
[77] Ibid, 210.

cultures confession does not bring relief; confession only leads to trouble. In a shame culture, public acknowledgement of wrongdoing is shameful. Shame cultures seek good luck, guilt cultures seek atonement.[78] For Japanese culture, ritualized suicide was the only way to expiate shame.

Shame arises from failure to meet one's duty or obligations. In shame cultures each individual has a specific place, specific obligations and expectations. Shame cultures are collectivist and the group is most important. Shame comes from the group, not from self. Self-respect comes from doing what is expected, not necessarily what is good.[79] Shame cultures rely on external sanction where guilt cultures rely on internal conviction.

Guilt arises from not meeting personal, internal morality; from violating one's conscience. Where feelings of shame are external, feelings of guilt are internal and do not need external validation. Guilt cultures emphasize atonement, punishment and forgiveness to restore personal moral order. Shame cultures stress humility and self-denial to restore social order.[80]

In the United States the early Puritans based their morality on guilt. Americans have finely developed consciences. Significant research has demonstrated a U.S. culture of an independent self.[81] Despite this, shame is also a function of American society and we are unequally torn between shame and guilt, with guilt the heavy weight on the fulcrum. American society uses shame, but it is not intrinsic to our nature. Shame is not fundamental to American morality.[82]

Return to the opening questions of this study: *Why does*

---

[78] Ruth Benedict, *The Chrysanthemum and the Sword* (London: Secker & Warburg, 1947). 222.
[79] Paul G. Hiebert, *Anthropological Insights for Missionaries* (Grand Rapids, MI: Baker Book House, 2006). 212.
[80] Ibid, 213.
[81] Wong and Tsai, 211.
[82] Benedict, 223.

the Navy remove commanding officers? Then move to the individual commander. A commander who thinks "I can't believe ***I*** ran the ship aground" experiences shame. The commander who thinks "I can't believe I ***ran the ship aground***" experiences guilt. Shame, while externally sanctioned goes against the individual failure. Guilt accrues from the external action.[83] Since individual commanders internalize guilt and shame, their experience with both influences how they later act when a subordinate commits a crime of command.

Wong and Tsai found that between the "dominant models of shame and guilt, guilt leads to reparative action, whereas shame does not." They found that in the United States experiencing guilt led to higher self-esteem, increased empathy and perspective. Shame oriented individuals were more likely to withdraw and avoid others, to experience inward anger and blame others.[84] However, individuals who more identified with groups were less likely to distinguish between shame and guilt than those who were more independent in their self-orientation.[85] Wong and Tsai never discussed military personnel, however when using Huntington's professional military ethic of a collectivist and team oriented profession, military personnel fit the former group, the group incapable of properly distinguishing between shame and guilt. Military personnel may make up a shame subculture within an overall American guilt culture. This is problematic as Western culture views shame as the "bad" moral emotion and guilt as the "good." Wong and Tsai found that some cross-cultural studies suggest that shame may have better and more adaptive consequences in collectivistic contexts[86] but they also predicted variation within cultural contexts as a result of different visions of the self.[87]

If shame is the dominant emotion for a collectivist

---

[83] Wong and Tsai, 210.
[84] Ibid, 211.
[85] Ibid, 212.
[86] Ibid, 216.
[87] Ibid, 218.

military society, and keeping shame secret and hidden precludes atonement, then virtue ethics based on doing good rather than hiding bad is indispensable. Furthermore, sin and mistakes may produce either guilt or shame, but the difference between guilt and shame lies in knowledge. The ignorant cannot sin, the knowledgeable are less likely to make mistakes. When deviance is normalized the individual does not know the difference between 'what is' and 'what ought' - especially when what 'is' has worked so well. How then can sin be differentiated from mistake? Should all mistakes be punished as sins?

For an act to be moral, we must consider the end, the means, and the circumstances[88] in their entirety - and this includes when acting to discipline someone for failure. In fact, acting morally in correcting failure may be more important than the moral failure being addressed. Shame, and guilt are considered "moral" emotions,[89] establishing the linkage with virtue ethics. Before one can feel shame or guilt one must have a concept of morality and a development of individual self that recognizes transgressions against either society or a personal moral code.[90] Where ethics is "figuring out the right way to do the right thing in a particular circumstance, with a particular person, at a particular time"[91] the theory of moral development explores the corollary question: *How does one decide what is right and what is wrong?*[92]

Moral development theory traces its roots to Swiss psychologist Jean Piaget and his 1932 book, *The Moral Judgment of the Child*. Piaget studied children and adolescents throughout his five-decade long career and advanced, and refined, a theory of cognitive development. In this theory, Piaget

---

[88] Toner
[89] Wong and Tsai, 210.
[90] Ibid
[91] Schwartz Sharpe, 5-6.
[92] White (1997), 46.

advanced the idea that children develop their own moral worldview from experience and reflection, not necessarily from direct teaching. Piaget established four stages of development - the sensorimotor (birth to age two), the preoperational (age two to seven), the concrete operational (age seven to eleven) and the formal operational (age eleven and onward).[93]

Modern child psychology springs from Piaget's work. Likewise, developmental psychology derives from child psychology in the same way that adults derive from children. Developmental stages support the overall concept of ethical individualism which in turn serves as a framework for personal behavior and social interaction.[94] For Americans, especially those ascribing to concepts of individualism, moral virtues arise from man's autonomy, the individual who acts based on choice and purpose.[95] Knowing one's personal identity means acknowledging who one is and what one wants to do in life; identity allows formation of goals, values, and beliefs.[96] The linkage between self-identity and ethical individualism leading to the development of moral judgment is the subject of psychologist Lawrence Kohlberg.[97] His work on moral development is foundational in understanding the linkage between self and virtue.

Kohlberg built his work on Piaget's early writings and also on another leader in developmental psychology, Erik Erikson, who expanded Piaget's four stages into eight. Erikson proposed that "as individuals advance they become more secure in their understanding of themselves, knowledgeable about their

---

[93] Jean Piaget, *The Moral Judgement of the Child* (New York: Harcourt, Brace and Company, 2013).
[94] Waterman, A. S. (1988) "Psychological Individualism and Organizational Functioning: A Cost-benefit Analysis" by Konstantin Kolenda, in *Organizations and Ethical Individualism* (New York: Praeger, 1988). 25.
[95] Gortner, 518.
[96] Waterman, 25.
[97] Ibid, 31.

values and analytic skills, and, therefore, sophisticated in dealing with the complexities surrounding ethical dilemmas."[98]

Lawrence Kohlberg focused on the development of moral maturity and proposed six stages of development related to understanding and handling ethical issues. At the lowest level, individuals are self-centered and amoral, focused on not being caught and punished. As individuals advance their values and moral decisions are more influenced by those around them. The highest stage of development consists of individuals who develop personal moral standards and principles, applying them in a universalistic manner.[99]

One challenge with Kohlberg is that his theory developed and changed over time. Some of his early writings conflict with later ones.[100] His theory, even though sound and paradigmatic, remains a theory, or methodology, to observe normative ethics and allows the observer to distinguish between moral progress and moral change. Kohlberg's work draws power from its interdisciplinary approach combining philosophy, psychology, education, political science, and other disciplines into his theory of moral development.[101] Kohlberg defined development as the "direct internalization of external cultural norms" where the individual "is trained to...conform to societal rules and values."[102]

Kohlberg developed three levels and six stages, or three levels of two stages each.[103] Preconventional is the first level wherein a child responds to rules and labels, but interprets them in relation to physical satisfaction or punishment. Within this level is Stage 1, where there is no underlying morality, simply

---

[98] Gortner, 511.
[99] Gortner, 511-2.
[100] James R. Rest et al., "A Neo-Kohlbergian Approach to Morality Research," *Journal of Moral Education* 29, no. 4 (2000): 382.
[101] White (1997), 51.
[102] Lawrence Kohlberg, *Stages of Moral Development as a Basis for Moral Education* (Cambridge, MA: Center for Moral Education, Harvard University, 1971). 30.
[103] Ibid, 86-92

selfish pleasure or avoidance of harm. In Stage 2 motivation continues to flow from avoiding punishment, but a nascent conscience recognizes concepts of fairness, sharing, and reciprocity but overall the individual remains focused on reward and punishment for decision making. Level II, the conventional level, supports maintaining what is expected, similar to the collectivist cultures. "Good behavior" is that which pleases the larger group - be it family, church, or other social collective. Conformity is central to this level. At Stage 3 social sharing and community value determine actions, actions are done to preclude disapproval rather than for reward or to avoid punishment. Stage 4 moves the orientation from family or community and towards authority, fixed rules, and larger social order. The right thing is that which derives from doing one's duty, respecting authority, and maintaining the social order.

Most military personnel fit within Level II, Stages 3 or 4. Rules are clear cut, group approval is desired, and authority is respected. Divine command theory, Rickover's actions towards subordinates, and the culture Chatham wrote about fit well within Level

II. The conventional level does not support higher order moral action. Following the rules does not in and of itself equate to moral behavior. While Rickover created Level II organizations, he did not operate at that level. In Level III, the postconventional level, the individual with a clear sense of self works to define moral values and principles at a personal level, separate from the group – as Rickover did when he studied after taps. Stage 5 is focused on respecting individual and general rights within a societal framework. Stage 5 accepts legal authority, but also seeks to change unjust laws. Stage 5 is the core basis or ideals of American morality, while individuals at Stages 3 and 4 are the core actors.[104] For example, during the Civil Rights movement, southern states and segregationists were

---

[104] Dan Simmons, *Carrion Comfort* (London: Quercus, 2010). 365-6

in Stages 3 and 4 while the marchers and their supporters were in Stage 5. Kohlberg found that only a minority reach Stage 4 by age 18. Fewer than 20% ever enter the postconventional level.[105]

Stage 6 is an aspirational stage. Kohlberg believed that only a few might ever attain Stage 6.[106] In Stage 6 the moral value of human life is separate and distinguished from rights. Principles are more abstract, like the Golden Rule, rather than concrete and specific, like the Ten Commandments. It is important to note that Kohlberg does not determine the morality or worth of individuals. Instead he sought to understand the mental processes in handling moral dilemmas.[107] He organized and defined moral

judgment according to how an individual reasons, not according to what the individual thinks.[108]

Kohlberg did believe that the stages were ordered and sequential. His research focused on ways of thinking rather than specific attitudes about specific situations. He also recognized that stages were not all inclusive and that

any individual is usually not entirely at one stage. Typically, as children develop they are partly in their major stage (about 50 percent of their ideas), partly in the stage into which they are moving, and partly in the stage they have just left behind. Seldom, however, do they use stages at developmental stages removed from one another.[109]

In 1995, psychologist Peter Langford wrote that the distinction between autonomy and heteronomy, between the conventional and postconventional levels, is far more complicated than Kohlberg theorized. Langford provided nine

---

[105] White (1997), 56.
[106] Ibid, 57.
[107] Ibid, 52.
[108] Ibid, 51.
[109] Kohlberg, 38.

ways to analyze the differences between heteronomous and autonomous individuals including freedom, mutual respect, reversability, constructivism, hierarchy, intrinsicalness, prescriptivity, universality, and choice. Table 2 provides more detail on Langford's ideas.[110] While some may see Langford as refuting Kohlberg, when using Langford's nine measures to examine the differences between Stages 3, 4, and 5, Kohlberg's ideas become richer.

Both Kohlberg and Piaget recognized autonomy as an important factor in developing moral judgment. Consistent with Kohlberg's logic, autonomy is a cognitive distinction indicating the ability of self-examination, individual reflection, and mental independence.[111] Exercising moral autonomy transcends rule following and rests instead with which rules to follow. For a decision to be moral, it must be free of coercion and done for moral reasons.[112] Whether rule following is voluntary or coerced, autonomous or heteronomous, is often a product of organizational design. Many studies in the past fifty years link organizational structure, ethical behavior, and moral development.[113] Echoing Admiral Carter's writing on rules-based ethics, Richard D. White wrote in 1997 that many organizations "identify and manage ethical behavior in a negative sense — when a member violates minimum ethical standards, sanctions are employed."[114]

---

[110] Peter E. Langford, *Approaches to the Development of Moral Reasoning* (Psychology Press, 2015). 107-8.
[111] White (1997), 111.
[112] Anthony C. Pfaff, "Five Myths about Military Ethics," *Parameters*, September 22, 2016. 68.
[113] White (1997), 6.
[114] Ibid, 7.

Table 2. Langford's distinctions between autonomous and heteronomous behavior

	Heteronomous	**Autonomous**
Freedom	reference to authority, law, and tradition	Law and authority inform rather than determine
Mutual Respect	Law and authority override mutual respect	show respect for cooperation between equals in coming to fair and just decisions
Reversibility	Law and authority provide only point of view	include differing points of view of all those involved
Constructivism	sacred, rigid, and inflexible view of rules and laws	Rules and laws are flexible formulations of the human mind designed for cooperation among equals.
Hierarchy	involve nonmoral and pragmatic considerations in thinking about a dilemma	clear preference for moral values and prescriptive duties
Intrinsicalness	People are a means to an end	People are ends in themselves
Prescriptivity	reflects an instrumental or hypothetical view of moral duty	Moral duty is binding regardless of inclinations of the actor or pragmatic considerations.
Universality	not explicit or universalized	Ethical concepts are universal
Choice	more likely to make dilemma choices that accord with Kohlberg's preconventional or conventional level	make choices that accord with the postconventional level

White's practical study supports the idea that a rigidly hierarchical organization contributes to unethical and immoral behavior of its members. White compared the moral development of military members with individuals in less-rigid organizations finding that "military members assigned to ships, where organizational hierarchy is most rigid, to be significantly lower than members assigned to less-rigid shore units."[115] In his study he wrote that:

> An example of a military hierarchy that severely restricts individual autonomy is a naval warship. Almost all decisions on board a warship are covered by a legalistic and comprehensive set of regulations, rules and standing orders, and the few discretionary actions are reserved only for the officers at the apex of the command pyramid. While such a rigid hierarchy leaves little room for error, there is also little room for autonomous behavior by the majority of the warship's crew. In *The Caine Mutiny*, Herman Wouk (1951) describes the rigid, legalistic and dehumanizing design of a naval warship. Through the eyes of a fictitious officer, Wouk's description of the naval organization provides little leeway for autonomy,[116]
> 'Whether it's the fragment of coding, the fragment of engineering, the fragment of gunnery — you'll find them all predigested and regulated to a point where you'd have to search the insane asylums to find people who could muff the jobs. Remember that one point. It explains and reconciles you to all the Navy Regulations, and all the required reports, and all the emphasis on memory and obedience, and all the standardized ways of doing things. The Navy is a

---

[115] Richard D. White, Jr., "Military Ethics," in *Handbook of Administrative Ethics*, ed. Terry L. Cooper, 2nd ed. (New York, NY: Dekker, 2001). 642.
[116] White (1997), 84.

master plan designed by geniuses for execution by idiots. If you're not an idiot, but find yourself in the Navy, you can only operate well by pretending to be one.'[117]

White determined that the "military profession must be organized in a hierarchy of obedience"[118] with "no opportunity for individual, autonomous behavior."[119] He mused "Incidents of sexual misconduct, discrimination, brutality and other immoral and amoral acts are not new or unique in the military. In fact, the research findings lead one to wonder why there are not *more* incidents of this type."[120] Presciently he also wrote that an "increased number of unethical incidents will occur in the area of sexual relations until [a gender-neutral organization] 'paradigm shift' is completed."[121]

Guilt and shame show their distinctions within both Kohlberg's and Langford's theories. Shame resides in the heteronomous Stage 3 or Stage 4 individual, while guilt tends towards the autonomous Stage 5. Ruth Benedict, writing decades before Kohlberg and Langford, predicted their theories when she wrote of the autonomous individualistic cultures that:

> The American assumption is that a man, having sized up what is possible in his personal life, will discipline himself, if that is necessary, to attain a chosen goal. Whether he does or not, depends on his ambition, or his conscience, or his 'instinct of workmanship,' as Veblen called it. He may adopt a Stoic regime in order to play on a football team, or give up all relaxations to train himself as a musician, or to make a success of his

---

[117] Herman Wouk, *The Caine Mutiny, a novel of World War II* (Garden City, NY: Doubleday, 1951). in White (1997). 84.
[118] White (1997), 78.
[119] Ibid, 78.
[120] Ibid, 167.
[121] Ibid, 167-8.

business. He may eschew evil and frivolity because of his conscience.[122]

In relation to the collectivist Japanese culture she wrote:
The Japanese assumption, however, is that a boy taking his middle-school examinations, or a man playing in a fencing match, or a person merely living the life of an aristocrat, needs a self-training quite apart from learning the specific things that will be required of him when he is tested....he needs to lay aside his books and his sword and his public appearances and undergo a special kind of training...Japanese of all classes judge themselves and others in terms of a whole set of concepts which depend upon their notion of generalized technical self-control and self-governance. Their concepts of self-discipline can be schematically divided into those which give competence and those which give something more. This something more I shall call expertness.[123]

If one replaces "American" with "individualist" or "civilian" and "Japanese" with "collectivist" or "military" we begin to see the moral development challenge for military personnel. If the majority of military personnel never rise above Stage 3, and few attain Stage 5 how can military personnel, even in Stage 4, determine what is right or wrong when rules are not comprehensive?[124]

First, and most importantly, we must recognize that not all military members can, or should, reach Stage 5 autonomy. Theorists insisting on rigid hierarchy and obedience, even when speaking in absolutes, also tend to think in generalities, conflating commanders with troops. Arleigh Burke repeatedly remarked that "a commander who fails to exceed his authority is not of much use to his subordinates." That concept speaks to autonomy, to consciously choosing which rules to follow but

---

[122] Benedict, 228.
[123] Ibid
[124] Toner

doing so in benefit of others and not oneself. Arleigh Burke was a product of a rigid military hierarchy, was a ship captain, and Chief of Naval Operations. At some point, military leaders must rise above Stage 3 and Stage 4, must lift themselves from heteronomy to autonomy; but woe is the autonomous leader who works for an adherent of heteronomous action.

How can the Navy engender more moral behavior? When groups make changes they tend to do so without thought. They improvise, guess, or make multiple changes without ascribing to either the scientific method or even simple patience. More specifically, psychologist Barry Schwartz wrote that we tend to use two tools: "a set of rules and administrative oversight mechanisms that tell people what to do and monitor their performance to make sure they are doing it…[and a] set of incentives that encourage good performance by rewarding people for it."[125] Rules, oversight, and incentives assume heteronomy and preclude autonomy. Schwartz goes on, saying that rules and incentives are insufficient and provides an alternative idea he calls "practical wisdom."[126] Practical wisdom builds on the same Aristotelian ideals Alasdair MacIntyre used in discussing virtue ethics.

Both agree and ethicists, philosophers, and psychologists support them on more than a few things. First, the quest for virtue is lifelong and "that happiness comes from learning to love the processes of a virtuous life rather than the chimera of achievement."[127] Second, that humans evolved as free beings, hence all moral actions must be free of coercion,[128] for doing good under threat only tells us that an individual is coerced through fear.[129] Therefore all journeys towards virtue must be

---

[125] Schwartz and Sharpe, 4.
[126] Ibid, 5.
[127] Hart, 139-40.
[128] Ibid, 140.
[129] Ibid

autonomous; they must reject determinism and compulsion - theological, cultural, or political.[130] Compelled virtue is not virtue. Finally, virtue must be pervasive. Leaders must act with virtue and ensure virtue undergirds the organization. Stage 5 autonomous individuals who feel compelled to create rules for Stage 3 and Stage 4 heteronomous followers should still act from virtue and not control.[131] In doing so, there are two areas which the Navy can adopt to enhance virtue - education and forgiveness. These ideas are not without challenge.

Seeking virtue is a lifelong quest. Movement from Stage 3 or 4 to Stage 5 is not simple, easy, common, or automatic. Development cannot rely on poorly remembered lessons from childhood. The basic tools of shared values and shared identity within the Navy are there, but they must be built and reinforced[132] similar to the way Rickover reinforced nuclear education. What should differ is how they are reinforced; the how is important. If done with virtue in mind, then the reinforcement will beget virtue. If the reinforcement or virtues are compelled, then the best result is compliance; the worst is malicious compliance. In order to be virtuous, the education and reinforcement must be well thought out. Kohlberg challenged the concept of moral education, citing the existence of a "hidden curriculum" where educators "engaged in moral education without explicitly and philosophically discussing or formulating its goals and methods." On the face of it, engaging in moral education without thinking about its goals and methods seems as dubious as it would be in intellectual education."[133]

Reinforcing values, and developing higher levels of moral development also requires one to constantly challenge current values and beliefs. Challenging the status quo is inherently non-heteronomous, non-collectivist, non-military. That challenge, however, does not always lead to change. When

---

[130] Ibid
[131] Ibid, 141.
[132] Carter, 5.
[133] Kohlberg, 29.

the values and virtues are correct and appropriate, the challenge will reinforce them. Where change is identified, then the change is necessary. Without constant challenge and an openness to new ideas, there is a risk that values and virtues will devolve to nothing more than personal biases.[134] Even heteronomous individuals will ultimately reject values based on nothing more than someone else's biases.

White's study of military hierarchy provided clear, and achievable, recommendations. First, he advocated continued civilian control of the military, to regulate the rigid hierarchy via external democratic processes by balancing the lower moral development with that of a higher development. Second, an increase in education, especially for higher ranking officers. He found that education is "the most significant determinant of moral reasoning and is also the most effective way of ensuring that senior military officials are in step with societal moral values." Moral education would "complement a leader's professional expertise with an increased ability to react to difficult moral dilemmas...education can help to mediate the conflict between [war-fighting ability and moral development].[135]

White also advocated replacing "blind obedience" with "informed obedience." This idea necessitates explaining orders rather than just expecting instantaneous compliance. Explaining orders, when possible, is shown to enhance subordinate development and increase their later autonomy.[136] The movement towards informed obedience would also give military personnel more opportunity for autonomous action and individual discretion. White recommended a military made up of fewer levels of bureaucracy and to not insulate the military

---

[134] Gortner, 524.
[135] White (1997), 171.
[136] Barry Schwartz, "Practical Wisdom and Organizations," *Research in Organizational Behavior* 31 (2011): doi:10.1016/j.riob.2011.09.001. 12.

from society. His final recommendation is exceptionally relevant to this study, especially in light of his prediction of increased immoral behavior until after a gender-neutral paradigm shift: "top military officials and civilian policymakers should not overreact to moral transgressions by making the hierarchy more rigid than necessary."[137]

While many military personnel eschew education in favor of training directly related to increasing their professional expertise, we know that virtue can be taught and it can be learned. We also know that moral expertise is an important part of professional expertise. Increasing that expertise means moving away from metrics-based education, from purely scientific or technological education, and reintroducing capabilities to evaluate good character.[138] Some of this lies in moving away from complicated rules and towards more general principles.

A 2001 study of successful firefighters found they followed four simple survival guides. The guides were broad principles which allowed the firefighters to have rules of thumb but also allowed opportunities for autonomous behavior and individual initiative. The study concluded "that it is better to minimize the number of rules, give up trying to cover every particular circumstance, and instead do more training to encourage skill at practical reasoning and intuition."[139] A different study of military officers found that junior officers given discretion and flexibility gained experience applying a limited number of guidelines, which in turn taught soldiers how to improvise in dangerous situations.[140]

Part of the education must be more than just ethics. In the same way that Kohlberg's theory is multidisciplinary,

---

[137] White (1997), 173.
[138] Hart, 144.
[139] Schwartz, 10.
[140] Schwartz, 12.

virtuous education must draw from across many disciplines. Individual self-examination, understanding one's own identity, is critical to autonomous virtuous action and crises of identity are likely to recur throughout adult life.[141] Military leaders must be self-aware enough to understand physical, psychological, and mental changes which affect moral development in themselves and others. To do this, military leaders must occasionally doubt themselves, an acquired trait that for some will be difficult to teach, learn, or accept.

While lifelong, the quest for virtue must not be incessant, nor the education periods long. White found that research indirectly suggested that changes in moral judgment may be quick acting, citing intervention studies which concluded that programs designed to stimulate moral judgment should be designed for periods of about 3 to 12 weeks. White then interpolated if moral judgment can improve, so can moral development.[142] By incorporating these programs into existing training and education processes, the military could easily improve the moral development of its senior leaders.

The Navy recognizes an issue with ethics education. The 2014 working paper from the U.S. Naval War College, pointing out the legalistic approach to ethics, also identified a series of other challenges and implications including:

> Navy ethics education and training must address internal motivations for ethical behavior, beyond the application of rules and policy. Comprehending the underlying impetus for ethical behavior and moral choice informs both the approaches to instilling, training, and mentoring on ethical standards as well as the policies and procedures intended to facilitate ethical behavior.[143]

---

[141] Waterman, 26.
[142] White, (1997), 158.
[143] Carter, 8.

Fundamentally, ethics is about choice. The decisions to adhere to core values, adopt prescribed morals, and act in accordance with ethical standards all revolve around personal choice.[144]

Complying with rules and policies is but one – and to some degree, limiting – factor that contributes to ethical decision making. Due attention, therefore, is needed to address the unenforceable domain of human action as well – specifically, discretion and moral judgment.

Tending to the moral development of Sailors such that ethical choices become routine helps establish a culture for Navy ethics, and in essence transforms the unenforceable into "enforceable". [145]

It is important to address poor moral choices early on, so as to be preventative (proactive) in addressing ethics behavior over time.[146]

None of these concepts address either Schwartz's intent to create "institutional practices that nurture practical wisdom"[147] or Kohlberg's concepts of moral development, but they are a start. Practical wisdom is about more than the job or position, but in allowing individuals to understand and internalize organizational aims, sometimes in spite of the official job description.[148]

Ethicists and philosophers from Aristotle on recognize that doing the right thing at the right time in the right way requires more than just knowledge, or facts. No rule or principle guarantees right behavior. Moral leadership requires moral example, which requires practice and moral skill;[149] something as important, if not more so, than technical expertise.[150] The

---

[144] Ibid
[145] Ibid, 9.
[146] Ibid, 10.
[147] Schwartz, 6.
[148] Ibid, 7.
[149] Ibid, 8.
[150] Kohlberg, 41.

institution must do more than educate. Which is why, while honor, courage, and commitment are important virtues, there is one virtue which the Navy, in fact all of society, should embrace. A virtue all too often forgotten about or sacrificed on the altar of accountability: forgiveness.

In the modern world, contrition is more important than forgiveness. The guilty, or even presumed guilty, are expected to apologize for their actions and seek forgiveness. Forgiveness is rarely given absent a meek and clearly repentant request, and coerced repentance defeats the idea of forgiveness. Since so many judicial or administrative decisions focus on the act and accountability without including a component of forgiveness, many transgressors simply choose not to seek forgiveness. Transgressors never demonstrate contrition because doing so is neither accepted nor rewarded, nor makes a difference in how they feel or are treated. Why bare your soul and seek forgiveness if others still treat you the same? There are arguments for contrition and forgiveness, but the perception of why someone might not seek either can be stronger those arguments.

The same problem exists within government. But should it? Can someone be held accountable, even punished, but also forgiven? Certainly. But how can a system do this and why should it? What lessons do they provide others? What virtues do those actions support? What good was achieved by holding the leaders accountable for their decisions? Or was their punishment simply retribution? Does the good derive from the example of their failure?

What if the Navy took a different approach, holding those officers accountable but with appropriate - not career ending - penance and also forgiving them? Many might think that forgiveness is anathema to military organizations, but there are many examples of officers who erred, were given penance, and forgiven. Two of the last three Chiefs of Naval Operations erred as junior officers, errors which they paid for but which were also forgiven.[151] But that is anecdotal, even if compellingly so. What about more scholarly considerations?

Almost a hundred years ago, psychologists Hugh Hartshorne and Mark A. May studied children and gave them the opportunity to lie, steal or cheat; to act selfishly or selflessly. They determined that almost everyone cheats some of the time; that cheating was distributed in a bell curve around a level of moderate cheating. Cheating in one situation did not mean that person would cheat in another. They also found that those who cheat disapproved of cheating as much, or more than, those who did not.[152]

In 2012 psychologist and behavioral economist Dan Ariely presented a compelling case for forgiveness in *The Honest Truth about Dishonesty*. Ariely walks through a series of examples of awkward ethics, like a father telling his son not to steal a pencil from school because the father can bring them home from work, and an experiment involving 30,000 people in which there were 12 people ("big cheaters") who stole a total of $150 and smaller thefts, spread among 18,000 people ("little cheaters") that resulted in a loss of $36,000. Ariely wrote: "the magnitude of dishonesty we most likely see in society is by good people who think they're doing good work, but in fact cheating just a little bit but because there's so many of them, of us, this actually has a tremendous economic impact."[153]

Hartshorne and May showed that people lie and cheat. Ariely's research expanded on this and showed three things – people cheat, people cheat less if they are repeatedly reminded of being good, and people who do cheat need the opportunity to reset themselves – to seek and receive absolution – or they will just keep cheating and increasing the scope of that cheating. This

---

[151] See "Greenert on Second Chances at Prison" TEDx Talk http://www.navy.mil/submit/display.asp?story_id=90265 and Admiral Mike Mullen at https://hbr.org/2012/06/admiral-mike-mullen
[152] Kohlberg, 75.
[153] Dan Ariely, *The (honest) Truth About Dishonesty: How We Lie To Everyone--Especially Ourselves*. RSA transcript. September 14, 2012.

latter idea Ariely refers to as the "what the hell" effect. If someone is already going to hell, why stop cheating?

The idea that once someone has done wrong, and absolution is not an option is also detailed in Dean Ludwig and Clinton Longenecker's "The Bathsheba Effect: The Ethical Failure of Successful Leaders." The idea draws from biblical King David and his seduction of Bathsheba, the arranged murder of her husband Uriah, and God's eventual punishment with the loss of two of David's sons, insurrection and turmoil. Longenecker and Ludwig found that "many of the ethics violations…result from a ready willingness to abandon personal principle – not so much a matter of ethics as of virtue and lack of fortitude and courage."[154] Further, they conclude that "living a balanced life reduces the likelihood of the negatives of success causing you to lose touch with reality."

Temperance, and prudence, are both virtues. As is honesty for we should note that while lust for Bathsheba was the proximate sin, the compounding of that sin by seducing her, arranging her husband's death, and then covering both crimes up were what brought pain to David. Had he been able to confide in a friend, seek counsel, or even seek forgiveness after lusting for or sleeping with Bathsheba he might never have ordered Uriah's death.

The New Testament also tells of forgiveness. During Jesus' travels he was invited to dinner by a Pharisee, Simon. A "sinful woman" met him there and washed Jesus' feet with his tears.

> Then [Jesus] turned toward the woman and said to Simon, "Do you see this woman? I came into your house. You did not give me any water for my feet, but she wet my feet with her tears and wiped them with her hair. You did not give me a kiss, but this woman, from the time I entered, has not stopped kissing my feet. You

---

[154] Dean C. Ludwig and Clinton O. Longenecker, "The Bathsheba Syndrome: The Ethical Failure of Successful Leaders," *Journal of Business Ethics* 12, no. 4 (1993):.

did not put oil on my head, but she has poured perfume on my feet. Therefore, I tell you, her many sins have been forgiven—as her great love has shown. But whoever has been forgiven little loves little."[155]

The relevant moral here is not that Jesus forgave, but rather the great value of forgiveness for great sins.

To move Navy culture, we must differentiate between personal and institutional forgiveness. Personal forgiveness, one person pardoning and absolving another, is what most of us think of as forgiveness. However organizational accountability provides little place or opportunity for institutional forgiveness.

Charles Eliot Loughlin made a mistake, killing thousands of innocent people. Even though he felt neither shame nor guilt, the Navy forgave him. Charles McVay felt both shame and guilt, finally expunging the shame the only way possible. His crew, aided by a teenage boy, fought and won institutional forgiveness.

This pattern repeated itself throughout the 1950s, 1960s, and into the 1970s. While some commanders were not forgiven, many others were. Somewhere in the 1980s the Navy lost its understanding of forgiveness. Much of that comes from the scientific approaches brought into Navy culture by Hyman Rickover.

At least one biographer attributes Rickover's lessons in responsibility to his first ship and the commanding officer's court-martial after running the ship aground, writing "the concept of personal responsibility was vividly impressed upon the young ensign."[156] Left out is the remainder of the story. Commander Herbert Emory Kays commanded USS *La Valette* (DD 315) from October 3, 1923, to October 1, 1925. The ship ran aground during Rickover's tour, sometime before January 1925, when Rickover reported to USS *Nevada* (BB 36).[157] It is

---

[155] Luke 7 36:50 *Holy Bible: New International Version* (Grand Rapids, MI: Zondervan, 2014).
[156] Rockwell, 23.
[157] Ibid

possible Rickover never knew the rest of the story, or that he did not tell his biographer, but two things are clear. First, while Commander Kays may have been court-martialed, he was not removed from command. Second, he was promoted to Captain before commanding USS *Chicago* (CL 29) from June 25, 1933, to August 30, 1934 and Destroyer Squadron Fourteen during 1938.[158] He retired, as a Captain, in 1940.

Rickover also forgave. Numerous stories exist attributing one removal or another to Rickover's temper. However, few are documented sufficiently to prove the legend. One story of both Rickover's temper, swift sword, and capacity for forgiveness occurred in the early 1960s. In 1962, Commander Ernest R. Barrett was removed from command of USS *Permit* (SSN 594) after the submarine ran into a freighter while on pre-commissioning trials. Transferred ashore, in 1964 Barrett reentered the command course, this time for nuclear missile submarines. Taking command of USS *Ethan Allen* (SSBN 608), he collided with a merchant ship in January 1965 and was again removed from command. He retired in 1961 as a Captain.[159]

This duality in the Rickover legacy is one of stated accountability but hidden forgiveness. Rickover retired in 1982 during the turn from a Navy that could still forgive to one that rarely, if ever, allowed redemption. Before 1982, at least a quarter of officers involved in an incident recovered in some form. Between 1982 and 1995 less than one in ten recovered and between 1995 and 2015, fewer than one in twenty. More tellingly, of the incidents before 1982, only three percent of commanders lost their command following an incident or crime of command, while since 1982 over 40% have. Since the beginning of the century, the number sits at 65%.

Commander Vavasseur did not lose her command, but she continues going through a drawn-out process hoping for

---

[158] *The Palm Beach Post*. West Palm Beach, Florida Issue Date: Friday, March 11, 1938: 7
[159] Polmar and Allen, 335

institutional forgiveness as she responds to the Secretary of the Navy withdrawing her promotion. For institutional forgiveness to hold she would be held accountable for her error in judgment, but the subsequent selection for Captain remain intact. By vacating that promotion, she is severely punished, outside of any judicial process, and the Navy loses any potential leadership lessons she could either implement or relate. Over the last thirty years, this loss is a price the Navy has paid, often without batting an eye.

Where should the military go from here? First and foremost, each general and flag officer must receive some real education in ethics and virtue, repeatedly. This education must then expand to all commanders, and potential commanders. Secondly, the many "ethics rules" which really pertain more to accepting gifts, lunches, use of position and so on should be renamed to "Standards of Conduct" so as to remove the idea that ethics is only concerned with who pays for what. Recognize these infractions for what they are – failures of standards of conduct. Finally, the services must begin evaluating how empathy and forgiveness can be integrated into service culture, even if it begins with something as simple as daily recitation of the Sailor's or Soldier's Creed – after they are properly rewritten to reflect virtues and not simple rule following. Even here, however, leaders must guard against such recitation becoming wrote compliance. Uninformed rote compliance degrades Ariely's idea of reminders and eventually casts the creeds, and the virtues they espouse, in a negative light.

None of these ideas will immediately solve any ethics problems present in the military or society, but change takes time and in order to really affect change we need to focus on the "little cheaters" more than the "big cheaters." The big cheaters will be caught and dealt with and include the expected level of publicity and academic dissection, but the little cheaters erode society one pencil at a time until the little cheaters are all big cheaters. To regain forgiveness, the Navy must create leaders who are neither big nor little cheaters.

Conclusion

On June 17, 2017, the *Arleigh Burke*-class destroyer USS *Fitzgerald* (DDG 62) and civilian containership ACX *Crystal* collided in the approaches to Tokyo Bay. The 29,000-ton containership stove in the destroyer's starboard side, puncturing two berthing compartments and crushing the captain's cabin. Seven sailors died.[1]

On August 21, 2017, the *Arleigh Burke*-class destroyer USS *John S. McCain* (DDG 56) collided with the oil and chemical tanker *ALNIC MC* in the Straits of Singapore. The tanker also punctured a berthing compartment, killing ten sailors.[2]

The Navy removed the commanding officers of both ships, as well as their executive officers and a number of other officers and enlisted personnel. On January 16, 2018 the Navy announced Article 32 hearings as precursor to courts-martial for the removed commanders and four others. Given the examples provided to this point, none of these actions are surprising or unusual for the 21st century Navy. What makes these cases unique are that the Navy included charges of negligent homicide against these officers. The pillory no longer, these captains, once pillars of leadership, face confinement for simply having command at the time of a fatal incident.

These were not the only two incidents in the Pacific Fleet during 2017. Commanders Sanchez and Benson were not the only officers removed from command; their charges are not the only unusual actions. On August 22, 2017, the Commander of

---

[1] United States, Department of the Navy, Chief of Naval Operations, *Report on the collision between USS Fitzgerald (DDG 62) and Motor Vessel ACX Crystal; Report on the collision between USS John S. McCain (DDG 56) and Motor Vessel Alnic MC* (Washington, DC, 2017). 4
[2] Ibid, 43

U.S. Seventh Fleet, Admiral Joseph Aucoin, was removed from command "due to a loss of confidence in his ability to command."[3] On September 18, 2017, Admiral Aucoin's replacement, Admiral Phil Sawyer, removed the subordinate commanders between Seventh Fleet and the ships, Commander Task Force 70, Rear Admiral Charles Williams and Commander Destroyer Squadron 15, Captain Jeffrey Bennett.[4]

The same week the Navy announced its intent to pursue negligent homicide charges it also announced that the Pacific Fleet administrative commander for ship, Admiral Thomas S. Rowden, resigned when his removal was recommended as part of the same actions leading to the negligent homicide charges. Admirals Rowden, Aucoin, and Williams are the first, and only, admirals removed from command for operational issues since World War II. While not facing courts-martial, these officers' careers will always carry this removal as a footnote to decades of service.

With this information one might readily accept that the Navy acted as expected given the changes since 1945. Of course, there is more to the story. *Fitzgerald*'s captain, Commander Bryce Benson, was asleep at the time of the collision and was almost killed by the impact. *John S. McCain*'s captain, Commander Alfredo J. Sanchez, was on the bridge as the ship operated in heavy ship traffic during a predawn transit. Captain Bennett and Admiral Williams were removed because they were in command of subordinate units who had problems. There were no indications of long term issues in those ships. No clear signs of troubled cultures or remediation actions available to Bennett or Williams before the fatal collisions. Their reliefs are from the culpability of command and their careers are ended.

---

[3] US Navy, "7th Fleet Commander Relieved Due to Loss of Confidence," news release, August 23, 2017, www.navy.mil, http://www.navy.mil/submit/display.asp?story_id=102073.
[4] US Navy, "CTF 70 and DESRON 15 Commanders Relieved Due to Loss of Confidence," news release, September 18, 2017, www.navy.mil, http://www.navy.mil/submit/display.asp?story_id=102464.

Admirals Rowden and Aucoin were also sacrificed on the altar of accountability, or so it appears. As usual, appearances are deceiving. While both admirals' careers now bear the taint and embarrassment of removal, this is the sum of their punishment. In both cases the removals occurred less than a month before an already scheduled change of command. Both replacements were already nominated, confirmed, and in place. Neither removal provided anything more substantive than a press release, and the public shame of removal, accompanied by grandiose statements on accountability and renewed quotations of "Hobson's Choice."

This study began seeking to explain the question, *Why does the Navy remove commanding officers and has the Navy always removed as many commanding officers as it does today?* The answer is complex, as are all answers in human systems. Before judging an incident, each case must be taken as an individual case and analyzed as an individual case - each on its own merits. Once each case is adjudicated, and many cases are reviewed, then we can formulate patterns and trends before proposing theories.

In 1945 the Navy court-martialed two commanders - Charles McVay for not zig-zagging and Eliot Loughlin for firing on a ship he could not see. Neither offense was singular to these officers, it was the results of their actions they were really tried for. McVay is today held up as one of the standards for both the Navy's accountability and its penchant for scapegoating. Loughlin, forgiven and promoted, is virtually forgotten.

Major fires aboard USS *Bennington* and USS *Ranger* - thirty years apart - show some of the changes from then to now. *Bennington*'s captain went on to command again, achieve flag rank and develop the Navy's Polaris missile program even though a hundred men under his command died. Arthur Fredrickson kept command of *Ranger* but faded into obscurity after six sailors died - because two other sailors improperly aligned a fuel system. While neither commander had direct knowledge or influence over the root causes of the incidents,

Fredrickson was found culpable in a way that Raborn was not.

The changing timeline of actions against commanders shows itself with USS *Stark*, USS *Cole*, and USS *William P. Lawrence*. *Stark*'s Glenn Brindel was held in command to complete the administrative and legal decisions. *Cole*'s Kirk Lippold was cleared by one chain of command, then condemned on the altar by a second. *William P. Lawrence*'s Jana Vavasseur met the same fate, though in less time than Kirk Lippold was subjected to.

Collisions between ships provide the richest cases, writings, and lessons. Collisions are seen as the most preventable of mishaps and there is some truth in that statement. Since 1945 collisions between ships have become exceptionally rare. In this century, naval ships collided twenty-one times; in 1967 alone, there were twenty collisions. In the seventeen years after World War II there were over a hundred. As the summer of 2017 shows, they still happen. When destroyers *Brownson* and *Charles H. Roan* collided, a sailor died but both commanders retained command and successively promoted and returned to command time and time again. The commanders of *Winston S. Churchill* and *McFaul* retained their commands after the collision, but rapidly retired from the Navy. The 2017 removals and negligent homicide charges hopefully mark the high water in the Navy's sacrifice of commanders to accountability but there is no starker difference in how these officers are treated than looking at *Brownson, Charles H, Roan, Belknap,* or *Frank E. Evans*. Despite the death and destruction in each of those cases, no commander was ever court-martialed for negligent homicide.

Then, why does the Navy remove commanding officers? Writ large, the Navy removes officers from command who violate the ideal and responsibilities of command. Sometimes those violations are for operational issues, crimes of command. Sometimes, and more often in recent decades, the removal is for personal misconduct.

Why does the Navy remove commanders so often? This

question does not need an answer because it is logically faulty. There are over 54,000 officers in the Navy; there are fewer than 2000 commands. At the height of removals, 2012 with 26 announced cases, which meant only 1.3 percent of commanders were removed. 26 averages one every other week. That can hardly be called often.

Neither answer is satisfactory, nor comprehensive. While one school of thought is that commanders should always perform to the acceptable standard, another is that if no commanders are removed then the Navy is hiding something.

Does the Navy remove commanders more often than it once did? The conclusion here is a categorical yes. While some might point to McVay and Loughlin's courts-martial, or even the resolution of the *Frank E. Evans, Belknap,* or *Stark* incidents they are specific cases removed from historical context. William Bainbridge committed a crime of command when USS *Philadelphia* grounded off Tripoli, and still went on to naval fame. John Barry and Chester Nimitz are not the only other commanders redeemed from crimes of command. In addition to those already identified Admiral Michael Mullen, former Chief of Naval Operations and Chairman of the Joint Chiefs of Staff; Admiral Jeremy Michael Boorda, former Chief of Naval Operations; and Admirals Robert J Natter, James F. Calvert, E. W. Cooke, John Morgan, and almost a hundred other commanders committed crimes of command and continued to advance in the Navy and reach Flag rank. Of over fifteen hundred catalogued incidents more than three hundred officers achieved redemption. In this century only twelve officers, across over four hundred incidents, received forgiveness and achieved redemption. Commanders today are removed more often, astronomically more often, than even thirty years ago much less seventy. The Navy is less forgiving, quicker to act, and the culture now eschews remorse and rehabilitation in favor retribution and removal. These modern actions are not permanent. The Navy can, and must, return to a time when a commander can commit a crime of command, be judged and afforded an opportunity to seek and receive forgiveness; an opportunity for redemption.[5]

To get there the Navy must reevaluate how modern responsibility and accountability are corrupted concepts and return them to their original meanings. Culpability must return as the standard for removal, not simple accountability. The Navy must let go of the idea that losing confidence in a subordinate is sufficient grounds for removal. A "loss of confidence" is such a vague and illusory term that it is the catchall for any manner of removal and often hides real impropriety on the part of the subordinate commander, or sometimes on the part of the senior who ordered the removal.[6]

The Navy must end the administrative fiat of one officer investigations and, if it cannot or will not return to courts-martial for crimes of command then approach the process from that of a professional review board. A professional review board would take the adjudication of crimes of command out of the hands of a potentially biased or self-interested superior commander and instead place the responsibility for action in the hands of a group of professional peers. Crimes of command require an accounting, but if the Navy seeks a righteous and virtuous officer corps then Navy leadership must act with right and virtue.[7] Navy officers should have rights when they are held to account, they should not be forced to fight the very institution they serve in.[8]

At the same time the Navy must also conduct a significant, and honest, review of the caveat to the Uniform Code of Military Justice that precludes individuals assigned to

---

[5] David Brown, "Why are COs getting the ax? Blame high tempo or a shrinking fleet, but the number of firings is way up," *Navy Times*, February 23, 2004.

[6] Matthew Dolan, "The Heavy Responsibilities of Command - Lessons to be Learned," *The Virginian-Pilot* (Norfolk), March 10, 2004.

[7] Greenbacker, 29.

[8] Dolan

sea duty the right to refuse nonjudicial punishment and instead be tried by court-martial.[9] The "vessel exception" had a place in the early years of the UCMJ, but those days are long gone and too many commanders abuse the privilege of nonjudicial punishment as a means to control the outcome. Doing so will continue to erode whatever positive virtues the concept of nonjudicial punishment affords. The arguments against lifting the vessel exception must be identified, studied, tested and modern technology inserted into the courts process. Anything less diminishes concepts of fairness and justice.

The Navy must remember that commanders, competent commanders, are in short supply.[10] The rarity of command in itself means that every commander has valuable, and rare, experience. By removing and discarding virtually all commanders who commit crimes of command the Navy wastes precious resources. Chester Nimitz' and William Raborn's contributions testify to the potential value lost when the Navy sent Kirk Lippold, Glenn Brindel, Walter Shafer, and over a hundred other commanders home over the last three decades rather than afford them an opportunity at redemption.

The Navy has changed, as has society. The rules today are different, less tolerant, than they once were.[11] As with all changes, some are positive, some not. There is little doubt that modern commanders are better educated and better prepared for command than their predecessors were. That they are better prepared for command today than those predecessors is a different question altogether. Modern command is significantly more complex than it was in 1945, or even into 1985.

So long as the Navy clings to antiquated concepts of command lifted out of their historical context the Navy will be incapable of change. As stirring as the words are in "Hobson's

---

[9] Dwight H. Sullivan, "Overhauling the Vessel Exception," *Naval Law Review* 43, (1996):57.
[10] Holloway, 349.
[11] Jim Frederick, *Black Hearts: one platoon's descent into madness in Iraq's triangle of death* (London: Pan, 2011).

Choice" or *The Cruel Sea*, leadership must focus on real people and real situations. Context matters as much as any ideal of command. We should accept traditions when they add value to the profession, not just because they strike a chord, or because they meet a need in the hearts and minds of culture, service, or law.[12] Leaders must do so from a position of virtue, of balancing one ethical challenge against another and doing so from a position of knowledge and experience. They must practice practical wisdom.

Navy leaders must stop looking at groups of commanding officers and telling them that "if you run a ship aground, if you have a collision at sea, or if through your negligence a member of your crew is killed, I'll relieve you, no questions asked,"[13] or to "look around the room. One of you will do something that will cause you to get relieved."[14] The speaker may feel better, but at what cost? Statements like this provide neither value nor virtue. How many new commanding officers went from looking forward to the challenge of command to looking over their shoulders?

As this is the first diagonal study of naval command and fully recognizing the limits of available data there are many areas available for further study. The most obvious is to complete the data set, locating commanding officer names, retirement ranks, and other important information about the thousands of reported incidents over the seventy years of the study.

The next area is to expand the case studies to include more aviation and submarine commands. Records for both communities are scant and difficult to locate, but may provide

---

[12] Elizabeth L. Hillman, "On Unity: A Commentary on Discipline, Justice, and Command in the U.S. Military: Maximizing Strengths and Minimizing Weaknesses in a Special Society," *New England Law Review* 50, no. 1 (Fall 2015):68.
[13] William Cole, "Fired Navy Officers Manage to Adapt," *The Honolulu Star-Advertiser*, April 28, 2013.
[14] Brown

an increased understanding of command, accountability, and culpability. Cold War incidents between and with submarines were handled in many different ways, especially when collisions were with Soviet submarines. Aviation commands in the 1950s through 1970s had abysmal safety mishap rates, but conventional wisdom is that commanders were rarely found culpable for them with blame instead placed upon the individual pilots. Aviation's changing approach to safety provides a number of areas for further study.

Another area is senior officer attitudes. As senior officers are the second most critical factor for whether or not a commander is removed following an incident (the incident being the most critical) studying the attitudes of senior officers towards command held by subordinates may provide interesting insights. Coupled with senior officer attitudes is the realization that very few admirals write biographies. The last Chief of Naval Operations to publish an autobiography was Admiral Holloway, and he retired in 1978. Admiral Frank Kelso, CNO between 1990 and 1994, provided an oral history but no autobiography. In the last two and a half decades no other Chief of Naval Operations leaves a written legacy in either autobiographical or biographical form. While retired Admiral James Stavridis wrote of both his commander command in USS *Barry* (DDG 52) and a later more holistic career autobiography in *The Accidental Admiral* there are scant other biographical writings from America's senior naval officers.

Linked to this is the appallingly poor submission rate for official command operations reports. These official reports summarize annual operations for ships and squadrons providing an index for researchers to identify issues which might then be delved into via individual daily logs. Research into why submission rates are so poor may allow the Navy to overhaul the program and provide a means to retain the important history that is being lost.

The Navy must abandon and bury the false idols of accountability. Tailhook was not the watershed for reliefs once thought, the process was already well underway. Alcohol and sex are not the primary downfall of modern commanders. The Navy must restore the balance between autonomy and accountability,[15] and authority and responsibility. A commander should only be held accountable for things within the scope of authority, and if authority is not absolute, then neither is accountability.

Ours is a maritime nation. We have always and likely will always depend upon the sea for commerce and defense. Maritime safety remains but how can we guarantee it? Secretary of Defense Donald Rumsfeld famously said we must go to war with the army we have, not the one we want. For the Navy it's no different, but the Navy we have is what ensures the freedom of the seas today and will be the one that must control the seas in time of war. We are unlikely to have the years of buildup we saw before Pearl Harbor, or the year of mistakes afterwards, before we could turn the tide in the Pacific. We must be ready today, but in being ready we must be honest, realistic, and redeemable. We must keep our captains as pillars, advocating for them instead of scorning them as we toss them into the pillory.

...stop.

---

[15] Hunt

Bibliography

"Comments and Observations regarding Lieutenant Commander Reo A. Beaulieu, USN, 565850/1100." Raymond W. Allen to Chief of Naval Personnel. April 12, 1967.

"Esquire's Official Court of Inquiry into the Present State of the United States Navy." *Esquire*, July 1969, 84-86.

"General court martial in your case," G. L. Russell to Commander David L. Martineau, U.S. Navy, May 2, 1951.

"George Dewey: Virtues of an "Ordinary" Naval Officer." Naval History Blog. January 23, 2011. Accessed January 17, 2018. http://www.navalhistory.org/2011/01/23/george-dewey-virtues-of-an-ordinary-naval-officer.

"Golden Eagles." Golden Eagles. Accessed August 18, 2017. http://www.epnaao.com/.

"Hard to Fix Blame in Awa Maru Sinking." *The New York Times*, July 15, 1945. Accessed March 23, 2017. Historical Newspapers.

"Hobson's Choice." *The Wall Street Journal* (New York), May 14, 1952.

"Informal investigation to inquire into the circumstances surrounding the fire on board USS RANGER (CV 61) which occurred in the Northern Arabian Sea on 1 November 1983." Crawford A. Easterling to Judge Advocate General. March 16, 1984. Naval Air Station, North Island, San Diego, California.

"Informal investigation to inquire into the circumstances surrounding the fire on board USS RANGER (CV 61) which occurred in the Northern Arabian Sea on 1 November 1983." Thomas R. Kinnebrew to Judge Advocate General. April 16, 1984. United States Pacific Fleet, Pearl Harbor, Hawaii.

"Letter of censure, proposed action concerning." F. G. Fahrion to Commander Eugene B. Henry, Jr. U.S. Navy. January 3, 1951.

"Letter of censure, reconsideration of action concerning." F. G. Fahrion to Commander Eugene B. Henry, Jr. U.S. Navy. January 25, 1951.

"Limited Punishment Signaled in Jet Downing." *The New York Times*, August 14, 1988.

"Memorandum for All Flag Officers and Officers in Command." Letter from J. L. Holloway, III. October 2, 1976. Washington, DC.

"National News in Brief." *United Press International*, April 10, 1984.

"Operational Propulsion Plant Re-Examination." Letter to Commanding Officer, USS Ranger (CV 61). July 7, 1983.

"Proposed Disciplinary Action." F. G. Fahrion to Commander Eugene B. Henry, Jr. U.S. Navy. December 29, 1950.

"Results of Inquiry into the Chain of Command Responsibility for the USS

Ranger (CV 61) Fire on 1 Nov 83." Letter to Commander in Chief, U.S. Pacific Fleet. July 16, 1984. Naval Air Station, North Island, San Diego, California.

"Results of Inquiry into the Chain of Command Responsibility for the USS Ranger (CV 61) Fire on 1 Nov 83." James D. Watkins to Judge Advocate General. November 9, 1984. Office of the Chief of Naval Operations, Washington, DC.

"Sinking of Japanese Ship AWA MARU; Report Of." C. E. Loughlin to Commander Submarine Force, Pacific Fleet. April 8, 1945.

"Statement in regard to proposed letter of censure; submission of." Eugene B. Henry, Jr. to Commander Destroyer Force, U.S. Atlantic Fleet. January 18, 1951.

"The skipper of the carrier USS Ranger vigorously denied..." *United Press International*, September 28, 1981.

"Theresa Jones, et al v. USA, et al." Justia Dockets & Filings. Accessed October 02, 2017. https://dockets.justia.com/docket/circuit-courts/ca9/17-55234.

"Two Damaged Destroyers Here After Collision in "High Speed Manoeuvres." *The Royal Gazette* (Hamilton, Bermuda), November 13, 1950.

"Vice Adm. F. E. M. Whiting, 87, Dies." *The New York Times*, June 7, 1978.

Abramson, Rudy. "Age-Old Tradition: Sea Skippers Must Answer for Tragedy," *Los Angeles Times*, June 6, 1981, accessed December 19, 2016.

Ageton, Arthur A. *The Naval Officer's Guide*. 1st ed. New York, NY: Whittlesey House, 1943.

Albion, Robert Greenhalgh. *Makers of naval policy: the American naval establishment 1798-1947.* 1950.

Ariely, Dan. *The (honest) truth about dishonesty: how we lie to everyone--especially ourselves.*

Arkin, William M., and Joshua Handler. *Neptune papers III; Naval nuclear accidents at sea.* Amsterdam: Greenpeace, 1990.

Bacevich, Andrew J. *The limits of power: the end of American exceptionalism.* New York: Metropolitan Books, 2009.

Barnes, Bart. "Md. Political Patron Irvin Kovens Dies at 71." *The Washington Post*, November 1, 1989. Accessed September 11, 2017. http://www.highbeam.com/doc/1P2-1220528.html?refid=easy_hf.

Barnett, Roger W. *Navy strategic culture: why the Navy thinks differently.* Annapolis, Md.: Naval Institute Press, 2009.

Benedict, Ruth. *The Chrysanthemum and the Sword.* London: Secker & Warburg, 1947.

Benjamin, Walter, Hannah Arendt, and Harry Zohn. *Illuminations.* New

York: Harcourt, Brace & World, 1968.
Bichowsky, F. Russell. *Is the navy ready?* New York: Vanguard Press, 1935.
Blair, Clay Jr. *Silent Victory*. New York: Bantam Books, 1975.
Borneman, Walter R. *The admirals: Nimitz, Halsey, Leahy, and King--the five-star admirals who won the war at sea*. New York: Little, Brown and Co., 2012.
Bray, Chris. *Court-martial: how military justice has shaped America from the revolution to 9/11 and beyond*. New York: W.W. Norton&Company, 2016.
Brown, David. "Why are COs getting the ax? Blame high tempo or a shrinking fleet, but the number of firings is way up." *Navy Times*, February 23, 2004.
Browne, Kinglsey. *Military Sex Scandals from Tailhook to the Present: The Cure Can Be Worse than the Disease*. Detroit: Wayne State University Law School, 2147483647.
Buell, Thomas B. *The quiet warrior: a biography of admiral Raymond A. Spruance*. Boston, 1974.
Caiden, Gerald E. "Dealing with Administrative Corruption." In *Handbook of Administrative Ethics*, edited by Terry L. Cooper, 429-55. New York, NY: Dekker, 2001.
Carter, Walter E. *Ethics in the U.S. Navy*. Working paper. United States Naval War College. 2014.
Chatham, Ralph. "Leadership and Nuclear Power." *Proceedings*, July 1978, 78-82.
Chisholm, Donald. *Waiting for dead men's shoes: origins and development of the U.S. Navy's officer personnel system, 1793-1941*. Stanford, Calif.: Stanford University Press, 2001.
Clark, J. J., and Clark G. Reynolds. *Carrier admiral*. New York: D. McKay Co., 1967.
Cohen, Dov, Richard E. Nisbett, Brian F. Bowdle, and Norbert Schwarz. "Insult, Aggression, and the Southern Culture of Honor: An "Experimental Ethnography"." *Journal of Personality and Social Psychology* 70, no. 5 (May 1996): 945-60.
Cole, William. "Fired Navy officers manage to adapt." *The Honolulu Star-Advertiser*, April 28, 2013.
Cooper, Kip. "Former Skipper Censured; CCUs Closed." *The San Diego Union*, October 27, 1982.
Cope, Harley F., and Howard Bucknell. *Command at Sea*. Annapolis, MD: United States Naval Institute, 1967.
Costagliola, Francesco. "Oral History Interview Capt. Francesco Costagliola USNA Class of 1941." Interview by Donald R. Lennon. *East Carolina Manuscript Collection*, March 30, 1990.
Cushman, John H., Jr. "Navy Forgoes Courts-Martial for Officers of Stark."

The New York Times, July 28, 1987.

Daland, Troy. "Home." The Military Code of Conduct: a brief history. February 09, 2011. Accessed January 16, 2018. http://www.kunsan.af.mil/News/Commentaries/Article/414344/the-military-code-of-conduct-a-brief-history/.

Dittmer, David Bruce. *The firing of Admiral Denfeld: an early casualty of the military unification process.* PhD diss., University of Nebraska at Omaha, 1995.

Dolan, Matthew. "The Heavy Responsibilities of Command - Lessons to be Learned." *The Virginian-Pilot* (Norfolk), March 10, 2004.

Dugan, Kathleen M. *Tailhook part III: the present aftermath.* Washington, DC, 1994.

Duncan, Francis. *Rickover and the nuclear navy: the discipline of technology.* Annapolis, MD: Naval Institute Press, 1990.

Duncan, Francis. *Rickover: the struggle for excellence.* Annapolis, MD: Naval Institute Press, 2011.

Dunn, Robert F. *Gear up, mishaps down: the evolution of naval aviation safety, 1950-2000.* Annapolis, MD: Naval Institute Press, 2017.

Esola, Louise. *American boys: the true story of the Lost 74 of the Vietnam War.* Temecula, CA: Pennway Books, 2014.

Eyer, Kevin. "Co-Ed Crew: Reality vs. Taboo." *Proceedings*, October 2012.

Eyer, Kevin. "Opinion: Why More Commanding Officers are Getting Fired." *USNI News*, October 1, 2013. Accessed October 25, 2017. https://news.usni.org/2013/09/30/opinion-commanding-officers-getting-fired.

Fidell, Eugene R., and Jay M. Fidell. "Loss of numbers." *Naval Law Review* 48 (2001): 202.

Francis J. Fitzpatrick to Reo Beaulieu. January 27, 1967. Washington, DC.

Frederick, Jim. *Black hearts: one platoons descent into madness in Iraqs triangle of death.* London: Pan, 2011.

Friedman, Norman. *U.S. Destroyers: an illustrated design history.* Annapolis, MD: Naval Institute Press, 2004.

From Staff, and Wire Reports. "CALIFORNIA IN BRIEF : SAN DIEGO : Skipper Not Guilty in Collision." *Los Angeles Times*, May 24, 1990. Accessed July 19, 2017.

Gallery, Daniel V. *Eight bells, and all's well.* [1st ed. New York: Norton, 1965.

Gallery, Philip D. "A Few Ideas of a Cruiser Skipper." *Proceedings*, 629th ser., 81, no. 7 (July 1955): 784-87.

Gelfand, H. Michael. *Sea change at Annapolis: the United States Naval Academy, 1949-2000.* Chapel Hill: University of North Carolina Press, 2006.

Gilmore, Daniel F. "Full Story Told of sinking of the Awa Maru." *United*

Press International, September 18, 1982. http://www.upi.com/Archives/1982/09/19/Full-story-told-of-WWIINEWLNsinking-of-the-Ava-MaruNEWLNMistakenly-torpedoed-by-US-sub-Mistakenly-sought-by-treasure-hunter/4980401256000/.

Gorski, Katherine. "Nonjudicial Punishment In The Military: Why A Lower Burden Of Proof Across All Branches Is Unnecessary." *National Security Law Journal* 2, no. 1 (2013): 83-110.

Gortner, Harold F. "Values and Ethics." In *Handbook of Administrative Ethics*, edited by Terry L. Cooper, 509-28. 2nd ed. New York, NY: Dekker, 2001.

Greenbacker, John E. "The Cruel Business of Accountability." *Proceedings*, August 1977, 24-30.

Grosenick, Leigh E., and Pamela A. Gibson. "Governmental Ethics and Organizational Culture." In *Handbook of Administrative Ethics*, edited by Terry L. Cooper. 2nd ed. New York, NY: Dekker, 2001.

Guy, Carol A. "Captains of USS Ranger CVA 61." USS Ranger CV/A 61 1957-1993. September 1, 2011. Accessed September 17, 2017. http://uss-rangerguy.com/captains_of_ranger.htm.

Hart, David K. "Administration and the Ethics of Virtue: In All Things, Choose First for Good Character and Then for Technical Expertise." In *Handbook of Administrative Ethics*, edited by Terry L. Cooper, 131-50. 2nd ed. New York, NY: Dekker, 2001.

Hart, Raymond J. "Surface Warfare Officers: The Need for Professionalism." *Proceedings* 102, no. 6 (June 1976).

Hartle, Anthony E. *Moral issues in military decision making*. Lawrence (Kan.): University Press of Kansas, 2004.

Hattendorf, John B., B. Mitchell Simpson, and John R. Wadleigh. *Sailors and scholars: the centennial history of the U.S. Naval War College*. Newport, RI: Naval War College Press, 1984.

Heggen, Thomas, and Edith Goodkind Rosenwald. *Mister Roberts*. Boston: Houghton Mifflin Co., 1946.

Heinl, Robert D., Jr. "Judge's Ruling Scuttles Accountability Law Of The Navy." *The San Diego Union*, June 4, 1976, sec. B.

Hibben, John Grier. *A Defence of Prejudice: and other essays*. Charles Scribner's Sons: New York, 1911.

Hiebert, Paul G. *Anthropological insights for missionaries*. Grand Rapids, MI: Baker Book House, 2006.

Hiebert, Paul G. *Cultural Anthropology*. 2nd ed. Grand Rapids, Michigan: Baker Book House, 1990.

Hillman, Elizabeth L. "On Unity: A Commentary on Discipline, Justice, and Command in the U.S. Military: Maximizing Strengths and Minimizing Weaknesses in a Special Society." *New England Law*

Review 50, no. 1 (Fall 2015): 65-72.
Hillman, Elizabeth Lutes. *Defending America*. Princeton, N.J.: Princeton University Press, 2005.
Hobsbawm, E. J., and T. O. Ranger. *The invention of tradition*. Cambridge: Cambridge University Press, 2010.
Holloway, James L., III. *Aircraft Carriers at War A Personal Retrospective of Korea, Vietnam, and the Soviet Confrontation*. New York: Naval Institute Press, 2011.
Holy Bible: New International Version. Grand Rapids, MI: Zondervan, 2014.
Hornfischer, James D. *Neptune's inferno: the U.S. Navy at Guadalcanal*. New York: Bantam Books, 2011.
http://www.epnaao.com/BIOS_files/REGULARS/Less-%20Tony%20A.pdf
Hull, Michael D. "Modest Victor of Midway." *World War II*, August 19, 1998.
Hunt, Robert B. "Monsarrat Was Wrong." *Proceedings*, February 1997.
Huntington, Samuel P. *The soldier and the State: the theory and politics of civil-military relations*. Cambridge: Belknap Press of Harvard University Press, 1957.
Janowitz, Morris. *The professional soldier, a social and political portrait*. Glencoe, IL: Free Press, 1960.
Joyner, James. "The U.S. Military's Ethics Crisis ." *The National Interest*, February 13, 2014.
Kaurin, Pauline. "Questioning Military #Professionalism – Pauline Kaurin – Medium." Medium. January 22, 2015. Accessed January 15, 2018. https://medium.com/@queenofthinair/questioning-military-professionalism-f00d34f6e1ac.
Keegan, John. *The mask of command*. New York, NY, U.S.A.: Viking, 1987.
Kerr, Alex Arthur. *The reminiscences of Captain Alex A. Kerr, U.S. Navy (Retired)*. Annapolis: U.S. Naval Institute, 1984.
Kerr, Andy. *A journey amongst the good and the great*. Annapolis, MD: Naval Institute Press, 1987.
Kohlberg, Lawrence. *Stages of moral development as a basis for moral education*. Cambridge, MA: Center for Moral Education, Harvard University, 1971.
Kolenda, Konstantin. *Organizations and ethical individualism*. New York u.a.: Praeger, 1988.
Lambert, Joe. "Rear Admiral David L. Martineau." *The Jolly Cholly* 18 (Spring 2015): 10-11.
Langford, Peter E. *Approaches to the development of moral reasoning*. Psychology Press, 2015.
Larson, D. R. "The Surface Line Officer: Some Conn, Some Can't." *Proceedings* 98, no. 7 (July 1972).
Lech, Raymond B. *The tragic fate of the U.S.S. Indianapolis: the U.S. Navy's*

worst disaster at sea. New York: Cooper Square Press, 2001.
Lederer, William J. *All the ship's at sea.* New York: Sloane, 1950.
Lehman, John F. *Command of the Seas.* Annapolis, MD: Naval Institute, 2001.
Lenahan, Arthur. "New Navy Film Dramatizes Collision of U.S., Aussie Ships." *Navy Times* (Tysons Corner), November 26, 1975.
Lerner, Barron H. *One for the road: drunk driving since 1900.* Baltimore: Johns Hopkins University Press, 2012.
Levinson, Jeffrey L., and Randy L. Edwards. *Missile inbound: the attack on the Stark in the Persian Gulf.* Annapolis, MD: Naval Institute Press, 1997.
Lewis, Skip. "M/V Steel Engineer - USMM Cargo Ship." Isthmian Lines. May 10, 2010. Accessed September 21, 2017. http://www.isthmianlines.com/ships/sm_steel_engineer.htm.
Light, Mark F. *The Navy's moral compass: commanding officers and personal misconduct.* Carlisle Barracks, PA: U.S. Army War College, 2011.
Lippold, Kirk. *Front Burner: Al Qaeda's Attack on the USS Cole.* New York, NY: Public Affairs, 2012.
Lockwood, Charles A., and Hans Christian. Adamson. *Hellcats of the sea.* New York: Bantam Books, 1988.
Lockwood, Charles A., and Hans Christian. Adamson. *Tragedy at Honda.* Philadelphia, PA: Chilton Co., Book Division, 1960.
Long, David F. *Gold braid and foreign relations: diplomatic activities of U.S. naval officers, 1798-1883.* Annapolis, MD: Naval Institute Press, 1988.
Long, Robert L. J., and Paul Stillwell. *The reminiscences of Admiral Robert L.J. Long, U.S. Navy (retired).* Annapolis, MD: U.S. Naval Institute, 1995.
Loudon, Wainright. "We Need Help...". *Life*, February 7, 1969, 15-23.
Loughlin, Charles Elliott. *The reminiscences of Rear Admiral Charles Elliott Loughlin, U.S. Navy (Retired).* Annapolis: U.S. Naval Institute, 1982.
Lucas, George R. *Routledge handbook of military ethics.* London: Routledge/Taylor & Francis Group, 2015.
Ludwig, Dean C., and Clinton O. Longenecker. "The Bathsheba Syndrome: The ethical failure of successful leaders." *Journal of Business Ethics* 12, no. 4 (1993): 265-73.
Machiavelli, Niccolò, Thomas More, Martin Luther, William Roper, Ninian Hill Thomson, Ralph Robinson, Robert Scarlett Grignon, and C. A. Buchheim. *The prince.* New York: P.F. Collier & Son, 1910.
MacIntyre, Alasdair C. *After virtue: a study in moral theory.* Notre Dame, IN: University of Notre Dame Press, 1984.

MacIntyre, Alasdair C. *Dependent rational animals: why human beings need the virtues*. Chicago, IL: Open Court, 1999.
Mack, William P. "The Exercise of Broad Command: Still the Navy's Top Specialty." *Proceedings* 83, no. 4 (April 1957).
Mack, William P., Albert H. Konetzni, and Harley F. Cope. *Command at Sea*. Annapolis, MD: Naval Institute Press, 1982.
Masland, John W., and Laurence I. Radway. *Soldiers and scholars; military education and national policy*. Princeton: Princeton University Press, 1957.
Mayo, Claude Banks. *Your Navy; Organizations, Customs And Traditions, Strategy, Tactics, The Nine Principles Of War, And The Place Of The United States Navy In National Security*. Los Angeles, CA: Parker & Baird Co., 1939.
McKearney, Terrance J. "The Path to Command." *Proceedings*, March 1978.
McKee, Christopher. *A Gentlemanly and Honorable Profession: the Creation of the U.S. Naval Officer Corps, 1794-1815*. Annapolis (Md.): Naval Institute Press, 1991.
Milgram, Stanley. "Obedience to Authority." *Rain*, no. 3 (1974): 9. doi:10.2307/3032069.
Moynihan, Daniel P. "Defining Deviancy Down." *American Educator*, Winter 1993/1994, 10-18.
Mullen, Michael G. "CDR Kirk Lippold." E-mail. August 15, 2006.
Nelson, Pete. *Left for Dead: A Young Man's Search for Justice for the USS Indianapolis*. Delacorte Press, 2002.
Nimitz, Chester W., and James M. Steele. *The Nimitz Graybook: the CINCPAC-CINCPOA running estimate of the situation, 1941- 1945*. Newport, RI: United States Naval War College, 2014.
Nomination PN698, confirmed by voice vote February 29, 1984
Oliver, Dave. *Against the tide: Rickover's leadership principles and the rise of the nuclear Navy*. Annapolis, MD: Naval Institute Press, 2014.
Peniston, Bradley. *No higher honor: saving the USS Samuel B. Roberts in the Persian Gulf*. Annapolis, MD: Naval Institute Press, 2006.
Persons, Benjamin S. *Court of Inquiry: "neglecting the possible"--U.S. Navy mistakes*. Manhattan, Kan.: Sunflower University Press, 2001.
Persons, Benjamin S. *Relieved of command*. Manhattan, Kan.: Sunflower University Press, 1997.
Pfaff, Anthony C. "Five Myths about Military Ethics." *Parameters*, September 22, 2016, 59-69.
Piaget, Jean. *The moral judgement of the child*. New York: Harcourt, Brace and Company, 2013.
Polmar, Norman, and Thomas B. Allen. *Rickover: controversy and genius: a biography*. New York: Simon and Schuster, 1984.
Potter, E. B. *Nimitz*. Annapolis, MD: Naval Institute Press, 1976.

Puryear, Edgar F. *American admiralship: the art of naval command.* Minneapolis, MN: Zenith Press, 2008.

Radiation safety and regulation: Hearings before the Joint Committee on Atomic Energy, Congress of the United States, eighty-seventh Congress, first session, on radiation safety and regulation, June 12, 13, 14, and 15, 1961. Washington, D.C.: United States Government Printing Office, 1961.

Reilly, Corinne. "Navy takes steps to combat poor personal choices." *Virginian-Pilot* (Norfolk, VA), June 18, 2012.

Rest, James R., Darcia Narvaez, Stephen J. Thoma, and Muriel J. Bebeau. "A Neo-Kohlbergian Approach to Morality Research." *Journal of Moral Education* 29, no. 4 (2000): 381-95.

Rickover, Hyman G. "Doing a Job." Speech, Columbia University, New York, 1982.

Rickover, Hyman G. "The Role of Engineering in the Navy." Speech, National Society of Former Special Agents of the Federal Bureau of Investigation, Seattle, Wa, August 30, 1974.

Rickover, Hyman G. "Thoughts on Man's Purpose in Life." Speech, San Diego Rotary Club Luncheon, San Diego, February 10, 1977.

Robinson, James T. *Initial Training of Surface Warfare Officers: A Historical Perspective from World War II to 2008.* Fort Leavenworth, KS: U.S. Army Command and General Staff College, 2008.

Rockwell, Theodore. *The Rickover effect: how one man made a difference.* Lincoln, NE: IUniverse, 2002.

Royster, Vermont. *My Own, My Country's Time: A Journalist's Journey.* Chapel Hill, NC: Algonquin Books, 1983.

Sacks, H. H. "Shoreside Checkout for Seagoing Destroyer Officers." *Proceedings,* February 1 1962.

Salzer, Robert S. "The Surface Forces." *Proceedings* 102, no. 11 (November 1976).

Schwartz, Barry, and Kenneth Sharpe. *Practical wisdom: the right way to do the right thing.* New York: Riverhead Books, 2010.

Schwartz, Barry. "Practical wisdom and organizations." *Research in Organizational Behavior* 31 (2011): 3-23. doi:10.1016/j.riob.2011.09.001.

Scott, Roger D. "Kimmel, Short, Mcvay: Case Studies in Executive Authority, Law And The Individual Rights Of Military Commanders." *Military Law Review* 156 (June 1998): 52-199.

Sheehan, Neil. "The 99 Days of Captain Arnheiter." *The New York Times,* August 11, 1968.

Sheehan, Neil. *The Arnheiter Affair.* New York: Random House, 1972.

Simmons, Dan. *Carrion Aomfort.* London: Quercus, 2010.

Skelton, William B. *An American profession of arms: the army officer corps,*

1784-1861. Lawrence, Kan.: University Press of Kansas, 1992.
Smith, Roy C. , IV. "Wanted - A Surface Line School for Junior Officers." *Proceedings* 89, no. 11 (November 1963).
Spector, Ronald H. *Professors of war: the Naval War College and the development of the naval profession*. Newport, RI: Naval War College Press, 1977.
Stanton, Doug. *In harm's way: the sinking of the USS Indianapolis and the extraordinary story of its survivors*.
Stavridis, James, and Robert Girrier. *Command at Sea*. Annapolis, MD: Naval Inst. Press, 2010.
Stavridis, James, and William P. Mack. *Command at Sea*. Annapolis, MD: Naval Institute Press, 1999.
Steele, Claire E. "Zero-Defect Leaders: No Second Chance? 3d Place 2001 MacArthur Writing Award Winner." *Military Review*, Sept. & oct. 2004, 66-70.
Stevenson, Jo. *In the wake: the true story of the Melbourne-Evans collision, conspiracy and cover-up*. Alexandria: Hale & Iremonger, 1999.
Stout, David. "Captain, Once a Scapegoat, Is Absolved." *The New York Times*, July 14, 2001.
Sullivan, Dwight H. "Overhauling the Vessel Exception." *Naval Law Review* 43, no. 57 (1996): 57-110.
Swartz, Peter M., and Michael C. Markowitz. *Organizing OPNAV (1970-2009)*. Center for Naval Analyses, 2010.
Syse, Henrik, and Martin L. Cook. "New Editors Introduction." *Journal of Military Ethics* 9, no. 1 (2010): 1-2. doi:10.1080/15027570903554490.
Taylor, Robert A. "Cat on a Cold Steel Dive Plane." *Naval History*, February 2010, 40-43.
The apology of Plato. Reprint. ed. New York: Arno Press, 1973.
Thompson, Roger. *Brown shoes, black shoes and felt slippers: parochialism and the evolution of the post-war U.S. Navy*. Newport, RI: U.S. Naval War College, 1995.
Thompson, Roger. *Lessons not learned: the U.S. Navy's status quo culture*. Annapolis, MD: Naval Institute Press, 2007.
Toti, William J. "The Sinking of the Indy & Responsibility of Command." *United States Naval Institute Proceedings Magazine*, 1160th ser., 125, no. 10 (October 1999): 34-38.
Tracy, Jessica L., Richard W. Robins, and June Price. Tangney. *The self-conscious emotions: theory and research*. New York: Guilford, 2008.
U.S. Cong. House. House Armed Services. *Readiness And Sustainment Of The Navy's Surface Fleet*. 111 Cong., 1st sess. Rept. 111-31. 2009.
U.S. Cong. Senate. Committee on Armed Services. The sinking of the U.S.S.

Indianapolis and the subsequent court martial of Rear Adm. Charles B. McVay III, USN: hearing before the Committee on Armed Services, United States Senate, One Hundred Sixth Congress, first session, September 14, 1999. 106 Cong. Rept. Washington: U.S. G.P.O., 2000.

U.S. Cong. Senate. Congressional record, vol. 130, proceedings and debates of the 98th Congress, second session. 98th Cong., 2d sess. Washington: Government printing Office, 1984.

U.S. Congress. Committee on Armed Services. The sinking of the U.S.S. Indianapolis and the subsequent court martial of Rear Adm. Charles B. McVay III, USN: hearing before the Committee on Armed Services, United States Senate, One Hundred Sixth Congress, first session, September 14, 1999. Cong. Washington: U.S. G.P.O., 2000.

United States Navy. Military Personnel Command. Results of an Assessment of the Navy Leadership and Management Education and Training (LMET) Prospective Commanding Officer Prospective Executive Officer (PCO/PXO) Course. By Margaret E. Minton, Katherine J. Saad, and Gloria L. Grace. Washington, DC: U.S. Navy, 1979.

United States Navy. USS William P. Lawrence Public Affairs. "USS William P. Lawrence Holds Change of Command Ceremony." News release, December 17, 2013.

United States, Department of the Navy, Commander, U.S. Pacific Fleet, Court of Inquiry Into The Circumstances Surrounding The Collision Between USS *Greeneville* (SSN 772) And Japanese M/V *Ehime Maru* That Occurred Off The Coast Of Oahu, Hawaii On 9 February 2001 (Washington, DC, 1954).

United States. Department of Defense. "Statement by Secretary of Defense Chuck Hagel Announcing His Senior Advisor for Military Professionalism." News release, March 25, 2014. Defense.gov. Accessed August 8, 2015.

United States. Department of Defense. Inspector General. *The Tailhook Report: The Official Inquiry Into the Events of Tailhook '91*. By Derek J. Vander Schaaf. Washington, DC.

United States. Department of the Navy. Central Command. Command Investigation Into the Actions of USS Cole (DDG 67) in Preparing for and Undertaking a Brief Stop for Fuel at Bandar At Tawahi (Aden Harbor) Aden Yemen on or about 12 October 2000. By James W. Holland, Jr. Washington, DC, 2000.

United States. Department of the Navy. Chief of Naval Operations. Report on the collision between USS Fitzgerald (DDG 62) and Motor Vessel ACX Crystal ; Report on the collision between USS John S. McCain (DDG 56) and Motor Vessel Alnic MC. Washington, DC, 2017.

United States. Department of the Navy. Commander Air Force, U.S. Atlantic Fleet. Court of Inquiry to inquire into an explosion and fire aboard the U.S.S. BENNINGTON which occurred 26 May 1954. Washington, DC, 1954.

United States. Department of the Navy. Commander Carrier Strike Group Twelve. *Investigation into the collision at sea of USS McFaul and USS Winston S. Churchill.* Washington, DC, 2005.

United States. Department of the Navy. Commander Cruiser Destroyer Group Two. Formal Investigation into the circumstances surrounding the attack on the USS Stark (FFG 31) on 17 May 1987. Washington, DC, 1987.

United States. Department of the Navy. Commander Cruiser-Destroyer Force, Atlantic Representative. Formal board of investigation to inquire into the circumstances surrounding the collision of USS Hartley (DE-1029) and motor vessel Blue Master and possible subsequent grounding of Hartley. Washington, DC, 1965.

United States. Department of the Navy. Commander in Chief United States Naval Forces Europe. Investigation to inquire into the circumstances surrounding the collision between USS John F. Kennedy (CV 67) and USS Belknap (CG 26) which occurred on 22 November 1975. Washington, DC.

United States. Department of the Navy. Commander Marianas. RECORD OF PROCEEDINGS OF A COURT OF INQUIRY CONVENED AT HEADQUARTERS, COMMANDER MARIANAS, GUAM BY ORDER OF COMMANDER IN CHIEF, UNITED STATES PACIFIC FLEET AND PACIFIC OCEAN AREAS TO INQUIRE INTO ALL CIRCUMSTANCES CONNECTED WITH THE SINKING OF THE USS INDIANAPOLIS (CA-35), AND THE DELAY IN REPORTING THE LOSS OF THAT SHIP AUGUST 13, 1945. Washington, DC: United States Navy, 1945.

United States. Department of the Navy. Commander, Seventh Fleet. Report of the Combined USN RAN Board of Investigation into the collision between HMAS Melbourne and USS Frank E. Evans convened by COMSEVENTHFLT and ACNB. By Jerome King. Washington, DC, 1969.

United States. Department of the Navy. Naval History and Heritage Command. The Sinking of USS Indianapolis: Navy Department Press Release, Narrative of the Circumstances of the Loss of USS Indianapolis, 23 February 1946. Washington, DC, 1946. July 8, 2016. Accessed June 1, 2017. https://www.history.navy.mil/research/histories/ship-histories/loss-of-uss-indianapolis-ca-35/investigation-and-court-martial.html.

United States. Department of the Navy. Naval Inspector General. *Report of*

Commanding Officers Detached for Cause. Washington, DC, 2004.
United States. Department of the Navy. *Naval Regulations*. Washington, DC, 1990.
United States. Department of the Navy. Office of the Judge Advocate General. *Manual of the Judge Advocate General*. Washington, DC: U.S. Dept. of the Navy, Office of the Judge Advocate General, 2012.
United States. Department of the Navy. *Ships' Data, U. S. Naval Vessels, 1911-*. Washington, DC: Government Printing Office, 1935.
United States. Department of the Navy. The Atlantic Command And United States Atlantic Fleet Headquarters of the Commander In Chief. *Record of Proceedings of a Court of Inquiry to inquire into all of the circumstances surrounding the collision between the USS Wasp (CV-18) and the USS Hobson (DMS-26) which occurred at or near Latitude 42-21 North Longitude 44-15 West on or about 27 April 1952*. Washington, DC, 1952.
United States. Department of the Navy. United States Pacific Fleet. Command Investigation into the Circumstances Surrounding a Class Alpha Mishap Involving HSC-6 MH-60B Aircraft, BUNO 167985, Which Occurred at N 22° 34' 18" E 037° 25' 29" Resulting in the Deaths of LCDR Landon L. Jones, USN and CWO3 Jonathan S. Gibson, USN on 22 Sep 2013. Pearl Harbor, HI, 2014.
United States. National Security Agency. *The Sinking and the Salvage of the Awa Maru*. Washington, DC, 1977.
United States. Naval Postgraduate School. *A Normative View of the Pre-Overhaul Planning Process*. By Michael Edward House. Monterey, CA, 1976.
US Navy. "7th Fleet Commander Relieved Due to Loss of Confidence." News release, August 23, 2017. Www.navy.mil. http://www.navy.mil/submit/display.asp?story_id=102073. Story Number: NNS170823-01
US Navy. "CTF 70 and DESRON 15 Commanders Relieved Due to Loss of Confidence." News release, September 18, 2017. Www.navy.mil. http://www.navy.mil/submit/display.asp?story_id=102464.
US Navy. "Navy Commander Pleads Guilty to Rape, Sex Assault." News release, October 28, 2011. http://www.navy.mil/submit/display.asp?story_id=63547.
US Navy. "Special and General Courts-Martial for February 2015." News release, March 17, 2015. http://www.navy.mil/submit/display.asp?story_id=86095.
Vion, Charles P. "The First Step Toward SWO Qualification." *Proceedings*, March 1978.
Vistica, Gregory L. *Fall from Glory: the men who sank the U.S. Navy*. New York: Simon & Schuster, 1995.

Voge, Richard G. "Too Much Accuracy." *United States Naval Institute Proceedings Magazine*, 565th ser., 76, no. 3 (March 1950): 257-63.

Waddle, Scott. *The Right Thing.* Integrity Publishers, 2002.

Watkins, James D. "Oral History." Interview by Gary Weir. *Oceanography: The Making of a Science People, Institutions and Discovery*, May 11, 2000.

Weber, Bruce. "William J. Lederer, Co-Author of 'The Ugly American,' Dies at 97." *The New York Times*, January 14, 2010.

White, Richard D. *Ethics and hierarchy: the influence of a rigidly hierarchical organizational design on moral reasoning.* 1997.

White, Richard D., Jr. "Military Ethics." In *Handbook of Administrative Ethics*, edited by Terry L. Cooper, 629-47. 2nd ed. New York, NY: Dekker, 2001.

Whitlock, Craig. "Bad behavior sinking more Navy officers' careers." *The Seattle Times*, June 17, 2011.

Wild, Payson Sibley. *International law documents: 1944-45.* Washington, DC: U.S. Government Print. Office, 1946.

Wolfe, Malcolm E., and F. J. Mulholland. *Selected readings in leadership.* Annapolis, MD: United States Naval Institute, 1960.

Wong, Y., & Tsai, J. (2007). *Cultural models of shame and guilt.*

Wouk, Herman. *The Caine mutiny, a novel of World War II.* Garden City, NY: Doubleday, 1951.

Wouk, Herman. *The winds of war: a novel.* Boston, MA: Little, Brown, 1971.

Wouk, Herman. *War and remembrance: a novel.* Boston: Little, Brown, 1978.

Zimmerman, Jean. *Tailspin: women at war in the wake of Tailhook.* New York: Doubleday, 1995.

Zumwalt, Elmo R. "A Course for Destroyers." *Proceedings*, November 1962.

Zumwalt, Elmo R. *On Watch.* New York: Quadrangle Books, 1977.